SpringerWienNewYork

Caramel

andreas russ-bovelino (ed)

architekten
katherl
haller
aspetsberger

SpringerWienNewYork

forget architecture,

schwätzen.

- pre / post
- vergänglich // transient
- abgehoben // uplifted
- schwarzbauten // in the grey zone
- bodenständig // down-to-earth
- luftschlösser // castles in the air
- mobil // mobile

inhalt / contents

schwarzbauten / in the grey zone

bodenständig / down-to-earth

luftschlösser / castles in the air

mobil / mobile

abspann / end titles

projekt // project
gebaut // built

essen. wohnen
büro
vorraum
zimmer.

nada, niente, rien, tipota, hiç, foyi – nothing, schätzchen!

»eigentlich sollte hier nichts stehen«, andreas bovelino

architektur ist narrativ, sie spricht für sich, sagen die architekten. diejenigen zumindest, die sich nicht aufs dampfplaudern verlegt haben, die zu recht selbstbewussten, deren arbeit aussage genug ist. wie diejenigen, um die's hier auf den nächsten 419 seiten geht. günter katherl, martin haller, ulrich aspetsberger – caramel architekten. vor zehn jahren gründeten sie ihr büro in wien und mischten von anfang an die szene auf. mit spektakulären bauten und wettbewerbsbeiträgen ebenso wie mit ungewöhnlichen performances. sie verpassten der österreichischen hauptstadt die schönste mistzentrale europas, deckten die kulturhauptstadt linz mit einem so rustikalen wie einladenden, gigantischen tischtuch und ließen das verblüffte biennale-publikum in venedig im regen stehen. doch egal mit welch spielerischer leichtigkeit sie scheinbar auch an die seriösesten angelegenheiten herangehen – nichts an ihrer formensprache ist verspielt, alles macht sinn. und ist ein deutliches statement. denn es stimmt: architektur ist narrativ, wenn man genau hinhört, erzählt sie sogar geschichten. wie das betriebsgebäude an der autobahn, das sich im schwarzen latexkleid so sexy fühlt, oder das haus an einem hang über der stadt, das so waghalsig auskragt und sich nicht um statische einschränkungen zu kümmern scheint, sondern fliegen will.
zwängt man architektur allerdings zwischen zwei buchdeckel, verschlägt es ihr oft die sprache. das ergebnis: ein architekturbuch. noch eines. schöne bilder zum durchblättern, alles sehr dekorativ, damit es sich gut auf dem regal macht. ein paar kluge texte von architekturkritikern für architekurkritiker, vom leben weitestmöglich entfernt, selbstreferenziell, satt, ermüdend. man mag sie kaum lesen, muss man auch gar nicht, im gegenteil, dafür wurden sie nicht geschrieben.

»nimmermehr!«, um einen nicht ganz unbekannten us-autor des 19. jahrhunderts zu zitieren, den man vielleicht nicht auf anhieb mit architektur in verbindung bringen würde. aber was wäre edgar allan poes prosa ohne seine atmosphärische beschreibung von gebäuden? und vor allem deren einzigartigem charakter? wären, um ein etwas weniger düsteres bild zu bemühen, die sexuellen und emotionalen verirrungen von john updikes protagonisten woanders möglich als in den hellen, sauberen holzhäusern des amerikanischen ostens? vielleicht ja, aber sie wären grundlegend anderer natur, völlig andere geschichten. so wie wir mit unseren vorlieben und abneigungen architektur beeinflussen, beeinflusst sie uns. jeden von uns. und geht jeden etwas an – nicht nur professionelle kritiker. den größten teil unseres lebens sind wir von architektur umgeben, ganz selbstverständlich. wenn wir reisen, dann von der uns gewohnten, zu einer fremden, ungewohnten architektur. wir leben, lieben, streiten, freuen uns und leiden »in architektur«. auch in dieser hinsicht erzählt architektur geschichten. spannende, sehnsüchtige, ungewöhnliche oder auch ganz alltägliche geschichten. höchste zeit, sie auch so zu präsentieren. und so über sie zu schreiben, dass es freude macht, über sie zu lesen. jedem der wohnt. jedem der lebt. eine revolution? ja genau, nichts weniger als das.

eine revolution, an der sich mit dem architekten friedrich achleitner auch ein legendärer kritiker als gast-autor beteiligt. und zwar überraschend lyrisch. sibylle berg träumt ihrerseits von der perfekten wohnung und erklärt ihren abscheu vor privaten essenseinladungen. bestseller-autorin doris knecht geht den feinheiten des städtischen zusammenwohnens auf den grund, otto lechner, der vielleicht beste akkordeonist der welt, findet parallelen zwischen spielen und wohnen. und beschreibt die tücken, mit denen ein mensch zu kämpfen hat, der räume hört und fühlt – aber nicht sieht. das von der musikkritik gefeierte punk-folk-rap-duo attwenger wirft einen blick auf die details des lebens und hat auch für architekten einen so scharfsinnigen wie entwaffnend simplen tipp parat. der surrealistische maler, lyriker und literat roberto yanez betancourt y honecker entwirft ein hochhaus, in dem wir uns auch sehr gut poes raben vorstellen könnten, der am ende eines langen, dunklen ganges mit unzähligen, geheimnisvollen türen sitzt und unbeirrbar vor sich hinkrächzt. langweilige architekturbücher? nimmermehr!

die wunderbare schauspielerin anne bennent schließlich erinnert sich an frühe reisen nach griechenland – und sehnt sich nach fliegenden häusern, die dieses buch erstaunlicherweise für sie bereithält, so wie es hoffentlich auch jedem leser die eine oder andere fantasie erfüllt...

dafür, dass hier eigentlich nichts stehen sollte, hat sich mittlerweile doch einiges an text angesammelt. trotzdem noch ein kleiner leitfaden zur benutzung dieses buches:

nehmen sie es nicht zu wörtlich.
nehmen sie alles wörtlich, vor allem – vergessen sie architektur, die sich selbst zu wichtig nimmt.
heben sie ab, wenn ihnen danach ist.
bleiben sie auf dem boden.
klammern sie sich nicht an die ewigkeit.
bleiben sie beweglich.
bringen sie nicht alle schwarzbauten, auf die sie stoßen, zur anzeige.
glauben sie an ihre luftschlösser.
der titel des buches hat keine sexistische konnotation.
der titel des buches hat eine sexistische konnotation, wenn sie es so sehen. sprechen sie deshalb möglichst viele menschen in ihrer umgebung möglichst geschlechtsunabhängig mit schätzchen an, um dem entgegenzuwirken.
genießen sie...

»actually there should be nothing here«, andreas bovelino

architecture is narrative, it speaks for itself, say the architects. at least those who have not resorted to hot air, who are justified in their self-confidence, whose work itself is statement enough. like the guys that the next 419 pages are all about. günter katherl, martin haller, ulrich aspetsberger – caramel architects. ten years ago they founded an office in vienna, and from the very beginning were involved with what was happening on the scene. with spectacular buildings and competition entries, as well as with unusual performances. they gave the austrian capital the finest waste disposal centre in europe, covered the cultural capital of linz with a huge rustic but inviting tablecloth and let a baffled biennale audience in venice stand out in the rain. yet despite the playful lightness with which they seem to approach even the most serious tasks, there is nothing playful about the formal language that they use – everything makes sense. and makes a clear statement. after all, it's true that architecture is narrative, and if one listens carefully, it even tells stories. like the company building on the motorway, which feels so sexy in its black latex dress; or the house on a slope above the city, cantilevered so audaciously that it seems to flaunt the restrictions of statics, and be trying to fly.

however, if architecture is forced between two book covers, it often becomes speechless. the result: a book about architecture. not another one! beautiful books for leafing through, very decorative, so that they look good on bookshelves. a couple of clever texts by architectural critics for architectural critics, as far removed from life as possible, self-referential, smug and tedious. one hardly wants to read them, indeed one does not have to, on the contrary, they were not written for that purpose.

»nevermore!« to quote a not exactly unknown 19th century US author, whom one would perhaps not immediately associate with architecture. yet where would edgar allan poe's prose be without its atmospheric description of buildings? the family usher without a house, a glass of amontillado in a garden full of flowers – something essential would be missing. or, to use a slightly less gloomy example: would the sexual and emotional aberrations of john updike's protagonists be possible anywhere else than in the bright, clean, wooden houses of the american east coast? maybe they would, but they would then be of a fundamentally different nature, and completely different stories. just as we influence architecture with our own likes and dislikes, so it influences us too. each of us. it affects each of us – not only the professional critics. for most of our lives we are surrounded by architecture, as a matter of course. when we travel, then it is from the architecture to which we are accustomed to a foreign, unaccustomed architecture. we live, love, quarrel, enjoy and suffer »inside architecture«. in this respect, too, architecture tells stories. exciting ones, stories of desire, extraordinary or quite mundane ones. it is high time to present them in that light. to write about them in such a way that they are enjoyable to read. for everyone who has a home. for everyone who lives. a revolution? right, nothing less than that.

a revolution which is also joined by the architect and legendary critic friedrich achleitner, as guest author. and, namely, as a surprisingly lyrical one. sibylle berg, for her part, dreams of the perfect apartment, and explains her horror of invitations to private dinners. bestseller authoress doris knecht delves into the intricacies of urban communal living. otto lechner, perhaps the world's best accordionist, finds parallels between playing and living. and describes the perils which a human being has to face who hears and feels rooms – but does not see them. attwenger, the punk-folk-rap duo acclaimed by the music critics, takes a look at the details of life, and offers architects and others an astute yet disarmingly simple tip. surrealist painter, poet and author roberto yanez betancourt y honecker designs a high-rise building in which we could well imagine even poe's raven, sitting at the end of a long, dark corridor with innumerable mysterious doors and croaking away to itself imperturbably. boring architecture books? nevermore!

finally, the wonderful actress anne bennent remembers her early travels to greece – and yearns for flying houses. astonishingly enough, this book provides them for her, just as it hopefully fulfils some fantasy or other for each and every reader …

considering the fact that nothing is actually supposed to be here at all, quite a bit of text has accumulated in the meantime. nevertheless, here are a few tips for using this book:

don't take it too literally.
take everything literally, above all: forget any architecture that takes itself too seriously.
get high if you feel like it.
keep your feet on the ground.
don't get fixated on eternity.
stay mobile.
don't press charges against any buildings that you bump into in the grey zone.
believe in your castles in the air.
the title of this book does not have a sexist connotation.
the title of this book does have a sexist connotation, if you want to see it that way. for that reason, address as many people as possible in your immediate environment, gender-blind, as »sweetie pie«, in order to counteract that fact.
enjoy…

vergänglich

transient

forget eternal, everything is vergänglich

»können wir das schaffen? ja, wir schaffen das!«, doris knecht

am donnerstag hat mich die hausverwaltung angerufen: ob bei uns zufällig eingebrochen worden sei, unten an der haustür sei die scheibe neben dem türknauf eingeschlagen worden, die wega sei bereits alarmiert. das ist... das ist saudeppert, weil die koinzidenz es will, dass mir der gatte abends zuvor berichtet hat, er habe beim heimkommen irrtümlich eine scheibe an der haustür eingedrückt, und ja, doch er werde die hausverwaltung umgehend, sofort und gleich informieren. dann kriegte er einen anruf, dann musste er sofort weg und etwas erledigen, jetzt ist er bei der arbeit, danke, das problem pickt nun also an mir und ich manage es bravourös mit vielen ähs, öhs und entschuldigen's.

ich erledige auch den kurz darauf via haussprech-anlage einlangenden auftrag, über die die nachbarin freundlich anfragt, ob wir, wenn wir schon das ganze haus in einbruchspanik versetzen, wenigstens bitte die scherben zammkehren könnten. sicher. können wir. kann ich. ich meine, ein normaler mensch, der irrtümlich eine scheibe im haus einschlägt, würde danach wieder hinuntergehen und das gescherbs entfernen. aber. man kann, wenn man ein mann im stress ist, ersatzweise auch zweimal drübersteigen, es dann vergessen und damit unseren ruf als beliebteste altbau-bewohner zementieren.

wir sind die, die bei der balkonwässerung hauswände, offene fenster und ungünstig geparkte cabrios mitgießen. wir sind die, in deren stockwerk aufgrund nachlässig geschlossener lift-türen immer der aufzug steckt. wir sind die, die den aufzug ruinieren, in dem wir widerrechtlich das wochenend-gepäck damit hinunterfahren lassen, worauf dieses zwischen zwei stockwerken umkippt, worauf der lift stecken bleibt, worauf der wochenendaufzugsnotdienst und so fort. wir sind die, die immer vergessene schlüssel vom balkon werfen, die dann nicht in unserem besitz befindliche autodächer eindellen; die cabrios parken in so einem fall zuverlässig woanders. wir sind die, die dafür verantwortlich sind, dass in allen blumenkisteln des hauses nur noch löwenmäuler in allen farben blühen. wir sind die, die morgens um halbacht alle, die das noch nicht sind, wach machen, weil sich erziehungsberechtigte und kinder durchs treppenhaus noch etwas nach- beziehungsweise retourzubrüllen haben. wir sind die, vor deren tür sich ein berg aus kaputten elektrogeräten, ausrangierten regalen, alten rollern und zu klein gewordenen kindergummistiefeln auftürmt, was, wie ich der nachbarin mit mäßigem erfolg klarzumachen versuche, einbrecher keineswegs anlocke, sondern final abschrecke. wir sind die, denen die architektonischen und sozialen umstände im haus stets feindlich gesonnen sind, und die, die beim ganz normal wohnen immer am meisten umstände machen, und lärm, und dreck.

insofern ist es überaus bedauerlich, dass die zwei depperten aus dem dritten stock letztes jahr ausgezogen sind und durch eine dezente, freundliche und ordentliche familie ersetzt wurden, die, anders als die zwei depperten, nicht beim kochen einschläft, nie die tschick auf der stiege austritt, nie nicht grüßt und nie nachts betrunken durchs treppenhaus marodiert. jetzt hängt es an uns, die allgemeine lebensqualität im haus konsequent zu nivellieren. und, yo, wir schaffen das.

»can we do it? yes we can do it!«, doris knecht

on thursday the apartment building management phoned me to ask whether, by any chance, we had had a burglary, because the window next to the handle on the front door of the building had been broken, and the special police unit had already been alarmed. that's... that's really stupid, because it so happened that my husband told me the evening before that when he came home he mistakenly broke a window by the front door of the building, and yes, of course he was going to inform the house owners as soon as he could, immediately, right away. but then he got a phone call, and had to leave immediately to do something, he's at work at the moment and so, thank you very much, now i'm stuck with the problem and am dealing with it valiantly with a great many ahs, ohs and i'm-very-sorrys.

i also deal with a demand made shortly afterwards via the building intercom, through which our neighbour amicably asks whether, since we have already created a state of panic in the whole building, we couldn't at least sweep up the pieces of broken glass. of course we can. i can. i mean, any normal person who accidentally smashes a pane of glass in a block of flats, would afterwards go down and clear up the broken pieces. nevertheless, as we all know, when a man is in stress, he will instead step over them, even twice, and then forget about them, thereby consolidating our reputation as the most popular inhabitants of the old apartment block.

we are the ones who, when we water the plants on the balcony, also water along with them the walls of the apartment building, and any open windows or unfavourably parked sports cars. we are the ones on whose floor the lift always gets stuck as a result of carelessly closed lift doors. we are the ones who ruin the lift because, against the rules, we send down our pieces of weekend luggage in it and they subsequently fall over between two floors, so that the elevator gets stuck, and so the weekend emergency elevator service has to be called and so on and so forth. we are the ones who are always throwing the keys that we have forgotten down from the balcony, and they then make a dent in the roofs of cars that do not belong to us; in such situations, the sports cars are always dependably parked somewhere else. we are the ones who are responsible for the fact that the only plant that blossoms in the building's flower pots are snapdragons of all colours. we are the ones who, at half past seven in the morning, wake up all those who are not already awake, because as parents and children we have to shout something afterwards or back down the staircase. we are the ones in front of whose door there piles up a mountain of broken electronic equipment, discarded shelves, old scooters and children's wellingtons that have grown too small, concerning which i try, with only moderate success, to explain to our neighbour that it would at any rate not tempt burglars, but rather scare them away. we are the ones who always have a hostile attitude to the architectural conditions and social circumstances in our block of flats, yet who always make the most trouble and noise and mess as far as the things of everyday life are concerned.

in this respect, it is most regrettable that the two idiots on the third floor moved out last year and were replaced by a decent, friendly and orderly family, who – unlike the two idiots – do not fall asleep while they are cooking, never stub out their cigarettes on the stairs, never fail to greet other people and never come home drunk at night, marauding up the staircase. now it is up to us to systematically even out the general quality of life in our block of flats. and, yes, we can do it!

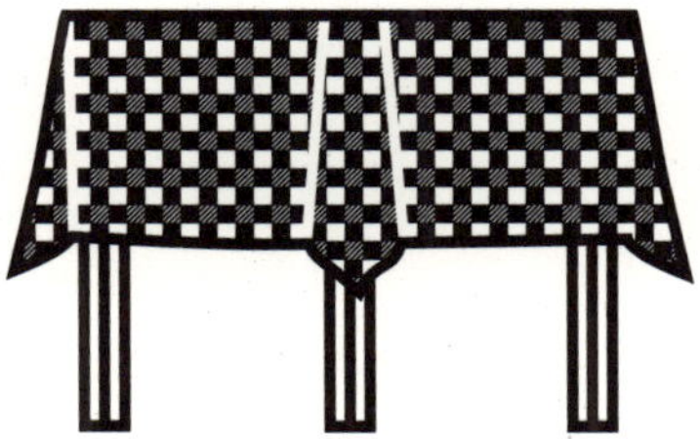

LINZ09 INFOCENTER

info_point linz09

linz kulturhauptstadt europas // linz cultural capital of europe

linz ist provinz; reimt sich und wurde schon oft und gerne gebraucht. und: es stimmt auch. das ist prinzipiell nicht schlimm. schlimm wird es nur, wenn versucht wird, aus diesem zustand heraus besonders urban oder »gestylt« aufzutreten. die antwort kann als augenzwinkernder verweis auf die regionalität verstanden werden; natürlich auch als einladende geste: das karierte tischtuch als symbol der gastlichkeit.
und mehr als dieses überdimensionale tischtuch tritt auch nicht in erscheinung. keine infos durch große beschilderung, durch fahnen oder fassadenbeschriftung; der infopoint soll sich selbst erklären...

der umgang mit dem physischen bestand:
vor der eigentlichen fassade befand sich eine massive steinwand, die als barriere gegen den besucher wirkte, diese wurde von den architekten mit einer vorgelagerten holzkonstruktion aus treppen und sitzstufen egalisiert. ganz ohne störendes beiwerk. dadurch wird der besucher zum betreten der künstlichen landschaft geradezu aufgefordert.

linz is province; it rhymes and has frequently been used. moreover, it's true. in principle, it is nothing bad. it would be bad if there were an attempt to use this fact to create an especially urban or stylish image. the answer can be understood as an eye-winking reference to regionalism; of course, also as a gesture of invitation: the checkered tablecloth as a symbol of hospitality. nothing more than this over-dimensional tablecloth is to be seen. no information using large-scale signposting, flags or lettering on the façade; the infopoint should be self-explanatory ...

the approach to the physical volume:
in front of the actual facade there was a massive stone wall that seemed to form a barrier against the visitors. the effect of this was mitigated by the architects, who placed a wooden construction in front of it, comprising steps and terraced seating. without the use of any disturbing accessories whatsoever. in this way, the visitor is virtually encouraged to step into the artificial landscape.

die linzer brückenkopfgebäude in denen der infopoint raum fand, sind die beiden einzigen realisierten projekte von hitlers geplanter »kulturhauptstadt« linz. sehr wichtig war es den architekten, mit dem historisch belasteten bestand möglichst »nicht in berührung« zu kommen. so wurde ein einziger neuer layer, einem tuch gleich, auf den bestehenden boden gelegt. dieser wölbt sich zu möbelstücken auf und endet letzlich als paravant mit distanz zum bestand.

the buildings of the linz bridge head, where space had been allocated for the infopoint, are the only two projects that were implemented when linz was being planned as hitler's »cultural capital«. it was a matter of great concern not to »come into contact« with the historically incriminating volume as far as possible. because of this, the only new layer, resembling a cloth, was placed on the existing floor. this arches up as pieces of furniture and finally ends as a folding screen at a distance to the volume.
infopoint linz09

das material der landschaft durchdringt die thermische fassade (wobei die ursprünglich kleinteiligen portalverglasungen gegen möglichst großflächige und profillose glaselemente ausgewechselt wurden) und bildet auch im rauminneren so etwas wie eine landschaft (pulte, präsentationsflächen etc). einerseits dringt so der hauptplatz in den infobereich ein, andererseits läuft der infobereich zum hauptplatz hin aus.

the material of the landscape is dominated by the thermal facade (the original fragmented portal glazing was exchanged for undivided glass elements of maximum size), and also forms something like a landscape on the inside of the space (lectern, presentation areas etc). on the one hand, the main square intrudes into information area, on the other hand, the information area emerges into the main square.

holzkonstruktion mit eingesetzten kunststoff-
elementen; außen osb mit polyurethanbeschich-
tung, innen mit epoxyharzbeschichtung
construction walls: wooden construction -
including the use of synthetic elements
floors: exterior osb, coated with polyurethane,
interior with epoxy resin

CaramelSYS
new game
score
shootings

ego shooter

häuserkampf, fsk 18+ // house-to-house fighting, fsk 18+

installation auf der »blickfang« im museum für angewandte kunst.
des bauherrn albtraum: die »caramelhäuser« mutiert, unter wasser, in vollbrand. die drei architekten auch ein wenig verändert; darunter ein videoschirm mit spielkonsole; der spieler bewegt sich durch gebautes und geplantes; allerdings immer auf der hut vor angreifern – und selbst schwer bewaffnet. nur die härtesten kommen durch. die etwas andere art von architektur-sightseeing …

installation on the »blickfang« at the museum of the applied art.
an owner's nightmare: caramel's houses mutated, under water, or fully ablaze; the three architects are also rather altered; a video screen with a game pad is included; the player moves through completed buildings and buildings that are in planning; however, always on the lookout for attackers – who may even be heavily armed. only the toughest survive. a rather different kind of architectural sightseeing …

wettbewerb / competition
transfusionsmedizin / transfusion medicine
1. preis / 1st prize salzburg 2001

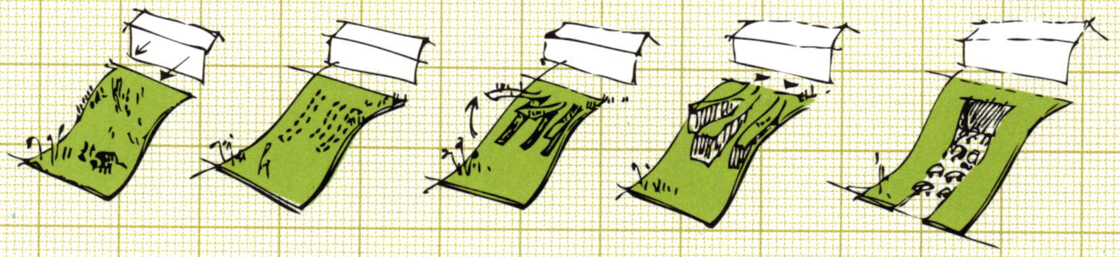

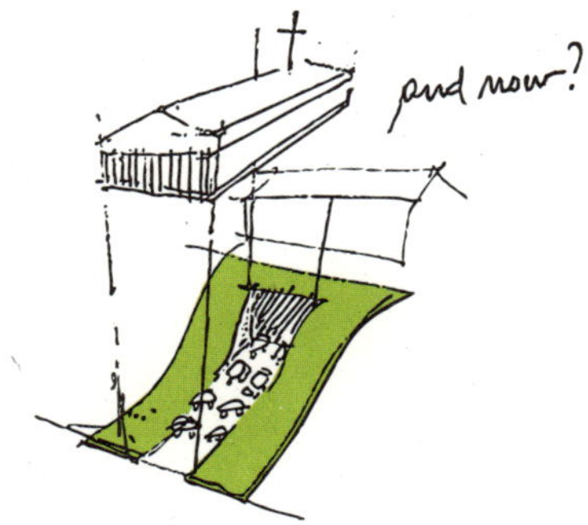
and now?

transfusionsmedizin

schade um den raren grünbereich; viel ist nicht mehr da am areal des salzburger langeskrankenhauses.
das wettbewerbsgrundstück liegt am zur bahnstrecke hin kaskadenartig abfallenden grünen rand; hau ruck, den böschungsverlauf aufgefaltet – schon gibt ein dach den nötigen raum für die transfusionsmedizin und die landesapotheke!
entlang des bestehenden unterirdischen ganges wird durch eine bohrpfahlwand die geländekante gesichert. die trennwände sind als leichtbauwände ausgeführt. die vorgehängte nurglasfassade besteht aus paneel- und glaselementen, die öffenbaren flügel sind flächenbündig in die paneelelemente eingesetzt.

pity about the sparse greenery; there's not much left on the site of the salzburg regional hospital.
the competition site lies on the green periphery that descends towards of the railway line like a cascade; heave ho! the line of the embankment unfolds – and already there's a roof to provide the necessary space for the institute of transfusion medicine and the local chemist's! along the existing underground corridor, the edge of the site is secured by means of a bored pile wall. the separating walls are executed as lightweight walls. the curtain-type glass-only facade consists of panels and glass elements, the casements, which can be opened, are set flush into the panel elements.

der tiefbau ist zwar aufwändig, aber rasch fertiggestellt; so wie die gesamte planung des bauwerkes, bis ins kleinste detail. nach einem jahr bauzeit überlegt es sich die politik dann anders...

excavation may be hard work, but it is soon completed; like all the planning for the building, right down to the smallest detail. then after a year's construction work, the politicians come up with a different idea...

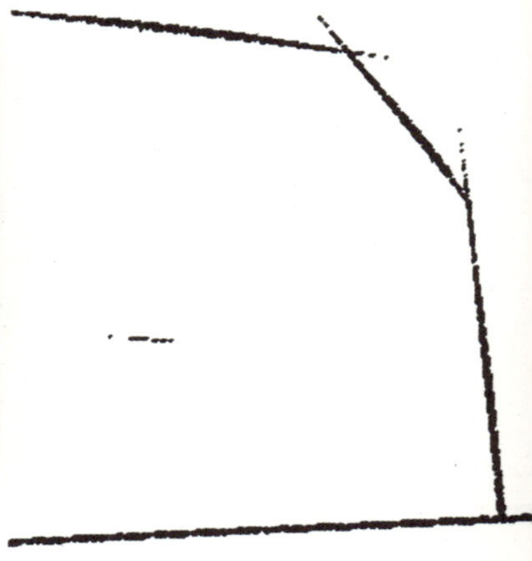

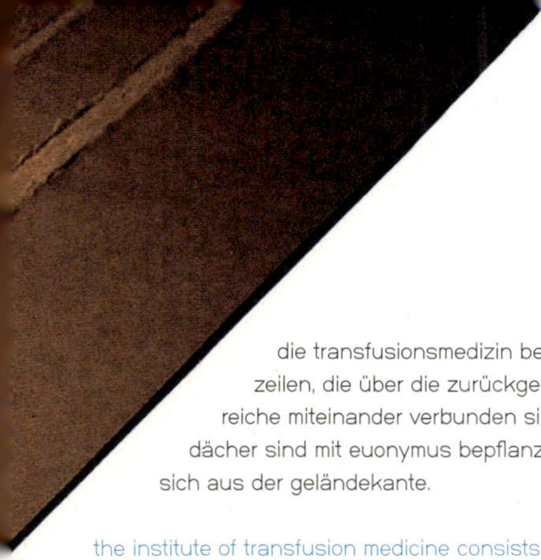

die transfusionsmedizin besteht aus drei wellenförmigen zeilen, die über die zurückgesetzten erschließungsbereiche miteinander verbunden sind. die aufsteigenden dächer sind mit euonymus bepflanzt und modellieren sich aus der geländekante.

the institute of transfusion medicine consists of three wavelike lines that are connected to one another via access areas that have been set back. the wavelike roofs have been planted with euonymus plants and modelled from the edge of the site.

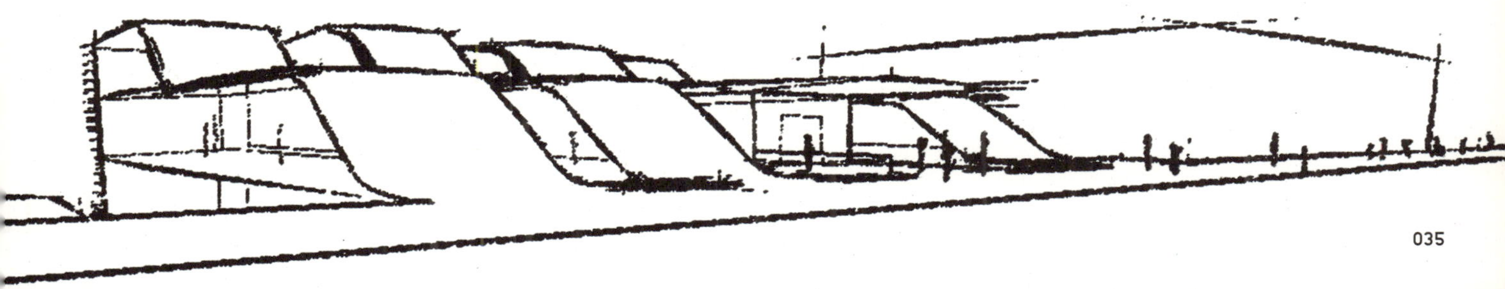

?
bubbles spielen

oxygen tents

ausstellungsgestaltung lentos kunstmuseum linz // exhibition design lentos artmuseum linz

die bisherigen präsentationen in basel, düsseldorf und rom beschränkten sich auf das ausstellen von modellen und plänen/grafiken: ohne austellungsarchitektur.
kritik: extrem »trockene« anhäufung von statischer information.
ziel der konzeption: mehrwert durch unerwartetes; dynamisieren ohne sich abgenutzter termini wie interaktivität zu bedienen, durch analoge animation materialien uminterpretiert; die eternitplatte wird zum sich bewegenden blatt. die starren modelle werden mit weichen beweglichen pneus umhüllt: pneumatische käseglocken.

previous presentations in basel, düsseldorf and rome were limited to the exhibition of models and plans/ graphic works, without any exhibition architecture.
criticism: extremely »dry« accumulation of statistical information.
aim of the concept: added value through unexpected elements; dynamisation without using outworn termini such as interaction, reinterpretation of materials through analogue animation; the eternit panel becomes a page that moves rigid; models are enveloped by soft moveable tyres: pneumatic cheese covers.

kurator / curator: andrea bina

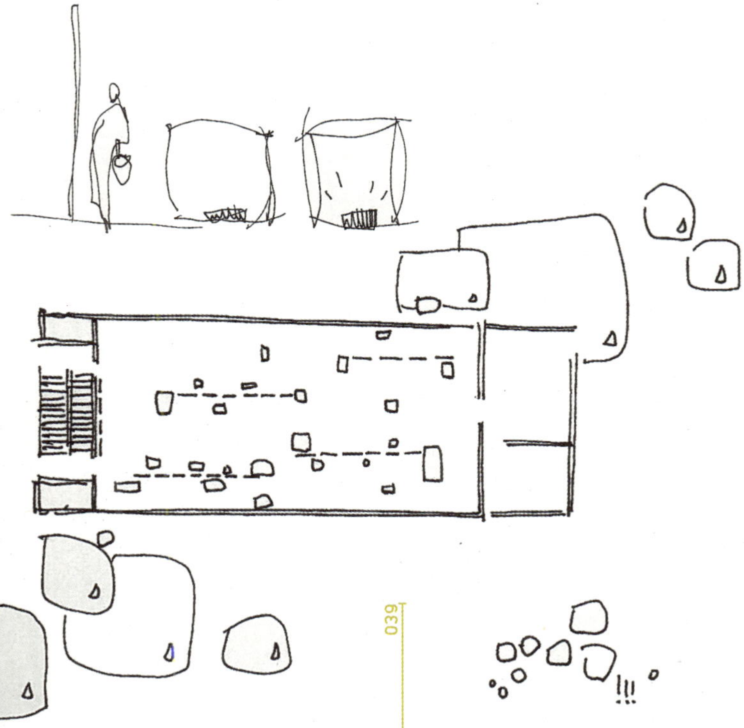

wettbewerb / competition
justizzentrum / court house wien 3
preis / prize wien 2008

justizzentrum wien 3

liebe grüsse aus dem knast! // greetings from prison!

nicht sühneanstalt – besserungsanstalt! mit licht und luft, freibereichen – und antidepressiva als fassade. städtebaulich fügt sich das gebäude in die straßenfluchten ein, bildet einen großzügigen, lichtdurchfluteten hof aus und schafft mit unterschiedlichen terrassen- und dachflächen nutzbare freibereiche. kein spaß. sondern das ernsthafte bestreben möglichst gute bedingungen für die insassen zu schaffen.

not a place of atonement – a place of improvement! using light and air, open-air spaces – and the facade as an anti-depressant. as far as urban development is concerned, the building fits in with the streetscape, forms a spacious well-lit courtyard, and creates utilisable open-air spaces by means of various terraces and roof areas. not a joke. rather, an earnest attempt to create the best possible conditions for the inmates.

die dachflächen werden als freiflächen genutzt. neben dem hofbereich dienen sie den insassen als bewegungs- und sportplätze.

the roof areas are used as open spaces. beside the courtyard area they serve the inmates as places for movement and sports.

wer erinnert sich an werbung von gestern? vergänglich die sujets – der entstehungsort blieb.

who remembers yesterday's advertising? the subject is ephemeral – but the location is retained.

reklame

umbau werbeagentur // conversion advertising agency

eines der ersten projekte von caramel entstand in einer ausgedienten lagerhalle am linzer hafen. eine werbeagentur benötigte mehr fläche. schnell, um wenig geld. die rohen stahlbetonstrukturen und der gussasphaltboden des lagerraumes wurden nicht nur erhalten, sie prägen den charakter des neuadaptierten innenraumes. mit einfachen industriellen materialien wurden räume für die bedürfnisse der nutzer geschaffen. ausgezeichnet im rahmen des landeskulturpreises oberösterreich.

one of caramel's first projects was executed in a disused warehouse on the harbour in linz. an advertising agency needed more space. quickly, at a low cost. the untreated reinforced-concrete structures and the mastic-asphalt floors of the warehouse were not only retained, but allowed to dominate the character of the newly adapted interior. using simple industrial materials, rooms suitable for the needs of the user were created. awarded a prize for regional culture by the province of upper austria.

in zusammenarbeit / in cooperation with friedrich stiper

wettbewerb / competition
seniorenheim / home for the elderly
preis / prize gaspoltshofen 2007

seniorenheim gaspoltshofen

warum sehen altenheime immer gleich aus? die frage können wohl nur die errichtergesellschaften beantworten; caramel kümmert sich nicht um »das ist halt so« und »das wurde immer so gemacht«, sondern entwirft einen neuen typus des seniorenwohnens: kleinteilige, lichtdurchflutete wohngruppen mit allgemeinbereichen, denen außenräume zugeordnet sind. die wohngruppen sind miteinander verbunden. die entstehenden einzelhäuser korrespondieren mit der umliegenden kleinteiligen bebauung.

why do homes for the elderly always look the same? the question can probably only be answered by the companies that build them; caramel disregards replies such as »that's just the way it is« and »it's always been like that«, and instead proceeds to conceive a new type of home for the elderly: apartment groups divided up into small sections, filled with light and including communal areas, to which outdoor rooms are also adjoined. the apartment groups are connected to one another. the ensuing individual buildings correspond to the surrounding small-scale development.

die elemente selbst liegen im park; der bildet gewissermaßen
auch die fassade aus – eine grüne vegetationsschicht
umhüllt die thermische fassade und bietet einen blühenden,
lebendigen sonnenschutz.

the elements themselves are situated in the park, which
virtually forms the façade, with a green layer of vegetation
enveloping the thermal facade and offering living, flowering
sun protection.

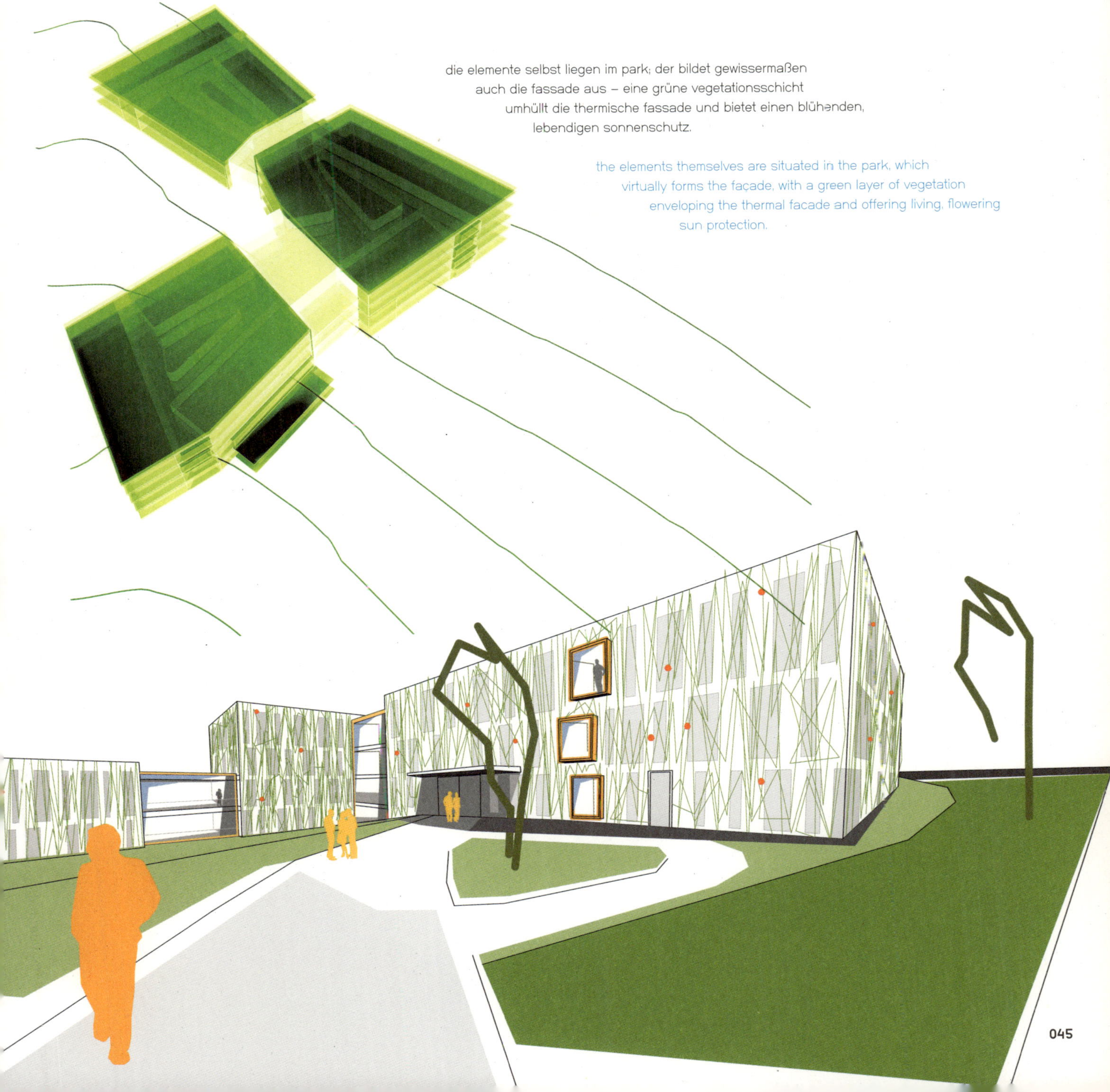

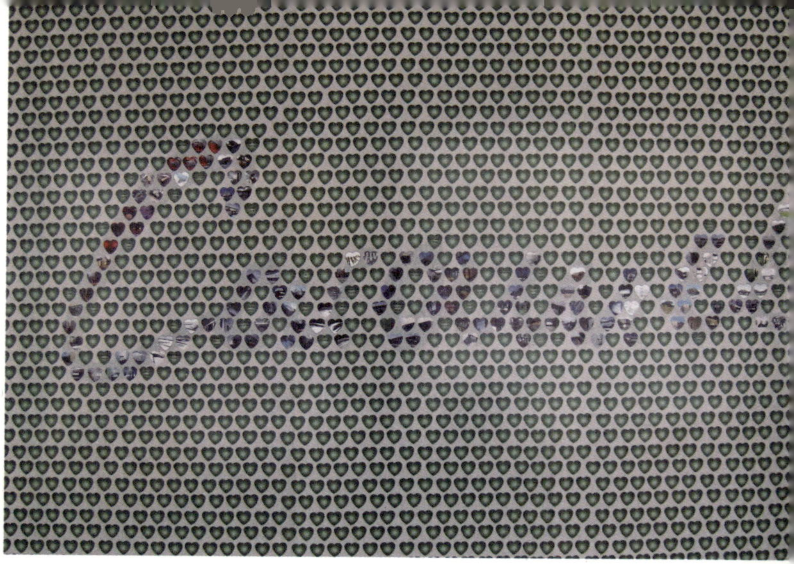

živi na Coca-Cola strani života
živi na Coca-Cola strani života

tapete belgrad

ein raum in belgrad // a space in belgrade

die architekturvereinigung belgrad lud caramel ein, ihre ausstellungsräume im zentrum der serbischen hauptstadt temporär zu gestalten.
statt schwere modelle aufzustellen, klatschten die architekten ihren herzensgruß an die wand.

the architectural association of belgrade invited caramel to create a temporary design for its exhibition rooms in the centre of the serbian capital.
instead of erecting heavy models, the architects slapped their own cordial greetings on the wall.

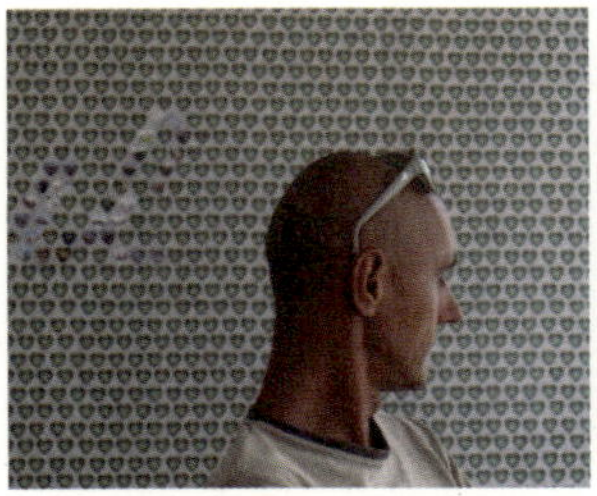

wettbewerb / competition
schulzentrum / school centre
1. preis / 1st prize krems 2002

schulzentrum krems

vergängliche freude // ephemeral pleasure

wettbewerbe gewinnen und dann nicht bauen – vieler architekten schicksal. dem 70er-jahre funktionsbau wurde im wettbewerbsbeitrag als erweiterung eine hübsche banane appliziert. nun erhielte die schule endlich ihren pausenhof, wohlverdient, nach 40 jahren.

winning competitions and then not building – the fate of many architects. in the competition entry, a pretty banana was added as an extension to the functional building of the 1970s. then, after 40 years, the school would finally have received its well-deserved school yard.

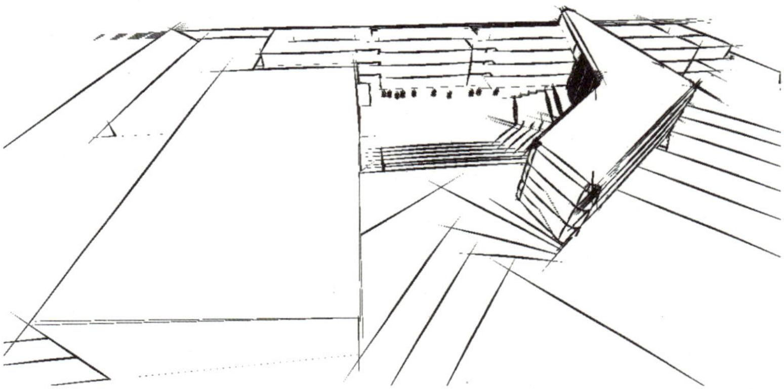

Caramel

mak nite

heiße luft // hot air

»heiße luft« ist das motto der architekturgruppe caramel, wenn sie im rahmen einer mak nite die große säulenhalle des museums mit 50.000 x luft füllt und optisch bespielt. durch den eintritt des besuchers in den wandelbaren raum wird die installation zum leben erweckt, quillt über und in angrenzende räume des maks und auf die straße. schlussendlich wird ganz wien überflutet – von lebendiger architektur.

(pressetext zur maknite im april 2001)

»hot air« is the motto adopted by the architecture group caramel when, as part of a mak nite at the museum for applied arts, the museum's great colonnaded hall is filled with 50,000 x air, into which optical effects are projected. the installation is brought to life by the visitors entering the transformable space, spilling over into the adjacent rooms of the museum of applied art and onto the street. in the end, the whole of vienna is flooded – with living architecture.
(press release for the maknite in april 2001)

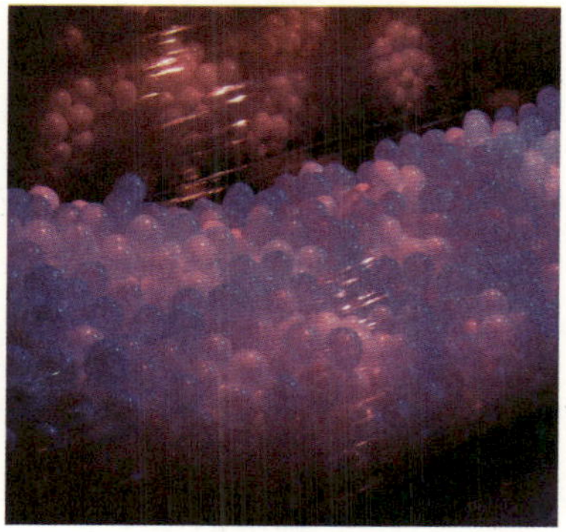

music & visuals:
lethemknowitsus

licht / light: heinz kasper, ars et lux
aufbau / assembly: caramel & lots of friends

abgehoben

uplifted

but don't forget abgehobenes, schätzchen

»träumen sie auch so oft von wohnungen?«, sibylle berg

sicher heißt das irgendwas, da ich aber ein schlichtes gemüt bin, nehme ich träume immer 1:1 und denke nach einem gelungenen wohnungstraum nur: potzblitz, ne hübsche wohnung war das wieder. finde ich im traum ein objekt, das mir gefällt, besuche ich es immer wieder. im moment ist es eine langgestreckte wohnung mit einem alten glasdach, schweren holzbohlen, bibliotheken, manufactum möbeln (oder so etwas in der art) und einem bach neben der tür. mit bachsitzplatz quasi.

im wirklichen leben wohne ich immer irgendwie und staune mithin, wenn ich bei erwachsenen zu besuch bin. dieses seltsame gefühl, das sich entwickelt, wenn man in einer besonders raffinierten straße vor einem speziell gelungenem haus steht. efeu, wintergärten, das volle programm. dann betritt man eine perfekte wohnung und das gefühl wird groß und mächtig und immer verwechsel ich es in den ersten minuten mit schlichtem neid. überwältigt stehe ich auf teakböden, große flügeltüren locken auf terrassen, die über den see blicken, wenn es warm wird, werden da vermutlich flauschige himmelbetten stehen – in der wohnung sicher ein zweites geschoss, wie kann man ohne zweites geschoss leben, italienische liegen, damastbettwäsche, luken in die man schmutzwäsche wirft, die gleitet dann wie ein luchs in eine waschküche, 230 m², das braucht man zu zweit, wir wollen uns ja nicht auf den wecker gehen, sagen die bewohner der perfekten wohnung, und alles klar, denke ich.

dann sitzt du da, an einem tisch, feuerlandkirsche, 50 kg, ein essen wird serviert, verschiedene gänge, die gastgeber sind auch brillante köche und reden über balsamico. das, was ich am anfang für neid hielt ist unterdes zur lähmung geworden. die wohnung, der lebensentwurf, alles scheint mich demütigen zu wollen. mit meinen nun bald 120 jahren lebe ich immer noch in einem ständigen provisorium. ich hatte noch nie eine perfekte wohnung, sondern nur immernur die, die gerade da war und dann wurde eine andere gesucht. wie jetzt gerade.

demütigung, sprach ich schon davon? erst auf der immobilienseite die feinsten kreise eingeben, im fall zürich: innenstadt. bahnhofstraße, altstadt, sowas eben. normal. wenn man 10 tausend franken im monat ausgeben möchte. nun mal nicht gejammert, wer sich die schweiz nicht leisten kann, soll getrost nach österreich ziehen. oder zurück nach deutschland. von da kommen jetzt eh alle, die einem die wohnungen wegschnappen. und schon wieder fast vergessen, über all meinem patriotismus, dass ich da auch mal herkam.

themenwechsel schnell. dass das zahlen von fetten mieten kein garant für wohnglück ist, hat uns frau kaas gelehrt, die 16 tausend für ein aquarium ausgab, in dem sie sich erstaunlicher weise beobachtet fühlte, weil gegenüber und links und rechts auch aquarien standen. mit unverhohlener schadenfreude sah ich die verhaltensauffällige frau kaas durch diese wohnung eiern, immer korrekt bekleidet, das licht aus. diese modernen gehäuse, die alle gleich aussehen, betonwände, offene küche, der prototyp ist in zürich über dem rif raf kino zu beobachten. ein oder zwei junge männer, es fällt mir schwer die auseinander zu halten, mit diesen immergleichen dummen haarschnitten, jeans, pullunder, scheinen da ein wohnprojekt zu machen. in voller beleuchtung spielen sie in ihrer wohnung e-gitarre, haben das zeug als einrichtung, das heute jeder hat, eames chair, usb haller zeug und witzige flohmarktklamotten (ich mixe immer markenkleidung mit flohmarktstücken), und darin bewegen sie sich, für jeden sichtbar. die lofts sind die reihenhäuser von heute.

wo war ich stehengeblieben? ich suchte ein jahr, solange wie ich in meiner jetzigen wohnung wohnte, eine andere. oh, dinge erlebt man da, über die ich nicht schreibe, denn die launigen aufsätze über teppichböden mit vertretereiweißflecken, bordellen im haus, und methadonausgabestellen im keller kennt man. wohin ich jetzt ziehe ist relativ egal, denn es wird wieder nicht die perfekte wohnung sein, und da offenbart sich etwas grundlegendes. es gibt menschen die sind für das ultimative gemacht, und andere, die sich bis zum ende durchfrickeln werden. gardinen annageln, weil man keine ahnung hat, wiedie dinger sonst halten sollen, möbel, wozu möbel? die muss man ja wieder in die nächste wohnung transportieren und, alter schwede, was manche menschen für ein zeug haben. männer kommen und schleppen klaviere. was für wundervolle witze es über klaviertransporte gibt, aber wozu ein klavier, wenn man nicht pianist ist? eine freundin fragte jüngst nach meinem esstisch. esstisch, mein mund öffnete sich, vielleicht rann ein wenig speichel aus ihm. esstisch, eine verrückte idee. nahrung wird zu bett oder auf dem boden eingenommen, und gäste in der wohnung werde ich nie verstehen. wozu menschen der schmach von zuviel intimität aussetzen, wenn es restaurants gibt. möglich, dass ich so etwas wie einen auf gäste und meine wohnung bezogenen waschzwang habe, mir ist es unangenehm, in den höhlen anderer leute zu stehen. zu intim, zuviel informationen, ich will nicht sehen, was sich andere ins gesicht schmieren, zahnbürsten mit speiseresten, toiletten wo klar wird, wie der gatte ausscheidet, knoblauchgeruch aus der spüle, und zu wissen, dass der staubballen unter dem bett sich aus hausschuppen geformt hat, spinne ich, oder geht das, was menschen in ihren höhlen machen, wirklich keinen anderen was an?

und dann muss man da sitzen, und stolz wird zeug aufgetischt, selber gekocht, und dann muss ich sagen, fleisch ess ich nicht, und alkohol an soßen ess ich nicht, und soßen ess ich nicht, und nein esst nur kleine lämmchen, das ist ok, ich nehme etwas von diesem rosenkohl, den ich hasse und weine wegen des lämmchens – ich hasse das. wer zu geizig ist in ein restaurant zu gehen und mich einzuladen, soll es doch grad alles sein lassen. nun, das tun die bekannten die ich habe dann auch, nach hundert absagen und nie erfolgten gegeneinladungen ist der ruf als kauz irgendwann manifestiert. je älter ich werde, um so eingerichteter werden meine bekannten. mit esstischen, abgezogenen parketts, neubezogenenen bauhausliegen, und eigenheimen. das ist das thema jetzt: wie, du willst nichts kaufen? das ist die beste anlage und die hypotheken so günstig im moment.
sehen wir davon ab, dass ich nicht weiß, was eine hypothek ist, verunsichern mich solcherlei fragen fast so wie die nach einem esstisch. muss ich jetzt etwas kaufen? wie soll man das bezahlen, ist nur eine frage. dann schaue ich mit schlechtem gewissen villen am comer see für ein paar milliarden an, aber ich glaube, so ist das nicht gemeint. die bekannten kaufen dreiraumwohnungen in orten wie forch, trödiswil und oberau.
der begriff: loftüberbauung. fällt oft. die bekannten ziehen also eine stunde außerhalb der stadt in so einen beton-aquariumkasten, stellen perfekte möbel auf, und sitzen da, für immer, und warten auf besuch zum abendbrot. (esstisch) das grauen endet in der regel mit dem ableben, und dann stehen die enkel in der bis dahin völlig unmodern gewordenen betonklitsche und müssen alte interiosofas entsorgen. aber daran denkt von den perfekteinrichtern natürlich keiner.

die sucht nach perfektion ist vermutlich nur der irrglaube, sich in der zeit zu manifestieren, für immer. je perfekter die oberfläche, um so unmöglicher scheint die unperfektion des späten alters und todes darin vorstellbar. siechen auf eileen grey? mit dem rollstuhl durch puls 5 buden brettern? (puls 5 für nichtzürcher: urbanes elend in beton, singles und junge paare überschuldet in glaskästen).

perfektes wohnen ist ein bisschen wie tot sein. was soll noch kommen, wenn alles schon da ist? doch vielleicht ist das gefühl, das ich in perfekten wohnungen empfinde, doch nichts weiter als neid. vielleicht würde ich wissen, wie glück wirklich geht, säße ich in dieser wohnung, von der mir immer träumt, mit bachsitzplatz. wer kann das wissen.

»do you dream about houses and flats as often as i do?«, sybille berg

it definitely must mean something, yet because i am of a simple nature, i always take dreams 1:1 and after a successful housing dream, all i can think is: wow, that was another pretty apartment! whenever i find a place in my dreams that i like, i visit it again and again. at the moment, it is an elongated apartment with an old glass roof, heavy timber planking, libraries, furniture from manufactum (or somewhere similar) and a stream outside the door. practically seated on a stream.

in real life, i always live any old how and am astonished when i visit grown-up people. that strange feeling that arises when one stands in tastefully designed streets in front of an especially successful house. ivy, a conservatory, the whole works. then one enters a perfect house and there is a feeling of grandeur and power, which i always confuse with simple envy during the first few minutes. i stand there on the teak flooring, overwhelmed, big double-wing doors enticing me to the terraces and the view of the lake, when it gets hot, fleecy four-poster beds are presumably put out there – there is certainly a second storey in the apartment, how can one live without a second storey, italian couches, damask bed linen, hatches into which one throws the dirty washing, so that it slides, like a lynx, down into a laundry room, 230 m², a couple needs that, in order to live together, we don't want to get in each other's hair, say the inhabitants of the perfect apartment, and i think to myself: say no more.

then you're sitting there, at a table, chilean cherry, 50 kg, a meal is served, various courses, the hosts are also brilliant cooks and talk about balsamico. what i at first perceived as envy has in the meantime become paralysis. the apartment, the lifestyle, everything seems to want to humiliate me. now almost 120 years old, i still live in a constantly makeshift way. i never had a perfect apartment, but rather always only those that happened to be there, and then i looked for another one. as is the case right now.

humiliation, have i already mentioned that?
first, type in the best districts on the property website, in the case of zurich: the city centre. bahnhofstraße, altstadt, something like that. normal. if one wants to spend 10 thousand francs a month. still, no cause for complaint, anyone who can't afford switzerland, can move to austria. or back to germany. after all, that's where they all come from now, they're the ones taking away all the apartments. almost forgotten again, for all my patriotism, that i, too, came here once upon a time. change the subject quickly. the fact that the figures of big rents are no guarantee for housing bliss we learned from frau kaas, who paid 16,000 for an aquarium, in which, astonishingly enough, she felt she was being observed, because opposite her and to her left and right there were also aquaria. with an unashamed sense of schadenfreude i saw behaviourly dysfunctional frau kaas, toddling round her apartment, always correctly dressed, with all the lights out.

these modern dwellings that all look the same, concrete walls, open kitchen, in zurich the prototype can be seen above the rif raf cinema. one or two young men, i find it difficult to tell them apart, they all have the same stupid haircuts, jeans and sleeveless pullovers, seem to be embarking on a communal living project there. with all the lights on, they play electric guitars in their apartment, and have all the furnishing objects that everyone has today, eames chair, stuff from usb haller and quirky clothes from the fleamarket (i always mix brand name clothing with fleamarket items), and they move about in them, visible to everyone. the lofts are the terraced houses of today.

now, where was i? i was looking for another apartment for a year, which is as long as i have lived in my present one. o the things that one then experiences, about which i shall not write, because one is familiar with all the humorous essays about carpets displaying the salesmen's protein stains, brothels in the building, and methadone distribution points in the basement. it doesn't really matter where i move to now, because it will once again not be the perfect apartment, and that is where something fundamental becomes evident. there are people who are made for the ultimate, and others who will always muddle their way through to the end. nailing up the curtains because one has no idea how the things are supposed to stay up, furniture, why furniture? it only has to be transported again to the next apartment and well, my old swede, what a lot of stuff some people do have. men come and carry pianos. what wonderful jokes there are about piano removals, but why have a piano if one is not a pianist? a friend of mine recently asked about my dining table. dining table, my mouth opened, perhaps a little bit of saliva dribbled out. dining table, a crazy idea. food is eaten in bed or on the floor, and i will never understand the idea of having guests in one's apartment. why subject people to the ignominy of too much intimacy, when there are restaurants. it is possible that i have something akin to ablutomania in relation to guests and my apartment, it makes me uncomfortable to stand in the caves of other people. too intimate, too much information, i do not want to see what other people put on their faces, toothbrushes with food leftovers, toilets where it is evident how the husband excretes, smell of garlic from the sink, and to know that the balls of dust under the bed are formed from house scurf, am i going bonkers, or is it really nobody else's business what people do in their caves?

and then one has to sit there, and the stuff is proudly dished up, homemade, and then i have to say – i don't eat meat, and i don't eat sauces with alcohol, and i don't eat sauces, no eat your little lamb, that's ok, i'll just have some of these brussels sprouts that i hate, and cry on account of the little lamb – i hate it. anyone who is too mean to go to a restaurant and treat me, should just forget it. well, that is what acquaintances of mine do, and i do still have some, even though, after a hundred cancellations and no forthcoming reciprocal invitations, one does gain a reputation for being a weirdo at some point or other. the older i get, the more furnished my acquaintances become. with dining tables, stripped parquet floors, newly upholstered bauhaus couches, and their own homes. that's the burning question of the day: what, you don't want to buy? it's the best investment, and mortgages are so reasonable at the moment. quite apart from the fact that i don't even know what a mortgage is, such questions unsettle me almost as much as the one about a dining table. do i have to buy something now? how should i pay for it? that is only one of my questions. then i look with a bad conscience at villas on lake como for a couple of billions, but i don't think that's what they really meant. these acquaintances buy 3-room apartments in places like forch, trödiswil or oberau. the term 'loft construction' is often heard. so the acquaintances move an hour out of town into a concrete aquarium, fit it up with perfect furniture, and sit there forever, waiting for a visit at suppertime (dining table). the torture generally comes to an end with one's demise, and then the grandchildren are left with the little concrete hole that has in the meantime become totally unfashionable, and it is they who have to dispose of the old interio sofas. yet of course, none of the perfect furnishers think about that.

the search for perfection is presumably only a popular misconception about attaining self-manifestation in time, for eternity. the more perfect the appearance, the more impossible does it seem to be to imagine the imperfection of old age and death behind it. to waste away on an eileen grey? to bomb through the dens of puls 5 in a wheelchair? (for non-zurich citizens, puls 5 is urban misery in concrete: insolvent singles and young couples in glass boxes).

perfect housing is a bit like being dead. what can still happen, if everything is already there? yet perhaps the feeling that i have in perfect apartments really is nothing more than envy. perhaps i would then know how happiness actually works, if i were sitting in that apartment that i am always dreaming about, with a bench overlooking a stream. who can know.

LECKER
CARAME

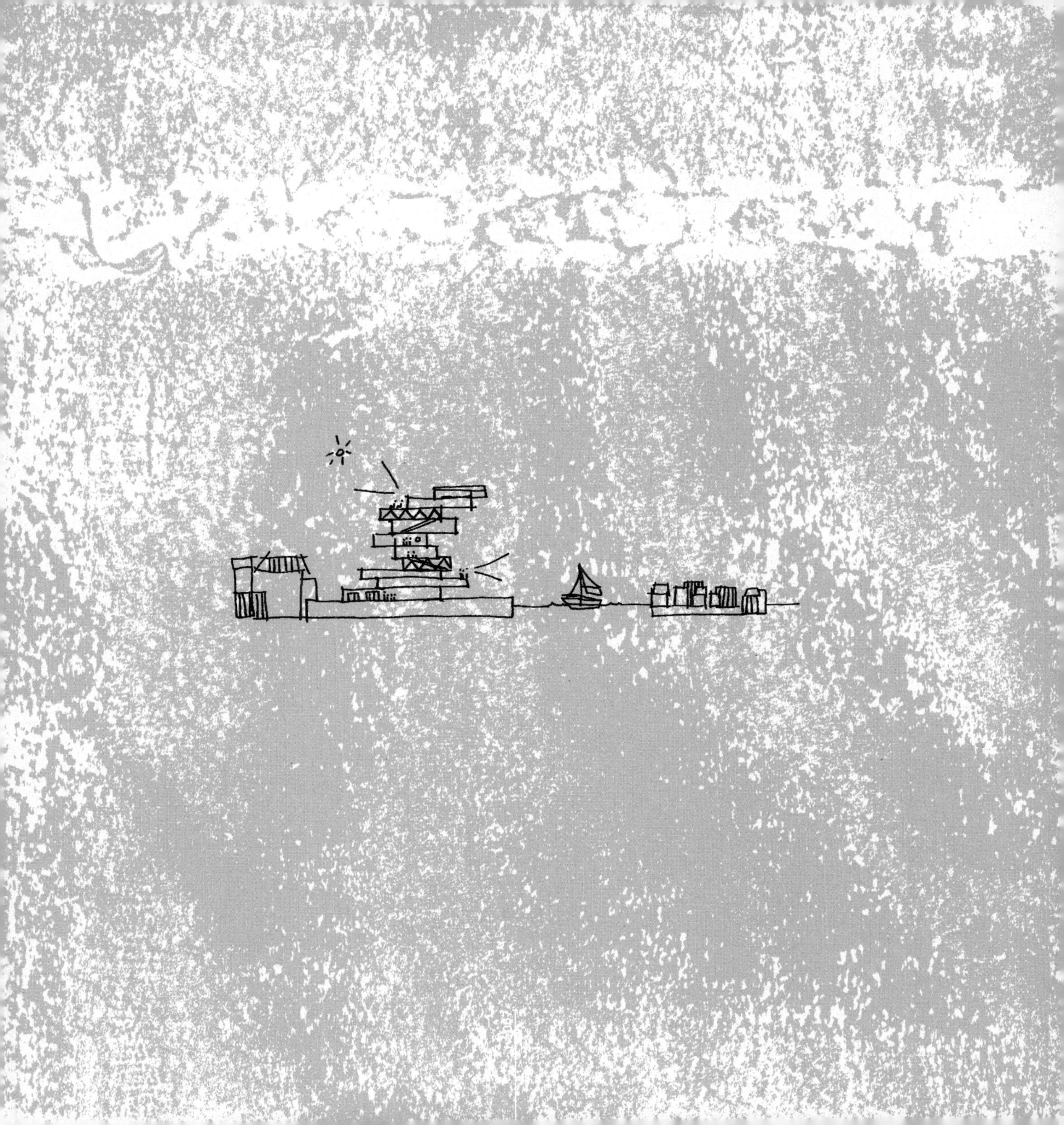

wettbewerb / competition
nationalmuseum / national museum
oslo 2009

cube twister oslo

am hafen von oslo wird auf dem gelände des ehemaligen bahnhofes ein neues nationalmuseum errichtet. zwischen dem bauplatz und der hafenpromenade soll das historisch wertvolle bahnhofsgebäude erhalten bleiben. der direkte bezug zum hafen ist somit durch ein dreistöckiges gebäude verdeckt.

mit dem cube twister schraubt sich hinter dem bahnhofsgebäude eine stapelung einzelner ausstellungskörper, vom hafen aus als sichtbares zeichen, in den himmel.

a new museum is being constructed on the site of the former station in the port of oslo. it is intended to maintain the historically valuable station building, situated between the building site and the harbour promenade. a direct connection to the harbour is thereby provided by a three-storey building.

with the cube twister, a stack of individual exhibition volumes behind the station building rises into the sky as a landmark that is visible from the harbour.

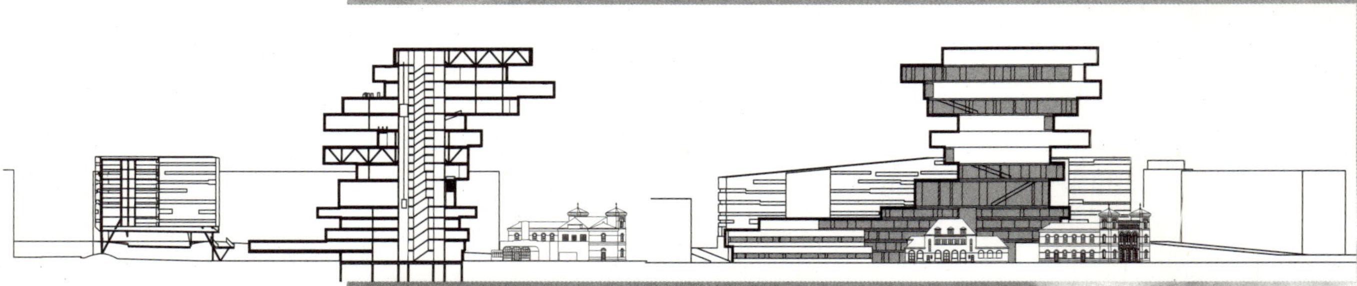

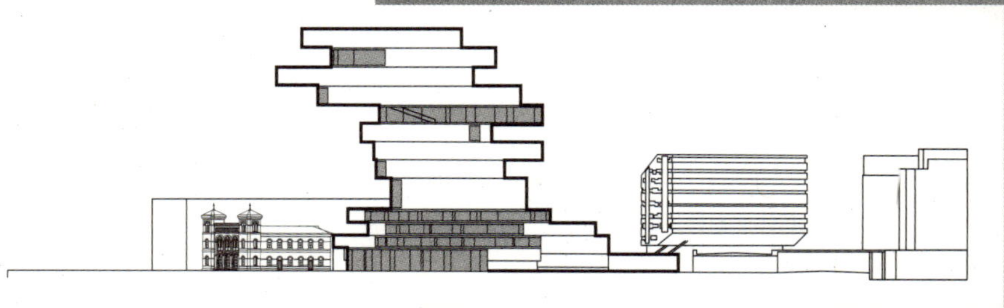

das freistehende gebäude ermöglicht den zugang aus allen umliegenden stadtbereichen und verdichtet die außenplätze zu einer höhenstaffelung aus einzelbaukörpern mit terrassen. der besucher bewegt sich in einer vertikalen drehbewegung durch die terrassierten ausstellungsgeschosse und erlebt so oslo aus allen denkbaren blickwinkeln und höhenlagen.

the free-standing building can be accessed from all the surrounding parts of the city and condenses the outside spaces into a staggered arrangement of the different heights of the individual building structures and their terraces. the visitor proceeds in a vertically circular movement through the terraced exhibition storeys, thereby experiencing oslo from every imaginable angle and height.

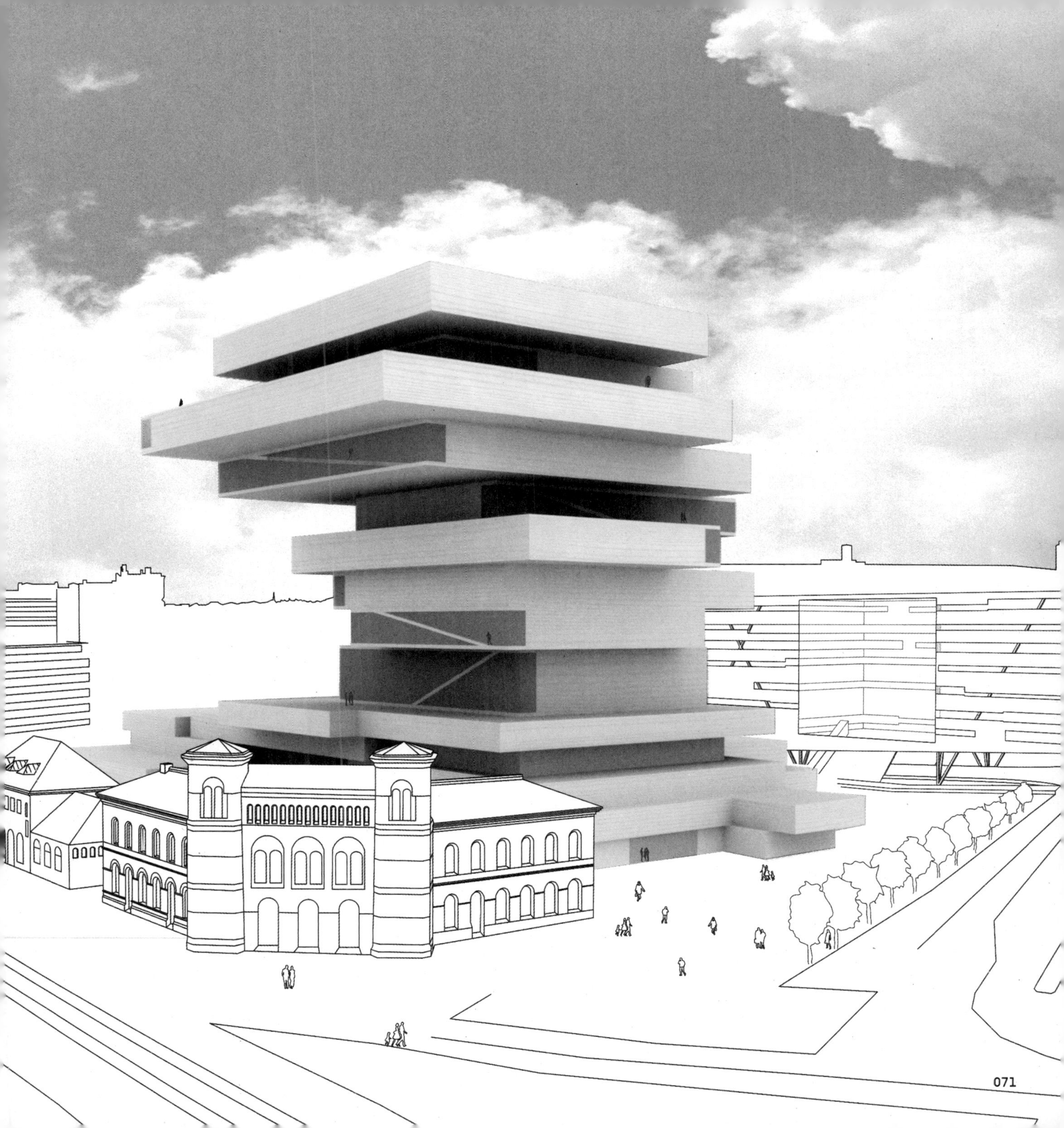

500 m^2 wohnzimmer

»schön wären 500 m^2 grundstück, 500 m^2 wohnzimmer und 500 m^2 mehrgeschossiger garten.« // »It would be great to have 500 m^2 of property, 500 m^2 of apartment space and 500 m^2 of multi-storey garden.«

eine familie mit einem kind und vielleicht auch noch mehr möchte von einer innerstädtischen wohnung an den stadtrand ins grüne ziehen. im traum spielen kinder auf der wiese, die eltern sitzen mit freunden dazwischen und ringsherum nur garten, bäume, freie natur. das erworbene grundstück ist ca. 500 m^2 groß und mit bäumen und wiese bewachsen.

um den charakter des unbebauten gartens zu erhalten, werden der wohn- und essbereich im erdgeschoss und der garten mit einer großen schwingungsbewegung vereint. dadurch entsteht atmosphärisch ein 500 m^2-wohnzimmer aus frei- und innenraumbereichen. die schwingung setzt sich im wohnmaßstab mit sitzgruben, geschwungenen möbeleinbauten, abgerundetem pool- und terrassenformen fort.

diese schwingungsbewegung im erdgeschoss besteht aus semitransparenten polycarbonatelementen. der flüchtige charakter des materials wird auch als fassade des obergeschosses eingesetzt, das dadurch einen luftigen, beinahe schwebenden charakter erhält.

darüber auf dem dach wird mit einer begrünten bürohügellandschaft das entnommene gartenstück des erdgeschosses als garten wieder eingesetzt.

a family with a child, or perhaps more than one, would like to move from their inner city apartment to the green suburbs on the edge of the city. they dream of the children playing in the fields, parents sitting there together with friends surrounded only by a garden, trees and nature. the purchased property is approx. 500 m^2 in size and is full of trees and fields.

in order to preserve the character of what is undeveloped in the garden, the living and dining area on the ground floor is unified with the garden in a vibrant sweeping movement. this creates an atmospheric 500 m^2 living room comprising an open space and interior areas. the vibrancy continues in the details of the living space, with cushion pits, curved built-in furniture, and the forms of the round pool and the terraces.

this vibrant movement of the ground floor is created by semi-transparent polycarbonate elements. while the fleeting character of the material is also employed in the facade of the upper storey, thereby creating a sense of airiness and even suspension.

above, on the roof, the garden character of the ground floor is once again employed for the landscaped of the mound of the office, which is covered with greenery.

auf drei oberirdischen und einem unterirdischen geschoss wurden insgesamt 300 m² wohnraum geschaffen.

a total housing area of 300m² was created on three overground levels and one underground level.

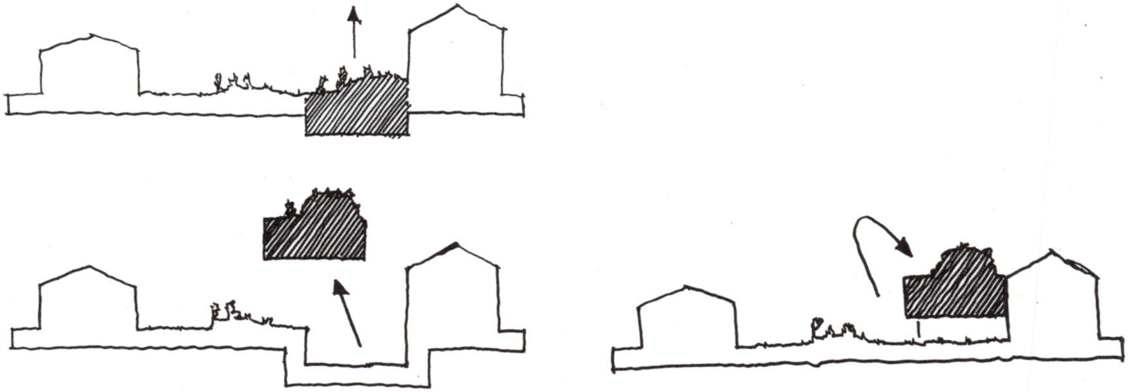

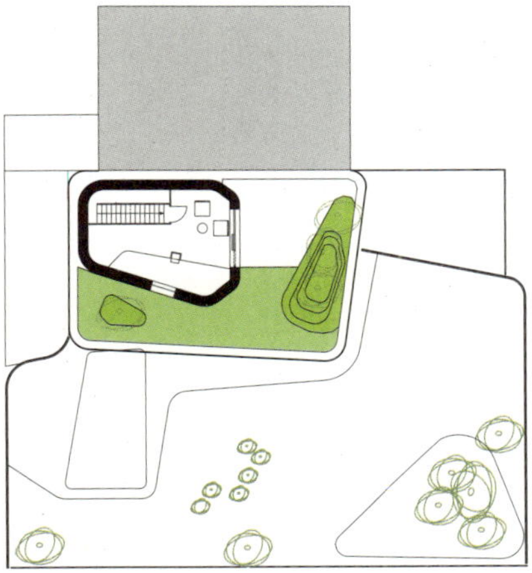

+2

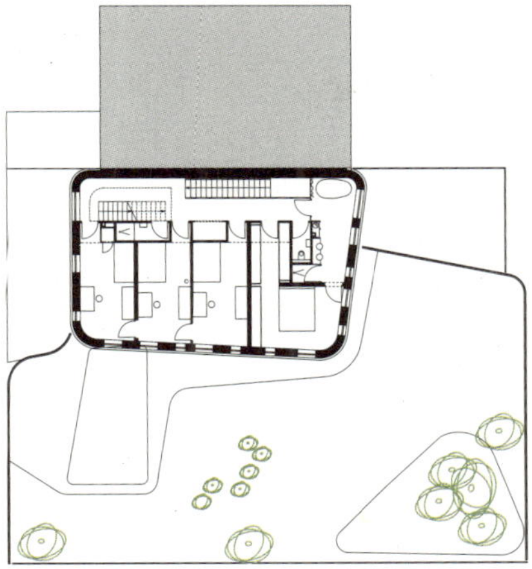

+1

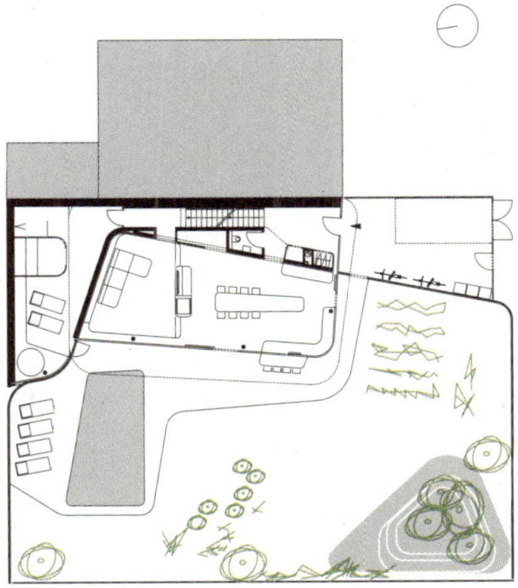

0

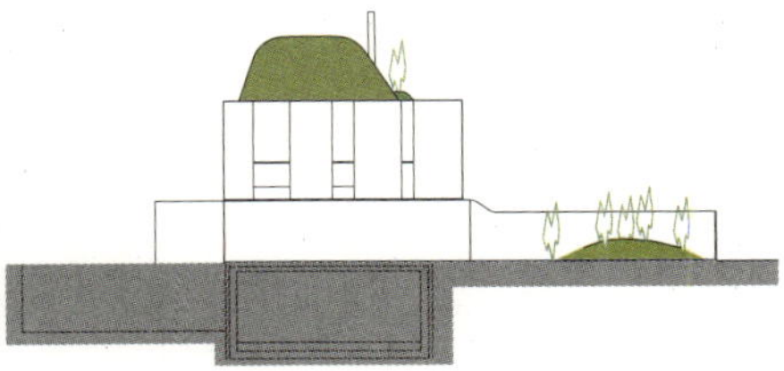

nord / north

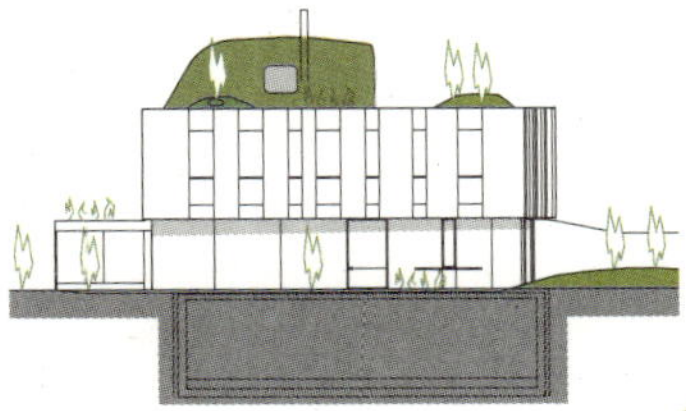

west

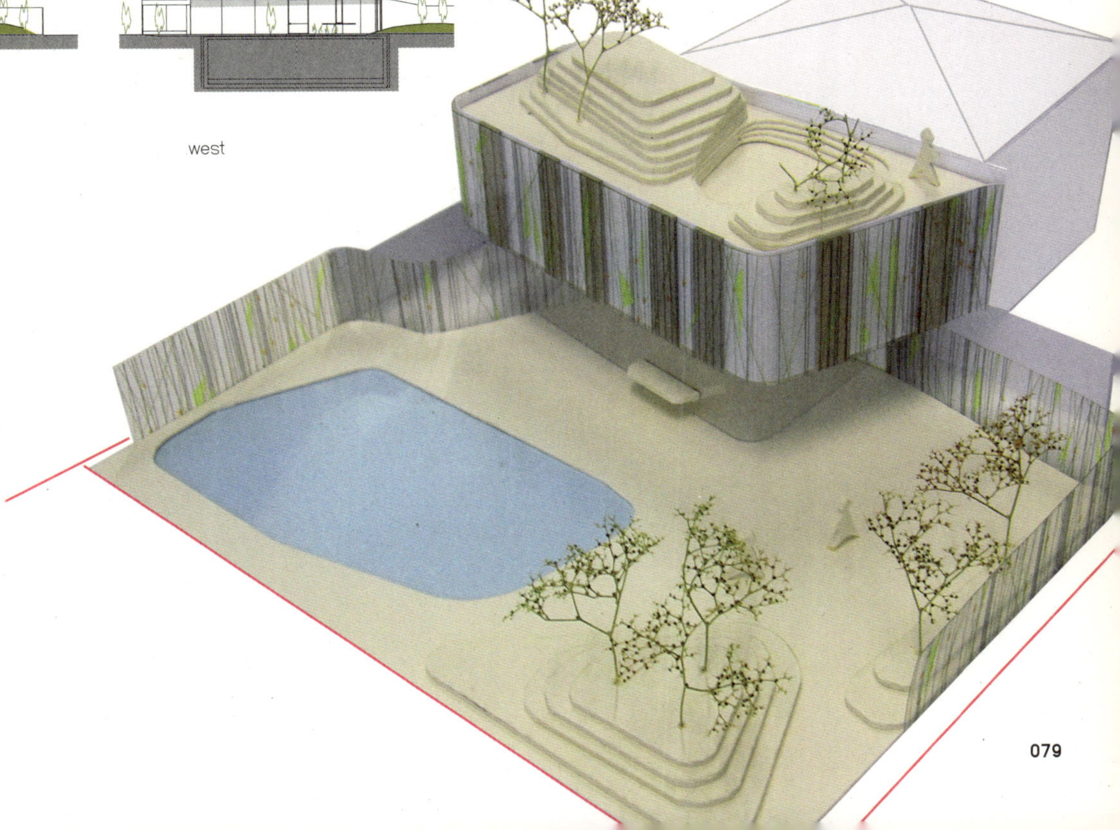

wettbewerb / competition
erweiterung schulzentrum / extension school centre
preis / prize hollabrunn 2005

a higher school

um den ohnehin nicht ausreichend vorhandenen außenraum der schule nicht noch weiter zu verkleinern, wird dem schulbau aus den 70er-jahren ein konsequent rationaler, zweigeschossiger baukörper appliziert; dieser, aufgeständert über pausenhalle und bestand, fungiert gleichzeitig als vordach und deckelung der neuen zugangshalle.

in order to avoid further reducing the size of the school's outdoor space, which was already insufficient, a thoroughly rational, two-storey volume was added to the school building, which dates from the 1970s; elevated above the recreation hall and the volume itself, the addition functions at one and the same time as a projecting roof and as a ceiling for the new entrance hall.

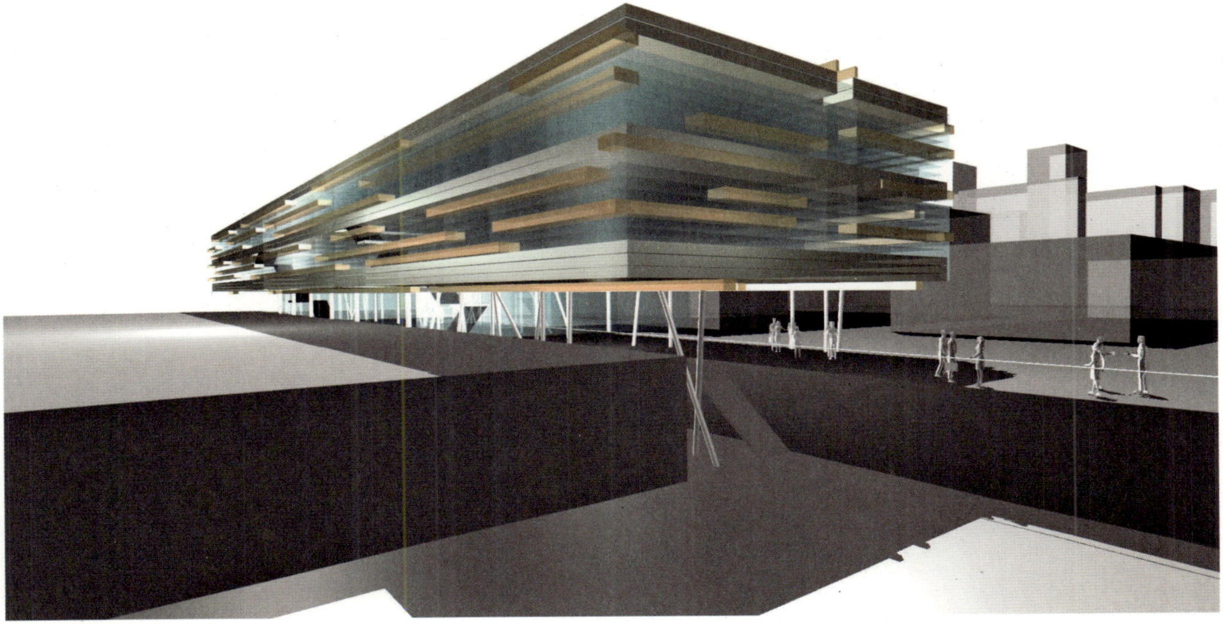

wettbewerb / competition
technologiezentrum / technology centre
preis / prize perg 2001

technologiezentrum

system mit erweiterungsmöglichkeit // system for potential extension

die funktionen »werkstatt« und »forschung / verwaltung« korrespondieren über eine gemeinsame gangzone mit gegenseitigen einblicken; der bereich forschung / verwaltung bietet als durchgehende und erweiterbare meanderstruktur maximale flexibilität; mit der möglichkeit, einzelne »kammzähne« als eigene einheiten abzuschließen. zwischen den kammelementen sind mitteltemperierte klimahöfe ausgebildet.

the areas for the functions of »workshop« and »research / administration« are connected via a common corridor area and have reciprocal views of each other; the area for research / administration has maximum flexibility as a result of its continuous and extendable meandering structure; it also includes the possibility of closing off individual »comb teeth« as individual units. between the comb elements are medium-temperature climatic courtyards.

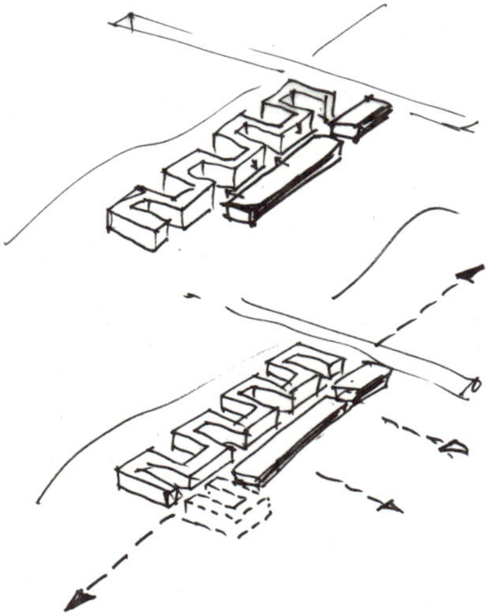

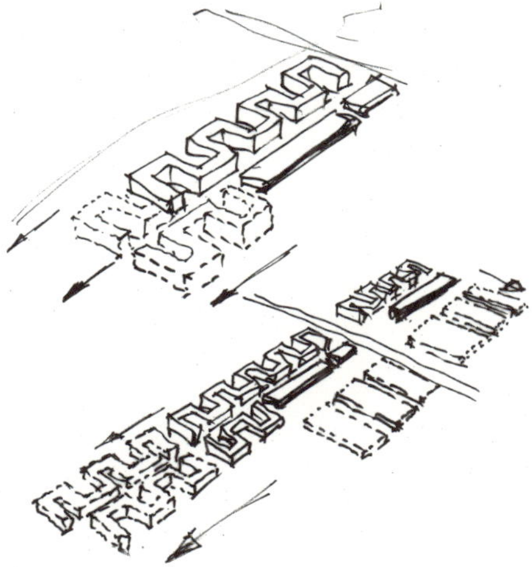

3

wettbewerb / competition
bundesschulzentrum / state school centre
3. preis / 3rd prize eisenstadt 2010

schule eisenstadt

ein bestehendes schulzentrum soll durch aufstockung des bestandes erweitert werden. interpretiert werden die vorhandenen, endlos umlaufenden bandfassaden als eigenständiger, fliegender riegel – mit ebenso endlos umlaufendem vertikalen strichcode. die schlanke gebäudeform lässt auf dem dach des bestandes ausreichend platz für freiklassen und ermöglicht einen direkten außenraumbezug für alle gebäudeteile.

die nötige erweiterung einer schule wird so zu ihrer neuen visitenkarte: der konsequent rationale baukörper bietet mit seiner außenraum / vorplatzüberdachung mehr als nur die deckung des klassenraumbedarfes. eingang und pausenhof werden durch den schwebenden riegel neu eingefasst und ebenfalls neu definiert.

an existing school centre to be extended by adding another storey. the existing seamless facades that completely surround the building are interpreted as an independent flying beam – with an equally endless, vertical barcode. the slimline form of the building leaves sufficient room for open-air classes on the roof of the building, and makes it possible to create a direct connection to the outside in all parts of the building.

in this way, the necessary extension of the school becomes its new visiting card: by roofing the exterior space/forecourt, the consistently rational volume satisfies more than simply the need for classroom space. the entrance and schoolyard are both re-enclosed and redefined by a suspended horizontal beam.

HTBLA

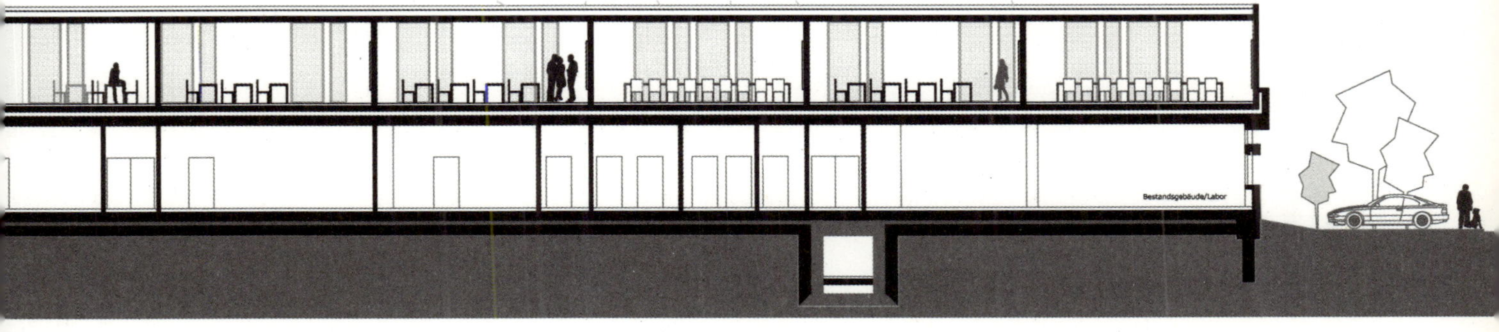
Bestandsgebäude/Labor

Z Z Z Z

LINZ

haus h

nur 46 m² »verbaut« // just 46 m² developed

teuer war's, das kleine grundstück am südosthang über linz. war also klar, die knappen freiraumressourcen ideal zu nutzen. so rückt das haus auf dem grundstück direkt an drei der vier gesetzlich bestimmten mindestabstandslinien, unterirdisch werden diese sogar unterschritten; die grundstücksform ist somit vorgabe für die baukörpersituierung.
die vertikale staffelung der funktionen führt außerdem zu höchst sparsamer »verbauung«; lediglich 46 m² des grundstückes sind nicht als freiraum nutzbar. der schlaftrakt wird von der großzügigen terrasse gedeckt, die (stützenfreie, 13,5 m lange) auskragung schützt den kinderspielbereich vor regen und sonne.

it was expensive, the small property on the south-eastern slopes above linz. it was therefore clear that the limited resources had to be used in the best possible way. for that reason, the house on the property was moved to three of the four legally stipulated lines of minimum distance – underground, these were even below the limit; the shape of the property therefore determined the conditions for positioning the building structure.
vertical staggering of the functions furthermore leads to a very economical »development«; only 46 m² of the property are not utilizable as free space. the bedroom section is covered by a spacious terrace, a projection (support-free, 13,5 m long) that protects the children's play area from the rain and the sun.

interieur: friedrich stiper

1|

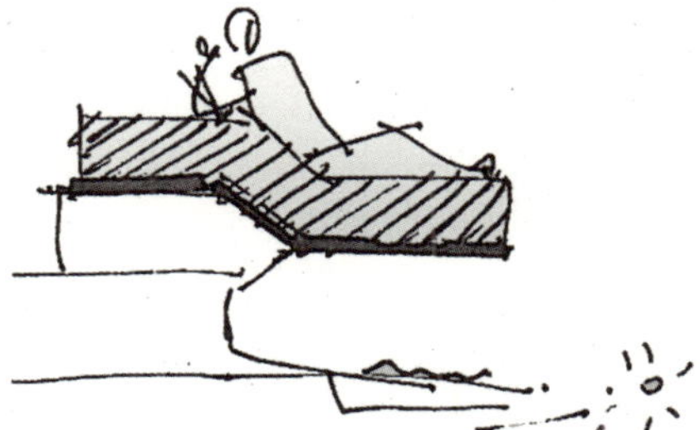

2|

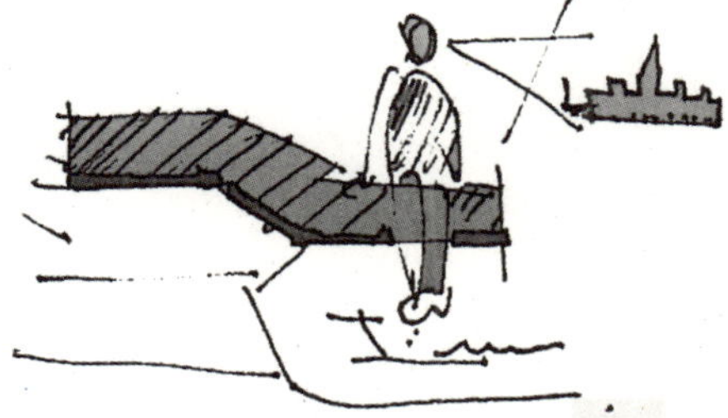

3|

ausgehend vom zentralen gebäudeknotenpunkt auf eingangsniveau, »küche+spielen«, entwickeln sich die raumbereiche wohnen, büro und schlafen als auskragende oder eingegrabene raumschleifen in die tiefe des grundstückes.
alle raumschleifenteile gehen ineinander über und haben einen direkten bezug zum knotenpunkt. der außenraum wird durch dieses raumgefüge jeweils entlang der schleifen bis zum zentrum geführt.
der knotenpunkt »küche+spielen« selbst artikuliert seine verknüpfende funktion durch ein geschossübergreifendes küchenmöbel mit bezug zu den verschiedenen nutzungsbereichen.

proceeding from the building's central point of intersection on the entrance level (»kitchen+play«) the spatial areas, office and bedrooms develop as projecting or submerged spatial loops in the depth of the property.
all the parts of the spatial loop run on from one to the next and have a direct relation to the point of intersection. the exterior space leads along this sequence of rooms or along the loop to the centre.
the »kitchen+play« intersection articulates its connecting function through trans-storey kitchen furniture and a connection to the various areas of utilisation.

die vorgehängte fassade des ebenerdigen schlaftraktes aus schichtstoffplatten birgt die außenliegenden schiebeflügeln aus demselben material; die gartenfassade lässt sich somit komplett schließen.

the curtain-wall facade of the ground-floor bedroom block made of laminated panels conceals the external sliding wings made of the same material; in this way, the garden facade can be completely closed.

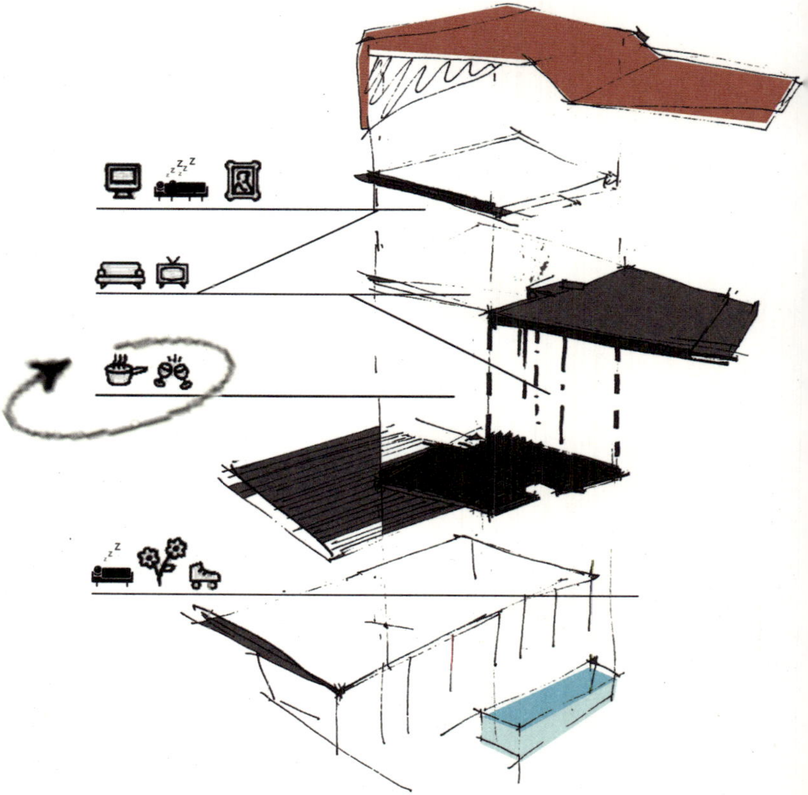

die homogene außenhaut des gebäudes (dach wie auch wände und untersicht) bildet eine polyurethan-folie, welche im spritzverfahren als letzte bauwerksschicht aufgebracht wurde. kein attikablech oder ähnliches stört die homogenität der hülle.

the homogeneous outer skin of the building (roof, as well as walls and lower soffit) forms a polyurethane sheet, which was put up with the last layer of the building by means of a spraying process. no parapet wall metal or anything like that disturbs the homogeneity of the shell.

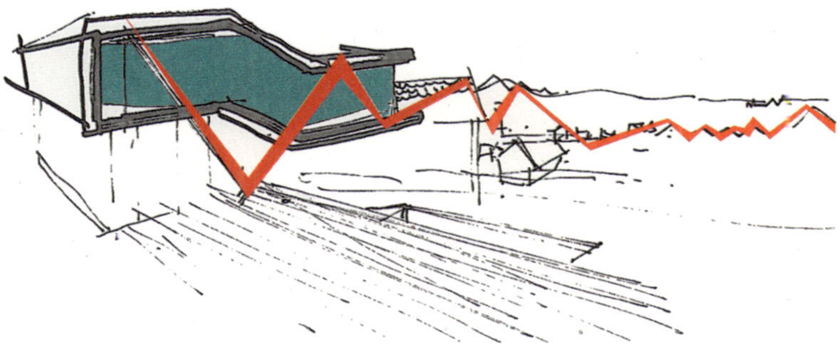

von der küche aus erreicht man einen halbstock höher den wohnbereich mit seiner spektakulären aussicht über linz bis hin zu den alpen.

from the kitchen one ascends one half-storey higher to the living-room area, with its spectacular view of linz and beyond to the alps.

vom wohnbereich aus gelangt man einen weiteren halbstock höher zu einer gemütlichen lounge und einem büroraum. die gesamte südfront ist durchgängig verglast und wird nur durch die statisch erforderlichen stahlträger akzentuiert.

from the living-room area, one reaches, a further half-storey higher, a comfortable lounge and office space. the whole of the south facade is continuously glazed and is accentuated only by the statically required steel beam.

der hauptzugang zum haus erfolgt westseitig über das mittlere geschoss. von hier erreicht man über eine treppe das untere stockwerk, dass, in den hang eingebettet, sich zum garten hin öffnet. hier befinden sich das elternschlafzimmer, drei kinderzimmer und zwei badezimmer. ein fitnessraum und der weinkeller schließen an die schlafräume an. im mittelgeschoss, gewissermaßen dem »knotenpunkt« der funktionen befindet sich neben dem haupteingang mit foyer die küche mit angeschlossenem (indoor) kinderspielbereich.

the main entrance to the house is located on the west side and accessed via the middle storey. from here, one reaches the lower storey, which is embedded in the slope and opens onto the garden. here are located the parent's bedroom, three children's bedrooms and two bathrooms. a fitness room and the wine cellar adjoin the bedrooms. in the middle storey, next to the main entrance and the foyer, is the kitchen, to a certain extent the »point of intersection« of the functions, with an adjoining (indoor) children's play area.

auf küchenniveau liegt auch die weitläufige terrasse, die sich durch die in einem stumpfen winkel zum unteren stockwerk gedrehten obergeschosse öffnet. darunter die geschlossene schlafzimmerfront mit ausgang zum pool.

also on the kitchen level is the wide-ranging terrace, which opens up onto the lower storey through the upper storeys, turned at an obtuse angle.
under it will be the closed bedrooom facade with exit onto the pool.

wettbewerb / competition
science center
preis / prize wels 2008

science center wels

wie ein stück erdreich ist das gebäude mit seiner rauhen schale aus dem untergrund herausgezogen. innen bieten ober- und untergeschoss einen parcours durch die exponate und versuchsanordnungen. im kontrast dazu steht das erdgeschoss, rahmenlos verglast, gewissermaßen ohne hülle. hier sind die öffentlichen funktionen wie empfang, kassen und restaurant angeordnet.

the rough shell of the building seems as if it has been pulled out of the ground like a piece of the earth. the interior presents a tour of the exhibits and experiments on display on both the upper and lower storeys. the ground floor provides a contrast to this by being glazed without a frame, and virtually without a shell. public functions such as reception, cash desks and restaurant are located here.

west

süd / south

2

wettbewerb / competition
pathologie / department of pathology
2. preis / 2nd prize feldkirch 2002

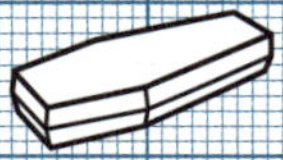

pathologie

pathologische abteilung landeskrankenhaus feldkirch // department of pathology, regional hospital feldkirch

eine zurückhaltende rauminsel im grünen als kontrapunkt zur massiven, vielgeschossigen bebauung des bestandes. oder: ein kleines ufo hat sich eingeparkt und beherbergt nun, abgekoppelt von den übrigen stationen des krankenhauses, die pathologische abteilung.

a restrained spatial island amid greenery as a counterpoint to the massive multi-storey development of the existing building. alternatively: a small ufo has parked here and now accommodates the department of pathology, which has become detached from the other wards of the hospital.

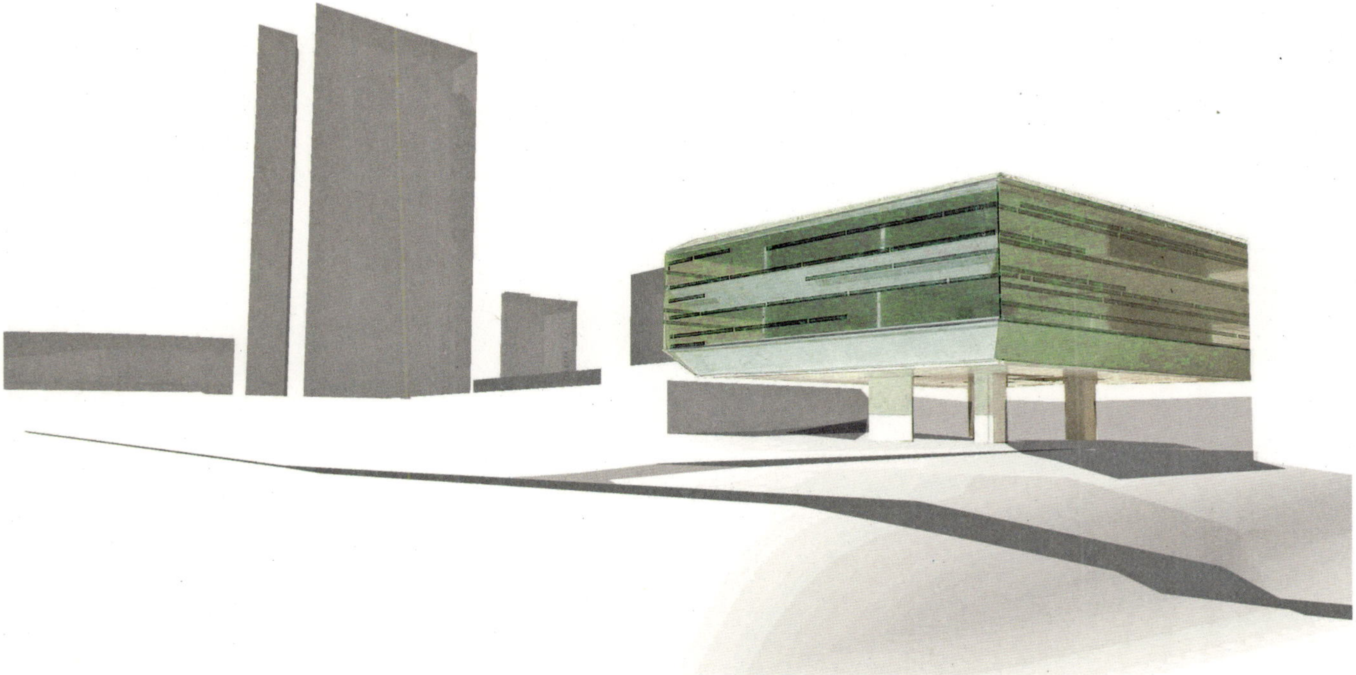

ein quadratischer sarg mit
auferstehungslöchern als letztes domizil
a rectangular coffin with resurrection holes
as the last place of residence.

wettbewerb / competition
»areal eichstraße«
stuttgart 2009

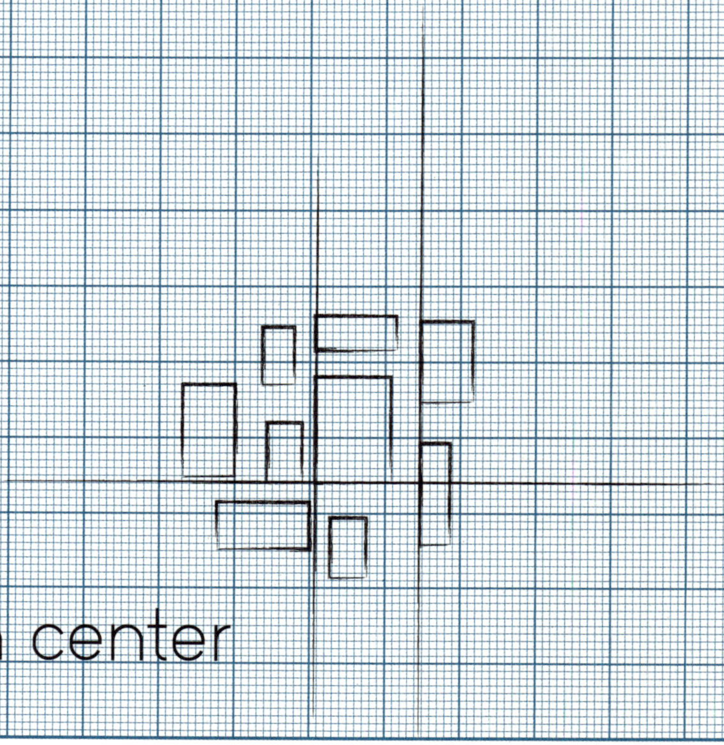

downtown center

aufgabenstellung: ein im zentrum gelegenes grundstück soll primär für die zwecke der regionalverwaltung bebaut werden; zusätzlich soll raum für cafes, nahversorger und ähnliches zur verfügung stehen.

das projekt übersetzt die kleinräumige historische innenstadtstruktur mit ihren als »menschlich proportioniert« empfundenen dimensionen in die gegenwart: eine durchlässige blockstruktur mit schmalen, verkehrsberuhigten gassen und kleinteilige, individualisierte fassadengestaltung.

brief: to develop a property, located in the city centre, primarily for the purposes of regional administration; in addition, space should be made available for cafes, local businesses and the like.

this project translates the small-scale historical structure of the city centre, with dimensions that are felt to be of »human proportions«, into a present-day setting: a permeable block structure with narrow, traffic-calmed streets and an individualized facade design divided into small sections.

amt stuttgart

casino und bank
umbau eines bestehenden gebäudes
aus den 60er-jahren.

casino and bank
conversion of an existing building
dating from the 1960s.

casino austria

spielst du mit? // are you playing?

ziel des umbaus ist ein rückbau diverser zubauten hin zur ursprünglich klaren gebäudezonierung und die erschaffung einer markanten neuen gesamtidentität. die entrümpelte erdgeschosszone wird mit einer großzügigen rahmengeste zu einer einheitlichen sockelzone zusammengefasst. die verschiedenen eingänge artikulieren sich als eigenständige raumeingriffe, eingebettet in die übergeordnete struktur. der bereich des obergeschosses wird bis zum dachaufbau durch eine vorgehängte glasfassade als einheitlich neu gestalteter baukörper hervorgehoben. eine auf die glasfassade folierte wellen- und flächengrafik spannt den assoziationsbogen von der gegenüberliegenden »unverrückbaren« plateaulandschaft des ifengebiets zu dynamischen bewegungen. durch die transluzente beschaffenheit der folie erscheint der gesamtkörper je nach den lichtverhältnissen selbstleuchtend, durchscheinend oder transparent und verändert sich somit im einklang mit dem jahreszeitlichen wechsel der umgebenden landschaft.

the aim of the conversion is to dismantle various additions in order to get back to the original clear zoning of the volume, and to create a distinct new overall identity. the cleared-out ground floor zone is concentrated into a uniform plinth area by means of a spacious framework gesture. the various entrances are articulated as independent spatial interventions, embedded in the overriding structure. the area of the upper storey is accentuated as a uniform newly designed structure by a suspended glass facade reaching right up to the roof superstructure. the graphic design with corrugated surface, which is laminated onto the glass facade, evokes a range of associations, from the »immovable« plateau landscape of the contrasting ifen region, to dynamic movement. through the diaphanous nature of the lamination, the whole volume seems to be luminous, translucent or transparent, depending on the light conditions, thereby changing in accordance with the seasonal changes of the surrounding landscape.

3

wettbewerb / competition
erweiterung stadthalle / town hall extension
3. preis / 3rd prize wien 2003

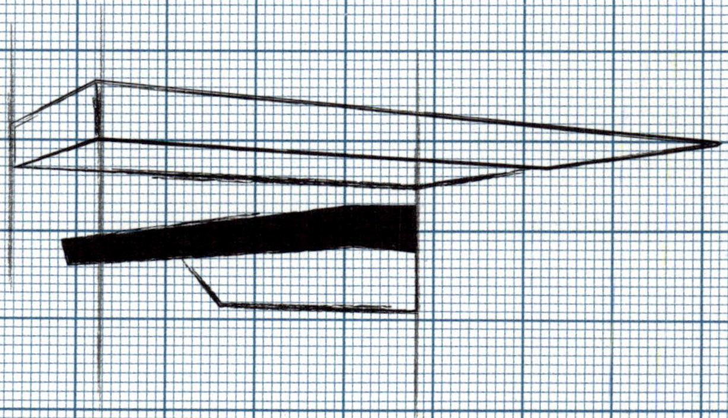

stadthalle wien

ein akzent in ehrwürdiger umgebung // an accent in a dignified surrounding

das ensemble des areals wiener stadthalle trägt die starke handschrift des großen architekten roland rainer. neben der bestehenden halle soll eine zusätzliche veranstaltungshalle mit nebengebäuden errichtet werden. caramel zeigt respekt und wölbt lediglich die platzoberfläche auf, um darunter raum für die erweiterungsfunktionen zu schaffen. in einer möglichen zweiten bauetappe wird ein leichter, schwebender baukörper als bindeglied zwischen neuen und vorhandenen bauteilen aufgebaut.

the ensemble of buildings on the property of the stadthalle in vienna bears the unmistakable signature of the great architect roland rainer. an additional events hall, including auxiliary buildings, was to be built beside from the existing hall. caramel showed its sense of respect by only arching the surface of the area upward, in order to create room underneath for the purposes of extension. in a possible second building stage, a lighter, suspended volume would be constructed as a connecting link between the new parts and the existing parts of the building.

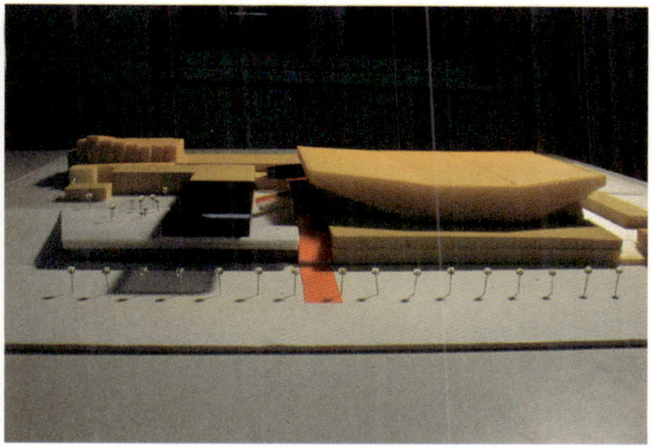

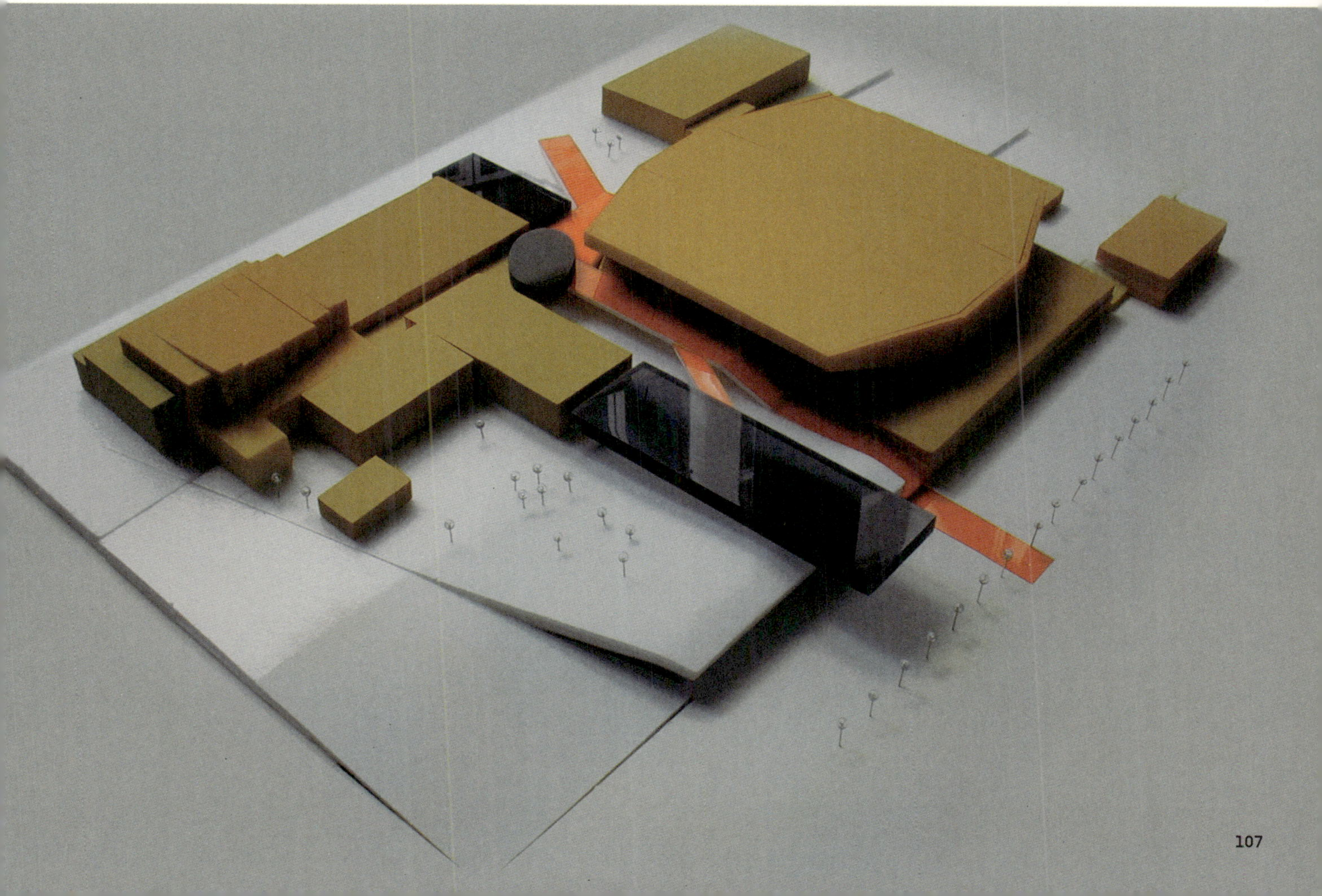

landesmuseum vorarlberg

ein neuer platz für bregenz //
a new square for bregenz

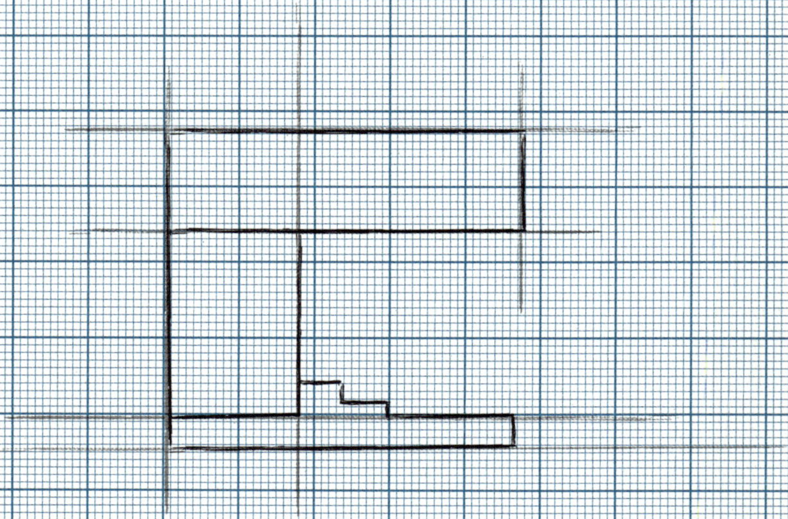

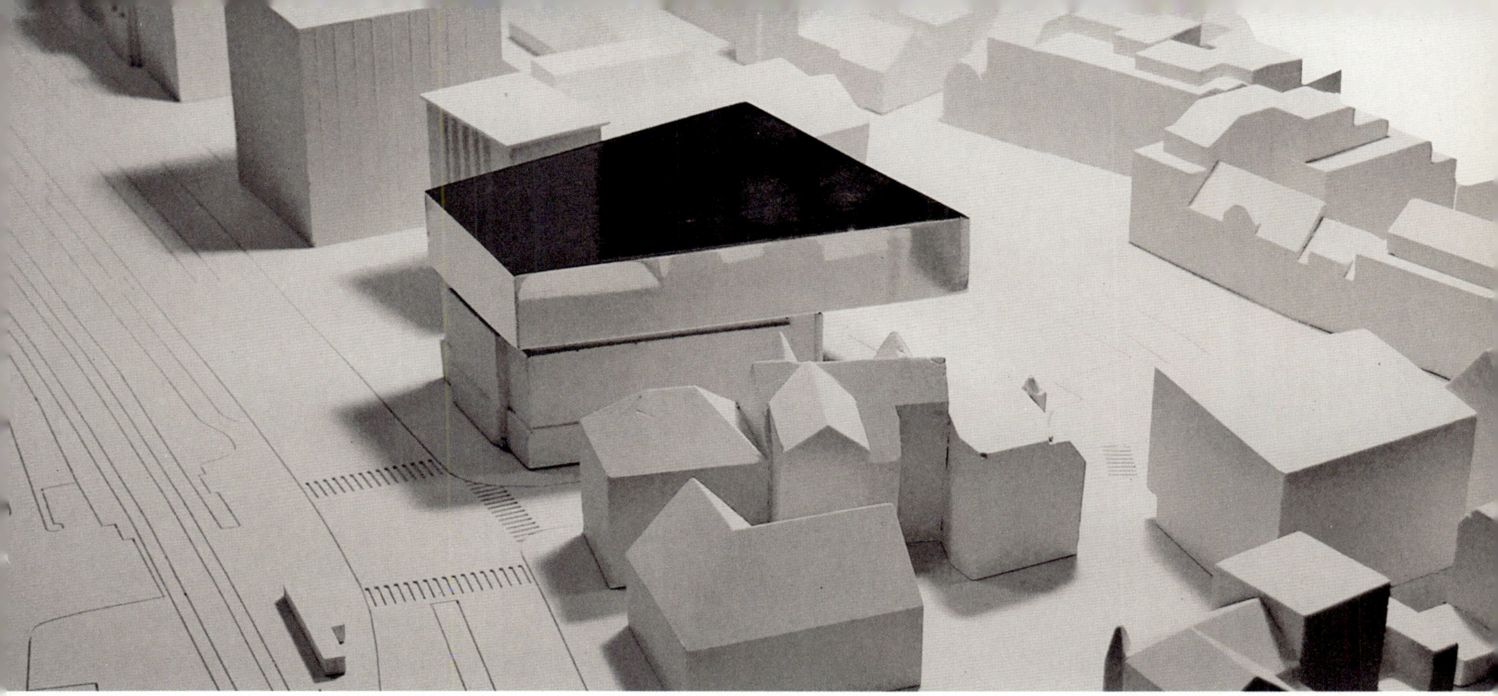

das alte landesmuseum vorarlberg soll abgerissen und neu errichtet werden. oder doch nur umgebaut? durch den abriss entstünde ein neuer großzügiger platz inmitten der stadt… caramel will den bauplatz als öffentlichen platz für die stadt erhalten. der historische gebäudeteil trägt das neue urbane implantat, wie die statische bemessung beweist. das ergibt nicht nur einen neuen platz, sondern auch noch eine platzüberdachung. und ja, vom museum im dach hat man ganz vorarlberg im blick. fast. ein neuer platz für bregenz!

the old regional museum of vorarlberg is to be pulled down and a new one built in its place. or should it just be altered? demolishing it would create a new spacious square in the middle of town… caramel wants to retain the building site as a public space for the city. the historical part of the building can bear the new urban implantation, as the structural measurements show. that produces not only a new square, but also a covering for the square. and yes, from the museum in the roof, one has a view of the whole of vorarlberg. almost. a new square for bregenz!

1. pause, it's time for a break

federieren // bouncing

der tisch wackelt nicht, herr architekt, der federiert. damit war nicht nur klargestellt, wer der meister und fachmann war, sondern dass sich in einem einfachen tisch zwei weltzustände manifestieren können: der einfache mechanische defekt, den ein tischler nie zulassen würde, und ein höheres prinzip der baukunst, das elastische schwingen, das prinzip des nachgebens und des sanften widerstands, das im schwingen des schilfs oder der weide, ja in jedem baum unübertroffen zum ausdruck kommt: eben das federieren. ich war beschämt und wollte möglichst elegant den hals aus der schlinge ziehen: aber meister, sagte ich ein wenig überheblich, das wackeln ist doch an sich nichts schlechtes, schließlich gibt es den berühmten wackelstein, und deswegen fahren sogar die wiener ins waldviertel. ja, antwortete er prompt, aber sicher keine tischler.

the table doesn't wobble, mr architect, it bounces. that not merely demonstrated, who the master and expert was, but also showed how in one simple table two states of the world can be manifest: the simple mechanical defect, which no carpenter ever would allow, and a higher principle of architecture, elastic vibration, the principle of giving way, of gentle resistance, which in the vibration of reed or willow, indeed in every tree, finds expression unexcelled: to wit, that »bouncing«. put thus to shame, i wished to pull my neck from the noose as elegantly as i could: yet master, i said a little arrogantly, wobbling in itself is nothing bad, after all there's the famous logan stone, even viennese drive to the waldviertel to see it wobble. yes, he replied promptly, but i'm sure not one of them's a carpenter.

friedrich achleitner

wettbewerb / competition
design school »zeche zollverein«
3. preis / 3rd prize essen 2003

design school zollverein

auf dem gelände der stillgelegten kohlenzeche zollverein in essen soll eine neue design school errichtet werden. das areal ist bestimmt durch ein netzwerk aus förderbändern, das die verschiedenen teile miteinander verbindet. einzelne zechengebäude werden bereits jetzt als neue kultureinrichtungen genutzt. die förderbänder könnten ohne gröberen umbau auch als schwebende fussgängerstege genutzt werden. caramel interpretiert dies als zentrales thema: die ausbildung eines netzwerkes mit kulturellen attraktoren als knotenpunkte. die besucher können sich auf den schwebenden stegen ohne störung durch den ebenerdigen fahrzeug- und schienenverkehr zwischen allen bauwerken frei bewegen. die neue design school ist ein knoten im netzwerk, der direkt am hauptzugang des areales liegt.

a new design school is going to be built on the site of the disused zollverein coal mine in essen. the site is determined by a network of conveyor belts, which connect the various parts of the mine. individual mine buildings are already being used as new cultural facilities. the conveyor belts could without any great alterations become suspended pedestrian footbridges. caramel interprets that as a central theme: the development of a network with cultural attractions as points of intersection. via the suspended footbridges, the visitors can move freely between all the edifices, without being disturbed by ground-level rail and vehicle traffic. the new design school is a point of intersection in the network, and is situated directly by the main entrance to the site.

netzwerk/network

3. netzwerkknotenpunkte // network intersections

1. bestand // existing structure

2. netzwerk bestehender förderbänder // network of existing conveyor belts

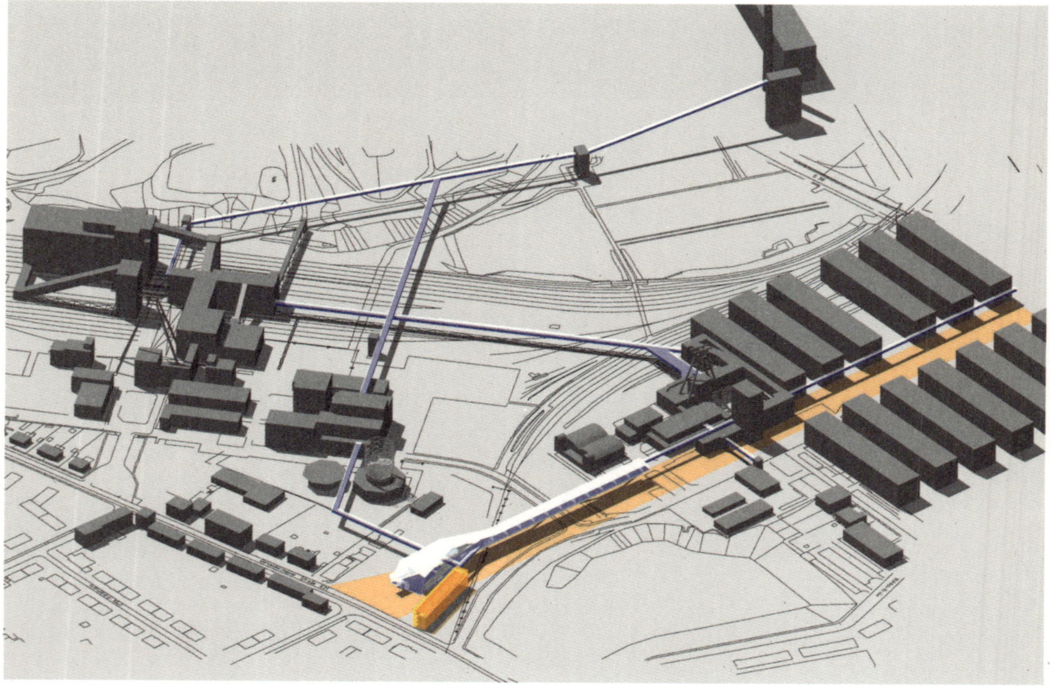

4. struktur aufdrehen //
untwisting the structure

5. ausbildung der knotenpunkte //
development of the intersections

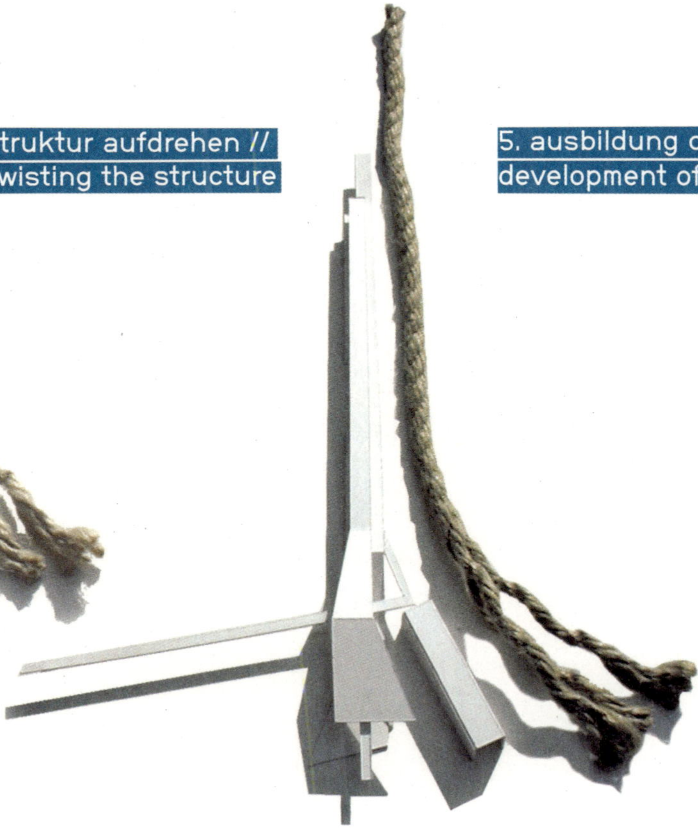

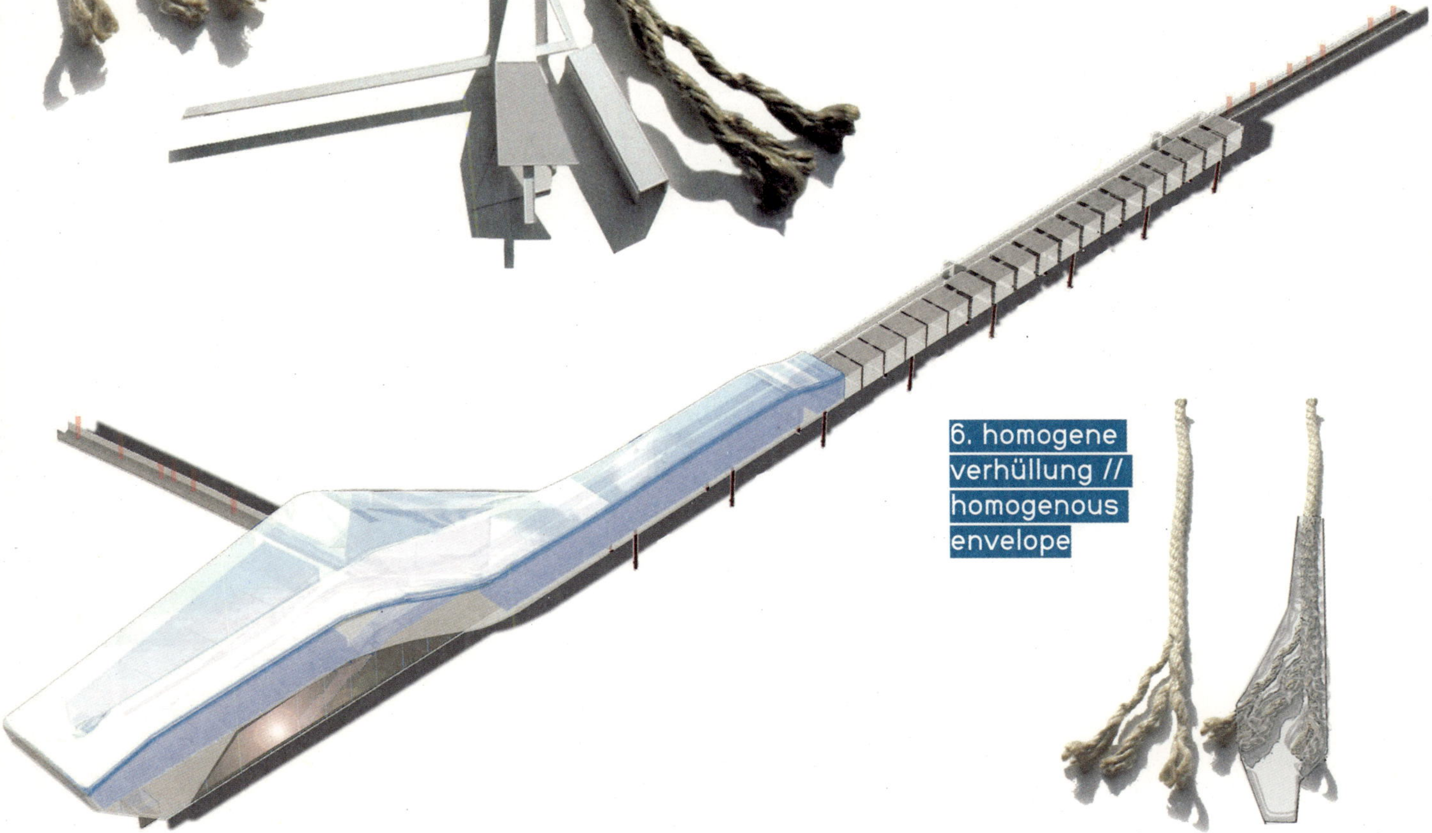

6. homogene
verhüllung //
homogenous
envelope

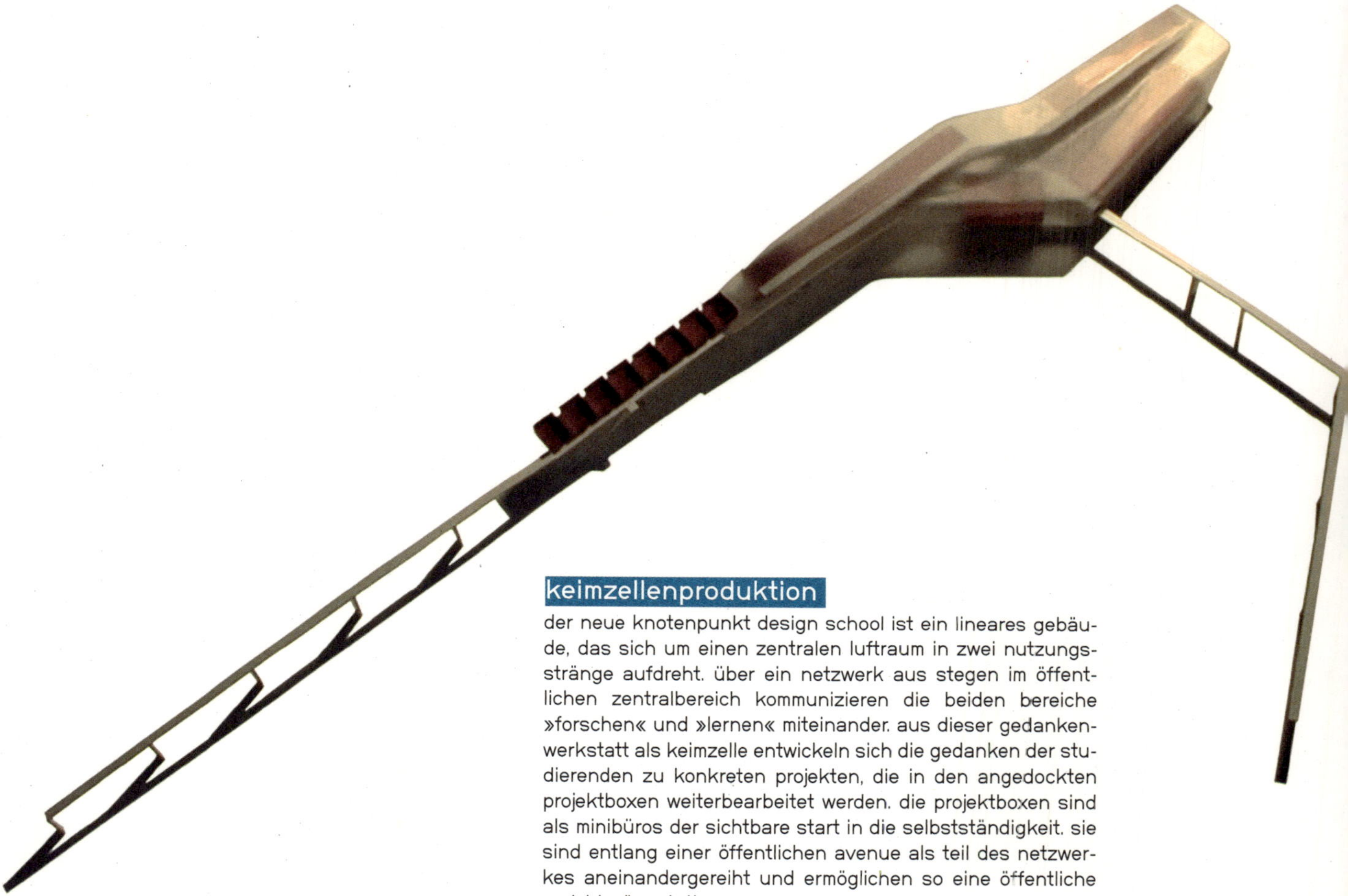

keimzellenproduktion

der neue knotenpunkt design school ist ein lineares gebäude, das sich um einen zentralen luftraum in zwei nutzungsstränge aufdreht. über ein netzwerk aus stegen im öffentlichen zentralbereich kommunizieren die beiden bereiche »forschen« und »lernen« miteinander. aus dieser gedankenwerkstatt als keimzelle entwickeln sich die gedanken der studierenden zu konkreten projekten, die in den angedockten projektboxen weiterbearbeitet werden. die projektboxen sind als minibüros der sichtbare start in die selbstständigkeit. sie sind entlang einer öffentlichen avenue als teil des netzwerkes aneinandergereiht und ermöglichen so eine öffentliche projektpräsentation.

breeding ground production

the new point of intersection, the design school, is a linear building that untwists two strands of utilisation around a central empty space. the two fields of »research« and »study« can communicate with each other by means of a network of footbridges in the public central area. this intellectual workshop serves as a breeding ground for ideas, enabling students to develop their own concepts into concrete projects, which are worked on further in the adjoining project boxes. as mini-offices, the project boxes are visible starting points on the road to independence. arranged in a row along a public avenue, they are part of the network, and make it possible to present the projects publicly.

wettbewerb / competition
landesmuseum / regional museum
linz 2007

schlossmuseum linz

auf dem schlossberg westlich der linzer altstadt liegt das namensgebende linzer schloss. markantestes zeichen zur altstadt hin ist die hohe historische schlossmauer, die den schlossplatz als aussichtsplattform zur altstadt abgrenzt. seit 200 jahren ist dieser platz dreiseitig durch das bestehende schloss eingerahmt, die seite zur altstadt ist offen. an dieser offenen seite soll laut auslober das neue schlossmuseum errichtet werden. caramel sieht die sache anders: der schlossplatz muss zur altstadt hin offen bleiben, die historische mauerkrone soll als solche ohne überbauung erhalten werden. daher schwebt das schlossmuseum als dachkörper frei über der schlossmauer und dient den besuchern der nach wie vor frei zugänglichen aussichtsterrasse als witterungsschutz. auf der ebene der plattform befinden sich lediglich eingangsbereich und restaurant. der wettbewerbsbeitrag wurde der jury aus formalgründen nicht zur bewertung vorgelegt.

on the castle hill, to the west of the old town of linz, lies linz castle, from which the hill takes its name. the most distinctive sight to be seen on the side facing the old town is the high historical castle wall, which encloses the castle square with a platform for viewing the old town. for 200 years, the square has been enclosed on three sides by the existing castle, while the side towards the old town has been open. it was on this open side that the client wanted the new castle museum to be built. caramel saw the matter differently: the castle square had to remain open towards the old town, the historical wall crest should be retained as such, without any superstructure. that is why the castle museum was freely suspended as a roof structure above the castle wall, providing protection from the weather for visitors to the panorama terrace, which is publicly accessible as before. on the level of the platform there is only an entrance area and a restaurant.
for formal reasons, the competition entry was not presented to the jury for evaluation.

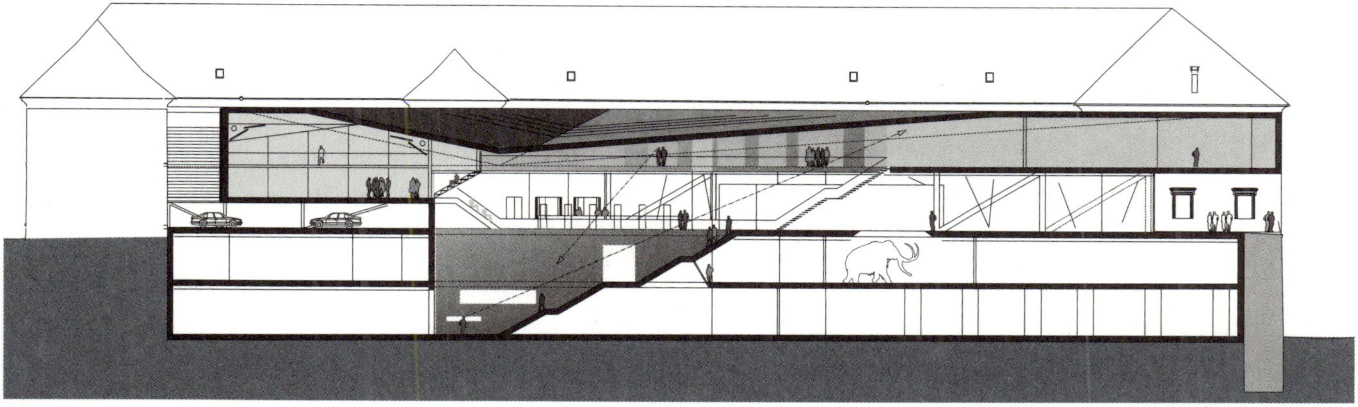

im vorletzten jahrhundert ist der südflügel des linzer schlosses abgebrannt. dieser entwurf stellt ihn als selbstbewusst zeitgemäßen baukörper wieder her.
in the last century, the south wing of linz castle burned down. this design restores it as a deliberately contemporary building structure.

3

wettbewerb / competition
oberstufengymnasium / sixth form college
3. preis / 3rd prize wels 2004

schule wels

die schule als brücke // school as a bridge

was tun mit einem grundstück, das viel zu klein ist für die vielfältigen funktionen eines schulbaus?
eine mögliche antwort gibt caramel mit dem entwurf dieser schule; die klassentrakte sind aufgeständert; der turnsaal ist – über die freihalle belichtet – eingegraben; so bildet sich ein großzügiger vorbereich mit eindeutiger eingangssituation aus; eine über das dach belichtete erschließungshalle verbindet die vier geschosse der schule nicht nur infrastrukturell, sondern auch in bezug auf kommunikation zwischen den funktionsbereichen.

what to do with a property that is much too small for all the various functions of a school building?
caramel supplies one possible answer with its design for this school; the classroom wings are mounted on pillars; the gymnasium is sunk into the ground – with natural lighting from an open hall; in this way, a spacious front area with a distinct entrance situation is formed; an access hall that is naturally lit from the roof connects the four storeys of the school not only infrastructurally, but also in relation to the communication between the functional areas.

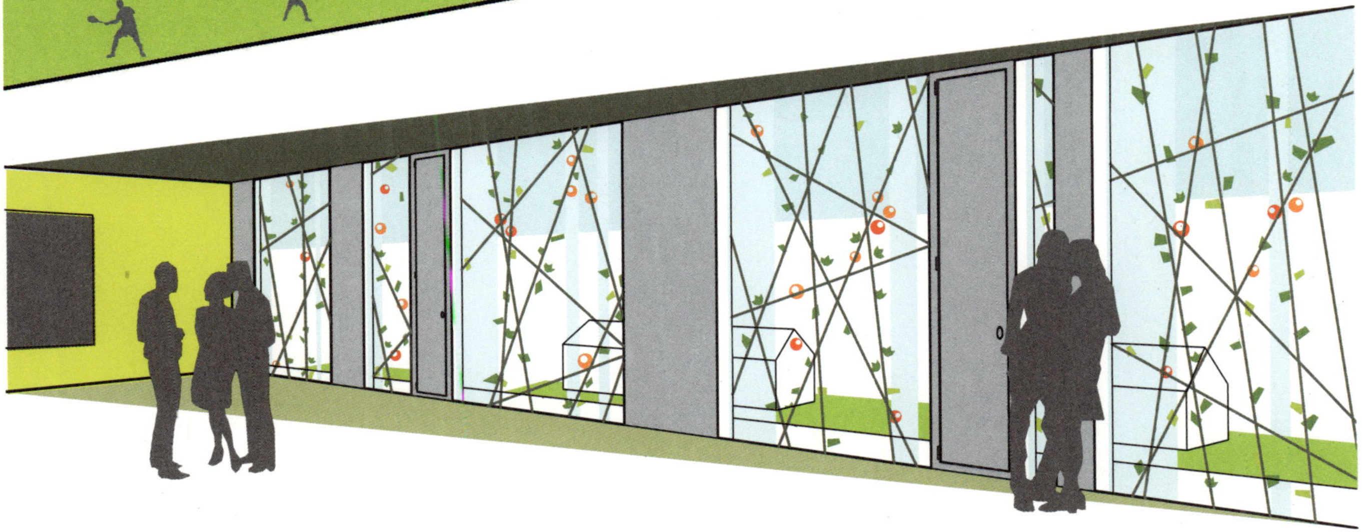

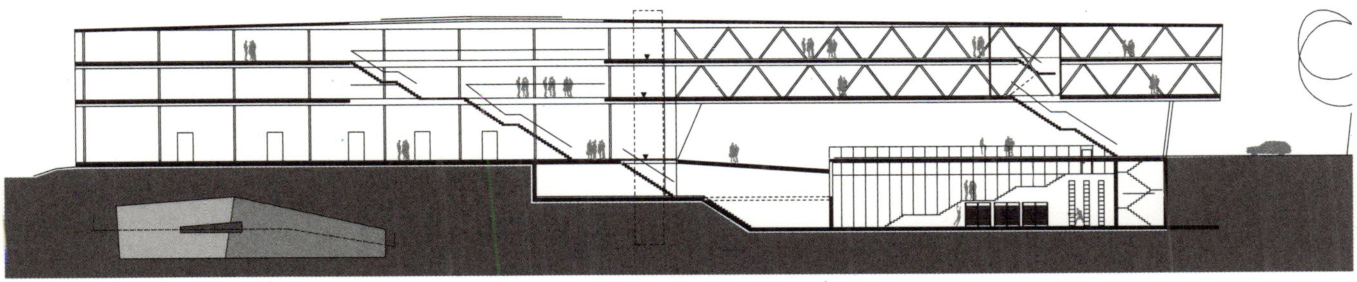

2

wettbewerb / competition
hauptbibliothek wien / main library vienna
2. preis / 2nd prize wien 2001

hauptbibliothek wien

lesen kann öffentlich sein und trotzdem ungestört ... // reading can go on in public and nevertheless be undisturbed ...

zwischen zwei lauten, dreispurigen stadtautobahnen und über einer offenen u-bahn station soll eine neue hauptbibliothek errichtet werden. die vordergründig als unpassend betrachtete betriebsamkeit des ortes macht sich caramel zu nutze und bildet den haupteingang als anziehungspunkt für den starken publikumsverkehr des ebenerdigen u-bahn zugangs aus.

a new main library situated between two loud, three-lane urban carriageways and above a public underground station. the bustle of the location, which at first glance seems quite inappropriate, is utilised by caramel so that the main entrance forms a focal point for the large numbers of commuters entering the underground station on the ground floor.

in zusammenarbeit mit / in cooperation with u.m.a.

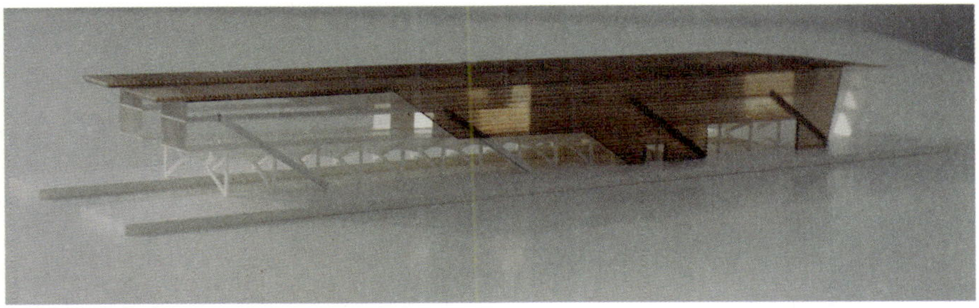

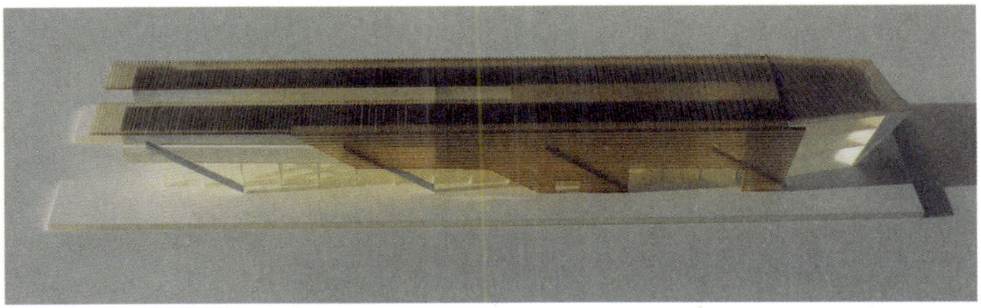

die außenlärmbelastung kann durch eine blickdurchlässige, schallabsorbierende holzlamellenhülle für die bibliothek vollständig ausgeblendet werden.

the noise pollution outside can be excluded from the library completely by means of an opaque, sound-absorbent covering of wooden slats. reading can go on in public and nevertheless be undisturbed.

wettbewerb / competition
kinderstation krankenhaus / children's hospital
4. preis / 4th prize schwarzach und st. johann 2009

krankenhaus schwarzach

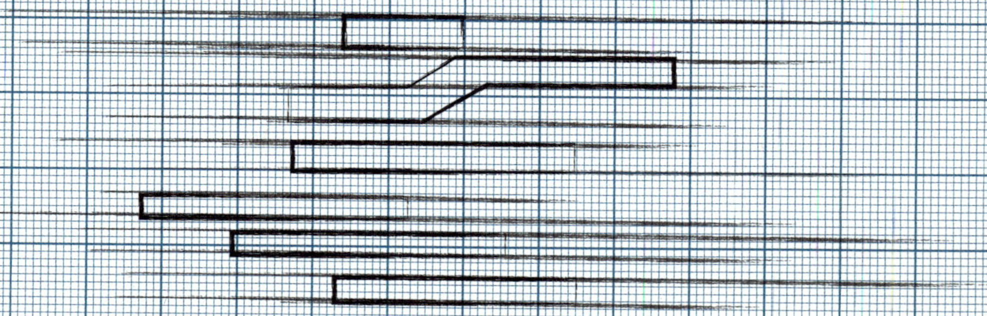

zwischen dem bereits bestehenden, geschlossenen gebäudekomplex krankenhaus schwarzach und dem dorf schwarzach verläuft ein bach mit einer schmalen grünzone. die neue erweiterung des krankenhauses soll genau auf dieser grünzone errichtet werden. statt diesen erholungsbereich zu verbauen, rückt der neubau vom bach ab und erweitert den bewuchs der uferzone in form vertikaler balkongärten vor den krankenzimmern. die patienten können so inmitten eines gartens gesund werden.

gebäudehöhe und gebäudeform des neubaus werden aus der bestehenden krankenhausstruktur weiterentwickelt und verbinden sich mit dieser zum neuen brückenkopf der gesamtanlage.

between the existing closed complex of buildings of schwarzach hospital and the village of schwarzach runs a stream with a narrow green area. it was intended to construct the new extension of the hospital precisely in this green zone. instead of developing this recreation area, the new building is moved away from the stream and extends the vegetation area near the bank of the stream in the form of vertical balcony gardens in front of the children's rooms. this enables them to get well again surrounded by a garden.

the height and form of the new building will be developed from the existing structure of the hospital, connecting with it as the new bridge head of the whole site.

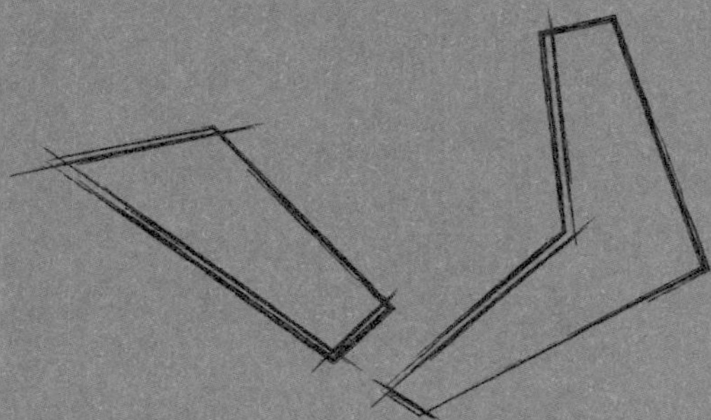

WIFI-Campus

wifi campus

neubau und erweiterung wirtschaftsförderungsinstitut bildungs- und wissenszentrum stadt dornbirn, vorarlberg // new construction and expansion of the institute for promotion of economic development, education and science (wifi)

mit dem projekt »wifi campus« wird durch erweiterungsbauten zum bestehenden bau eine neue städtische struktur zwischen bahnhof und stadtzentrum geschaffen. das vorhandene baugrundstück zwischen grabenweg und bahnhofstraße wird durch zwei dynamisch geknickte, sichelförmige baukörper als quartier entlang der außengrenzen umhüllt.

durch die teils schwebende ausführung der baukörper und das offen gehaltene zentrum des neuen quartiers entsteht ein mehrfach durchlässiger außenraum zwischen den baukörpern als neuer öffentlich-städtischer freiraum.

die gebäudehülle und die großflächigen wandelemente der bereiche gastronomie und veranstaltungsraum bilden als grundlayout in anlehnung an den fluss der raumelemente einen dynamisch linearen strichcode aus.

by adding on to the extant building, the »wifi campus« project creates a new urban structure between the railway station and the city center. tracing the border of the building site between grabenweg and bahnhofsstraße, the campus is formed by two dynamically bent, sickle-shaped building volumes.

executed in part as floating building volumes and left open at the center, the permeable exterior space between the building volumes of the new campus gives rise to a new public-urban open area.

in allusion to the dynamics of the spatial elements, the basic design pattern of a dynamic linear barcode runs along the building shell and the expansive wall elements in the restaurant and function room.

nettonutzfläche oberirdisch ca. 6500 m² // unterirdisch ca. 10.000 m²
tiefgarage dreigeschossig (250 pkw) // kubatur 28.000 m³

planungsbeginn 2003 // baubeginn 06/2005 // fertigstellung 06/2008

net useable area above ground approx. 6,500m² // below ground approx. 10,000 m² 3 levels underground garage (250 cars) // cubage 28,000 m³

planning start 2003 // construction start 06/2005 // completion 06/2008

WIFI-Campus

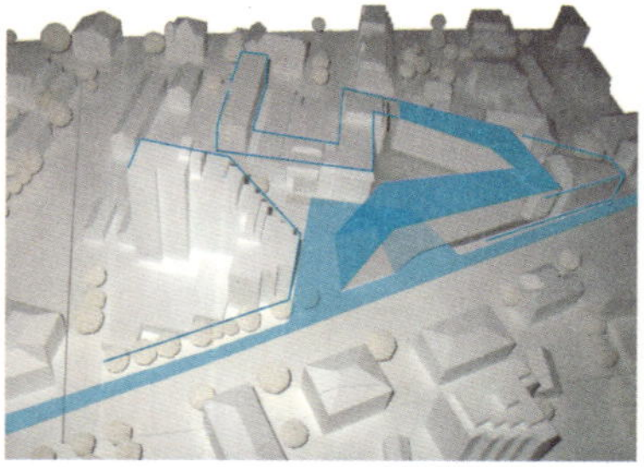

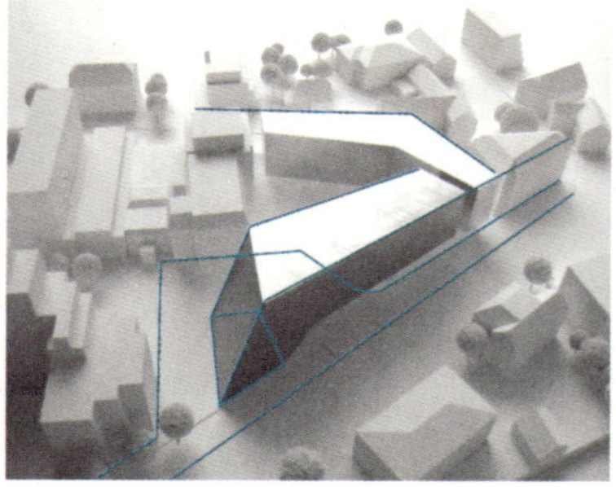

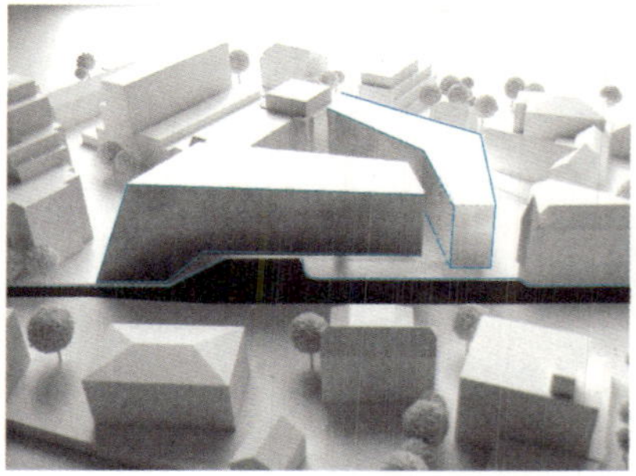

die außenräume folgen in ihrer oberfläche dem faltungsprinzip der baukörper und machen so den offenen raum zwischen den bauten auf unterschiedlichsten ebenen erlebbar.

in their folded surface, the exterior spaces trace the folded principle of the building volumes and in this way allow the user to perceive and experience the open spaces between the buildings on different levels.

als großzügige eingangsgeste zum quartier fungiert der zweigeschossige freiraum, der vom baukörper entlang der bahnhofstraße als portal umschlossen wird. dieser »portalbereich« wird öffentlich als gastgarten genutzt und verteilt als zentrum die besucher zu den eingängen wifi, gastronomie und mietpartner.

on the bahnhofstraße side, a two-story open space enclosed by the building volume creates a generous entry gesture that leads into the complex. this »portal area«serves as an outdoor café and as a central hub that directs visitors to the wifi, restaurant, and tenant-partner entrances.

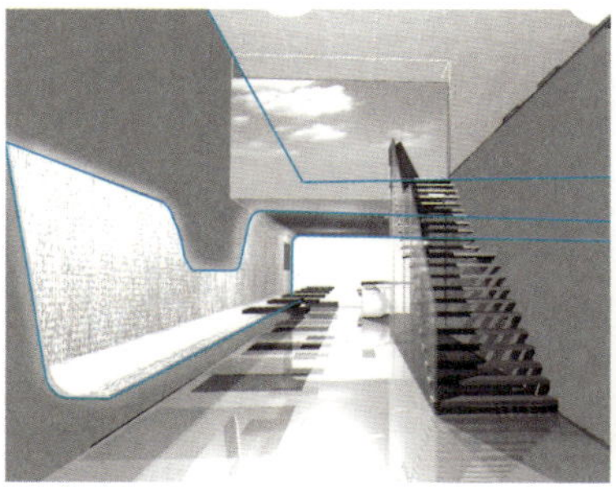

im inneren der anlage wiederholt sich das system der städtebaulichen raumverschränkungen.
im zentrum steht die veranstaltungshalle und die zweigeschossige gastronomie. durch übergänge von ein-, eineinhalb- und zweigeschossigen raumkörpern auf unterschied-lichen ebenen wird der innen- und außenraum von jedem blickwinkel aus mehrfach erlebbar.
die inneren raumzusammenhänge erschließen sich dem betrachter gesamtheitlich.

the inside of the complex echoes the folded design of the structure in its urban planning context. at the center are the function room and the two-story restaurant. the transitions of one-and-a-half and two-story spatial volumes on different levels let the user experience interior and exterior spaces from multiple angles, affording an overall impression of coherency of the interior spaces.

analog zur einrahmungsgeste des »portals« wird das gesamte volumen des zentralen gastronomiebereiches von einem raumgreifenden decken-wand-sitzelement eingefasst.

analogous to the framing gesture of the »portal«, the entire volume of the centrally located restaurant area is enclosed by a vast ceiling-and-wall encompassing seating element.

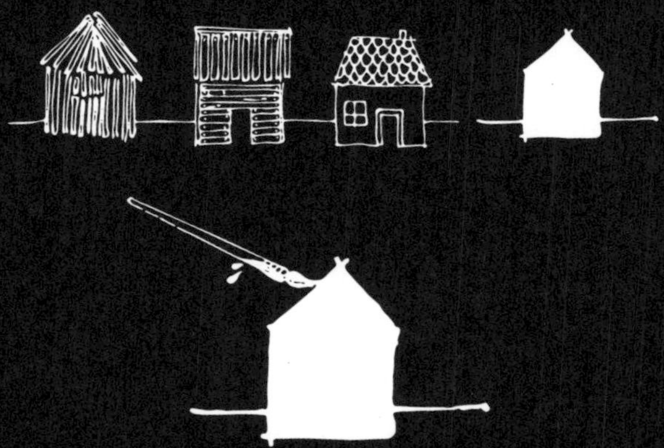

schwarzbauten

in the grey zone

and please do not forget schwarzbauten, schätzchen

»die position im raum«, otto lechner

au, ein zu schneller, oder zwei sich überschneidende gedanken genügen, und ich habe meine position im raum vergessen. da, wo ich mich gerade noch befand, verfinde ich mich; ich habe mich nicht verirrt, weil noch gar nicht bewegt, sondern eben verfunden. kann leicht passieren, denn, ich seh ja nichts. das verfinden allein ist nicht so gefährlich; mit händen, füßen oder ohren lässt sich in ruhe wieder ein orientierungspunkt erkunden. wenn aber jene gedanken einen bewegungsimpuls enthalten haben, dann steigt die wahrscheinlichkeit, mir den kopf anzuhauen, anzustoßen, auf-, ja blutigzuschlagen, sprunghaft. dabei darf ich mich nicht einmal zu sehr ärgern, sonst passiert's gleich nocheinmal. da würden sie mir natürlich ein schirmkapperl empfehlen, aber das mag ich nicht, weil es die akustische wahrnehmung zu sehr beeinträchtigt. auch ein leichter haushelm verträgt sich nicht wirklich mit meinen vorstellungen von lebensqualität. die meisten dieser behelfe zur verringerung der verletzungsgefahr schränken zugleich unsere wahrnehmemöglichkeiten ein.
da heißt es also einerseits, kühlen kopf zu bewahren, und andererseits beim gestalten von räumen vorsorge zu treffen; aber wie?

aufgrund meiner erfahrung bin ich zum beispiel ein fan von schiebetüren; die ragen nicht einfach in beliebigem winkel in den raum, sind platzsparend und lassen sich im idealfall so einstellen, dass sie entweder ganz offen, oder wirklich geschlossen sind. renovierst du aber ein altes haus, so musst du bald erkennen, dass die schiebetüre an ihre grenzen stößt; sie fordert rechtwinkeligkeit, einen geraden boden und gerade wände, sonst will sie nicht recht funktionieren. außerdem ist sie so praktisch, dass sie schon deswegen vielen leuten nicht gefällt, und die meisten tischler haben keine erfahrung im umgang mit ihr.
kurz gesagt: unsere zwei schiebetüren funktionieren schlecht und sind nicht schön.
bei dieser gelegenheit möchte ich dem weitverbreiteten vorurteil, eine schiebetür könne man nicht zuknallen und sie sei deswegen für ein einfamilienhaus nicht brauchbar, entgegentreten: mit etwas kraft und technik lässt sich das ohne weiteres lautstark bewerkstelligen. dafür tut die schiebetür jetzt etwas, das der intention des türschlägers meist nicht entspricht; sie öffnet sich gleich wieder.

die renovierung eines alten hauses setzt voraus, dass man seine form versteht. für mich als musiker ist dies mit der bearbeitung eines werks vergleichbar: kenne ich das original, seine form und seine besonderheiten gut, so kann es sich mir begreiflich machen; es zeigt, was es braucht. möglicherweise will es ja auch abgerissen werden, aber diesen spezialfall will ich hier beiseite lassen.

die erstbesichtigung unserer kleinen villa ließ bei mir ein zauberhaftes gewirr von räumen, schwellen, treppen, terrassen, ein- und ausgängen zurück, das für mich die vorstellung eines schlösschens ergab. allerhand verwirrendes gerümpel stand im wege und beim ständigen ausweichen verlor ich immer wieder die orientierung. vieles schien verwinkelter, als es war. erst mit der gründlichen entrümpelung kam die klarheit, eine vorstellung vom neben- und übereinander der räume, ein gefühl für die größenverhältnisse.

hier, und eigentlich nur hier, ist der punkt, an dem sich der blinde hausmitbesitzer an der planung und gestaltung beteiligen kann, denn wenn einmal die handwerker da sind, wird vieles wieder unbegehbar und unbegreiflich.
so erklärt sich auch, warum ich große bauliche veränderungen nach möglichkeit vermeiden möchte, da sich mir durch eine baustelle mein territorium entfremdet. aber auch der jazzmusiker in mir reagiert auf ähnliche weise: ist man im jazz mit einem stück nicht zufrieden, so verändert man nicht gleich die form, sondern arbeitet an der interpretation; man spielt es anders. umgelegt auf ein haus würde das also bedeuten: bevor ich alles umbaue, versuche ich das haus besser zu bewohnen.

wie nun ein haus aussehen würde, das ich mir nach meinen vorstellungen und bedürfnissen bauen lasse, ist schwer zu sagen. das geheimnis des schlösschens, von dem zuvor die rede war, kann man sich ja nicht selber herstellen. freilich scheint es reizvoll, räume mit unterschiedlichen raumhöhen und akustischen verhältnissen zu kreieren und einen rhythmus für die raumabfolge zu finden. aber hier muss ich wieder zur musikanalogie zurückkommen: ich halte mich selbst für keinen wirklich interessanten komponisten; und so überlasse ich die planung eines hauses lieber den architekten. ich spiel es dann.

»the position in space«, otto lechner

ow, one thought too fast, or two overlapping thoughts are all it takes, and i've forgotten my position in space. here, where i found myself just before, is where i find myself; i have not gone wrong, because i haven't even moved anywhere yet, i've just found myself elsewhere. can easily happen, because of course i can't see anything. finding oneself elsewhere is not so dangerous; with the use of hands, feet or ears, a point of orientation can be calmly ascertained once more. yet if those thoughts included an impulse to movement, then the probability of knocking, banging or even bloodily cracking open my head increases in leaps and bounds. all the same, i musn't get too annoyed, otherwise it will happen again straightaway. of course, you would probably recommend that i use a protective cap, but i don't like them, because they impair acoustic perception too much. even a light home helmet is not really compatible with my idea of quality living. most of these aids for minimizing the danger of injury at the same time limit our perceptual potential.
and so, on the one hand, it is necessary to keep a cool head, and on the other hand to take precautions when designing rooms; but how?

as a result of my experiences i am, for example, a fan of sliding doors; they do not simply rise up arbitrarily in any particular corner of the room, they save space and, ideally, can be adjusted in such a way that they either open completely, or really are closed. however, if you are renovating an old house, you will soon see sliding doors coming up against their limits; they require right-angles, a level floor and straight walls, otherwise they will not want to work properly. furthermore, they are so practical that some people don't like them for that very reason, and most carpenters have no experience in working with them. to put it briefly: our two sliding doors work badly and are not very fine.

at this juncture, i would like to counter the widespread prejudice that a sliding door does not bang shut and for that reason is not suitable for a single-family home: with a bit of power and technique that could easily be solved vocally. however, the sliding door then does something that is not usually in keeping with the intention of door bangers; it opens again right away.

the renovation of an old house presupposes that one understands its form. for me, as a musician, that is comparable to the treatment of a piece of music: if i know the original, its form and its particularities well, then it can become comprehensible for me; it shows me what it needs. it possibly even wants to be torn down, but this special case i will leave aside here.

the first visit to our small villa left behind the impression of an enchanting entanglement of rooms, thresholds, staircases, terraces and entrances and exits, which for me created the idea of a little castle. all kinds of bewildering junk stood in the way and, in constant avoidance of this, i repeatedly lost my orientation. it all seemed more labyrinthine than it actually was. only after a thorough clearout had occurred, did clarity emerge, an idea of the juxtaposition and superposition of the rooms, a feeling for the dimensions.

here, and actually only here, we come to the point where the blind co-owners of a house can participate in the planning and design, because once the workers have arrived, many things become inaccessible and incomprehensible again. that would also explain why i like to avoid large-scale architectural changes as far as possible, because my territory becomes alienated from me when it becomes a building site. but the jazz musician in me reacts in a similar way too: in jazz, if one is not satisfied with a piece, then one does not immediately alter the form, but rather works on the interpretation of it; one plays it in a different way. applied to a house, therefore, that would mean: before rebuilding everything, i ought to try to improve the way i live in the house.

it is difficult to say what a house would look like if i could have it built according to my ideas and needs. one cannot oneself produce the secret of the little castle that i was talking about earlier. of course, it would seem tempting to create rooms of different heights and acoustic conditions and to find a rhythm for the sequence of rooms. yet here i must once again return to the analogy of music: i do not regard myself as a really interesting composer; in the same way, i prefer to leave the planning of a house to architects. i will then play it...

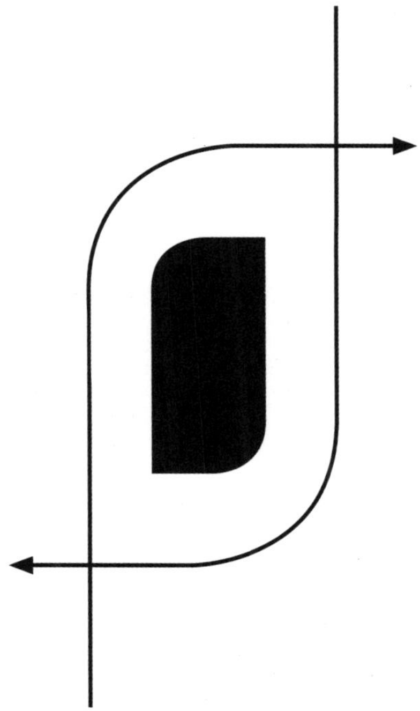

ma 48

büro und garagengebäude wien // office & garage building vienna

zwei runde und zwei scharfkantige ecken angepasst einzig und allein an die verkehrssituation des rege befahrenen betriebsgeländes.
einfach nur »funktionsgebäude«? nein. sondern neue identitätsstiftende, sehr starke, kraftvolle, kubische, kompakte baukörper, deren plastizität durch den flächenbündigen fenstereinbau und die materialität unterstrichen wird. gewählt wurde ein antrazitfarbenes, samtig wirkendes kupfertitanzinkblech, das durch die feinen unregelmäßigkeiten lebendig wirkt und durch die sehr dunkle farbe eine präsenz bekommt. kontrast dazu und wichtiges gestaltungselement ist ein großes, gebogenes schaufenster, das durch den einbau bis zur attikaoberkante wie eingeschnitten wirkt. spannung wird durch das einzige ausbrechen aus der flächenbündigkeit durch eingestellte rolltorboxen im erdgeschoss erzeugt.

bauweise:
stahl-/stahlbetonbau mit stahlbetonkernen und hinterlüfteter metallvorhangfassade.
die werkstatthalle ist durch geschosshohe stahlbetonscheiben im og und verbundstützen an den einfahrseiten stützenfrei und dadurch sehr flexibel. an den querseiten sind betonkerne angeordnet, welche die queraussteifung sicherstellen.

projectmanger sandra scheffl

two rounded and two sharp-edged corners adapted solely to the very busy traffic situation of the factory premises.
just »service buildings«? no. but structures that create a sense of identity. the stark lines of the compact cubic structures are enhanced by flush windows and anthracite-coloured cladding made of copper-titanium-zinc alloy. the very dark colour of the velvety metal sheets gives solid presence to the building, and slight surface irregularities add an element of liveliness. an important contrasting design feature is the large floor-to-ceiling window on the top floor. the clear run of glass up to the top line of the building creates a cut-out effect. the inset rollup doors on the ground floor provide visual tension, as they are the only planes that are not flush with the exterior building wall.

construction:
steel/reinforced concrete construction with concrete cores and rear-ventilated metal-cladded facade.
the workshop floor (ground floor) is designed as a column-free space, providing maximum flexibility. columns are placed at the entry side of the workshop hall. concrete cores on the transverse sides ensure adequate transverse stiffening.

das tiefgeschoss ist in betonbauweise errichtet und über bohrpfähle fundiert. um während der bauphase die zufahrt zu ermöglichen, wurde die baugrube durch bohrpfähle gesichert.

the underground floor is built in concrete, based on drill-foundation piles. to provide vehicle access during the construction stage, the excavation is secured with drill-foundation piles.

wichtiges gestaltungselement ist ein großes, gebogenes schaufenster, das durch den einbau bis zur attikaoberkante wie eingeschnitten wirkt.

an important contrasting design feature is the large floor-to-ceiling window on the top floor.

2

wettbewerb / competition
finanz landesdirektion und gendarmeriekommando
regional finance authorities and police headquarters
2. preis / 2nd prize innsbruck 2001

fld & lgk

das mekka der verwaltungseinrichtungen // a mecca of spruced-up administration buildings

aufgabenstellung des wettbewerbes war die erweiterung von verwaltungseinrichtungen; und zwar für die tiroler finanzlandesdirektion und das landesgendarmeriekommando. im innenhof der umgebenden bestandsgebäude wird ein freistehender schwarzer würfel, die ka'aba, positioniert. als konzentrationspunkt verbindet er über brücken alle gebäudeteile miteinander.

the brief for the competition was to provide an extension for administrative offices; namely, for the headquarters of the tyrolean regional finance authorities and for the regional police headquarters. positioned in the inner courtyard, and surrounded by the already existing buildings, is a free-standing black cube, the kaaba. as a point of concentration, it connects together all the parts of the building by means of bridges.

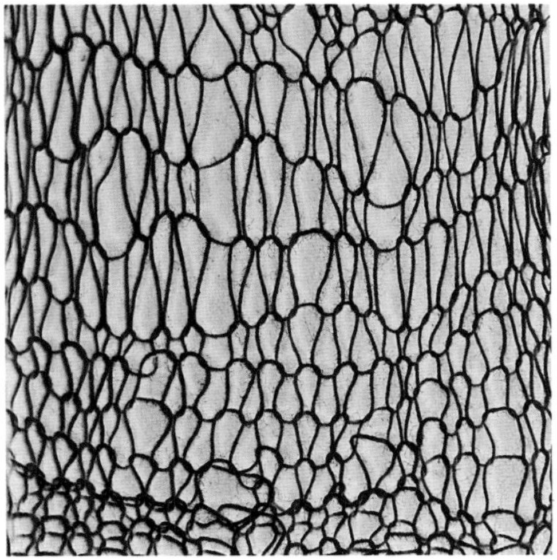

projekt / project
so_oke für / for »palmers«
wien 2001

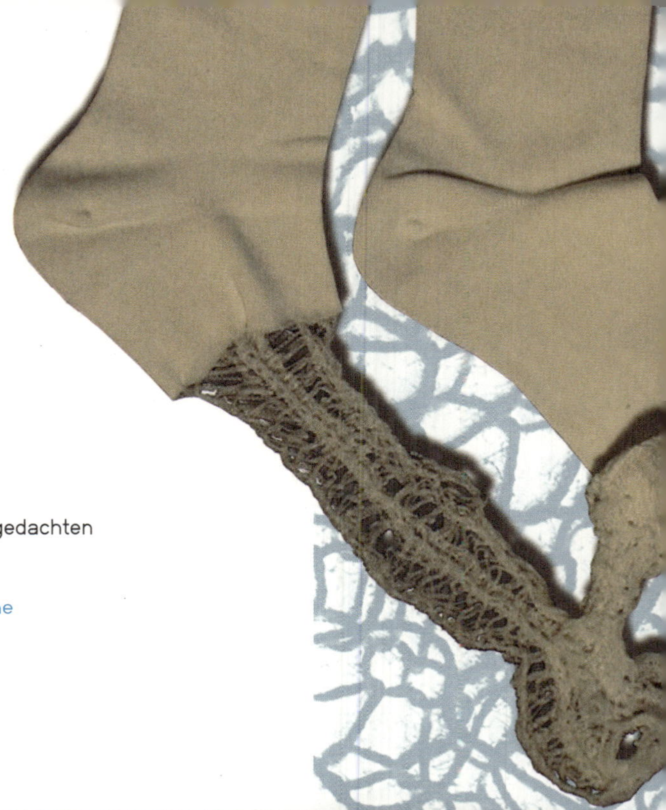

so_oke
»prendre son pied...«

sooke – verringerung der gedanklichen dichte führt zur erhöhung der gedachten geschwindigkeit. garn. ichts.

sooke – a reduction of the mental density leads to an increase in the imagined speed. zip.

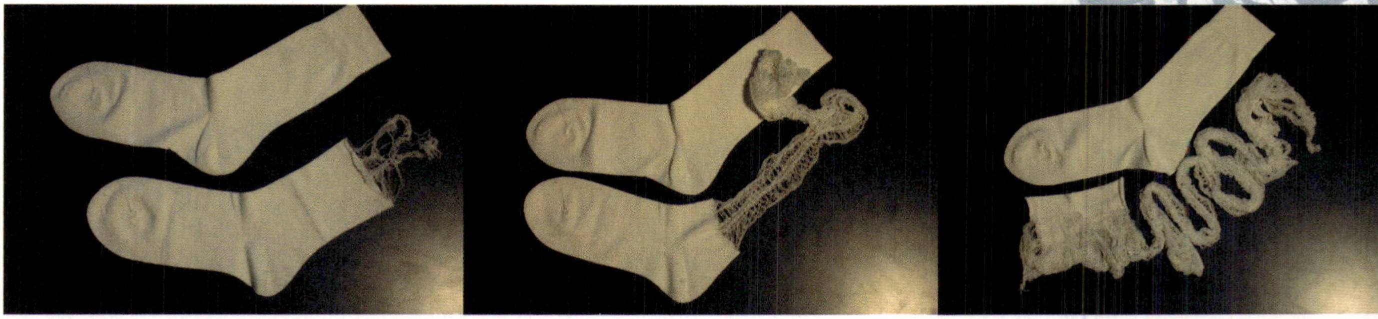

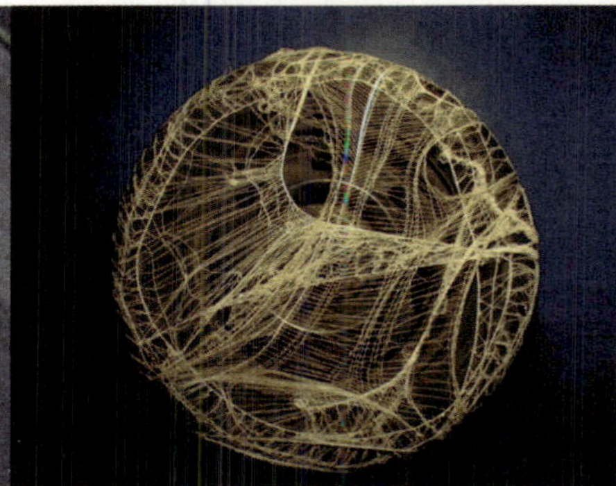

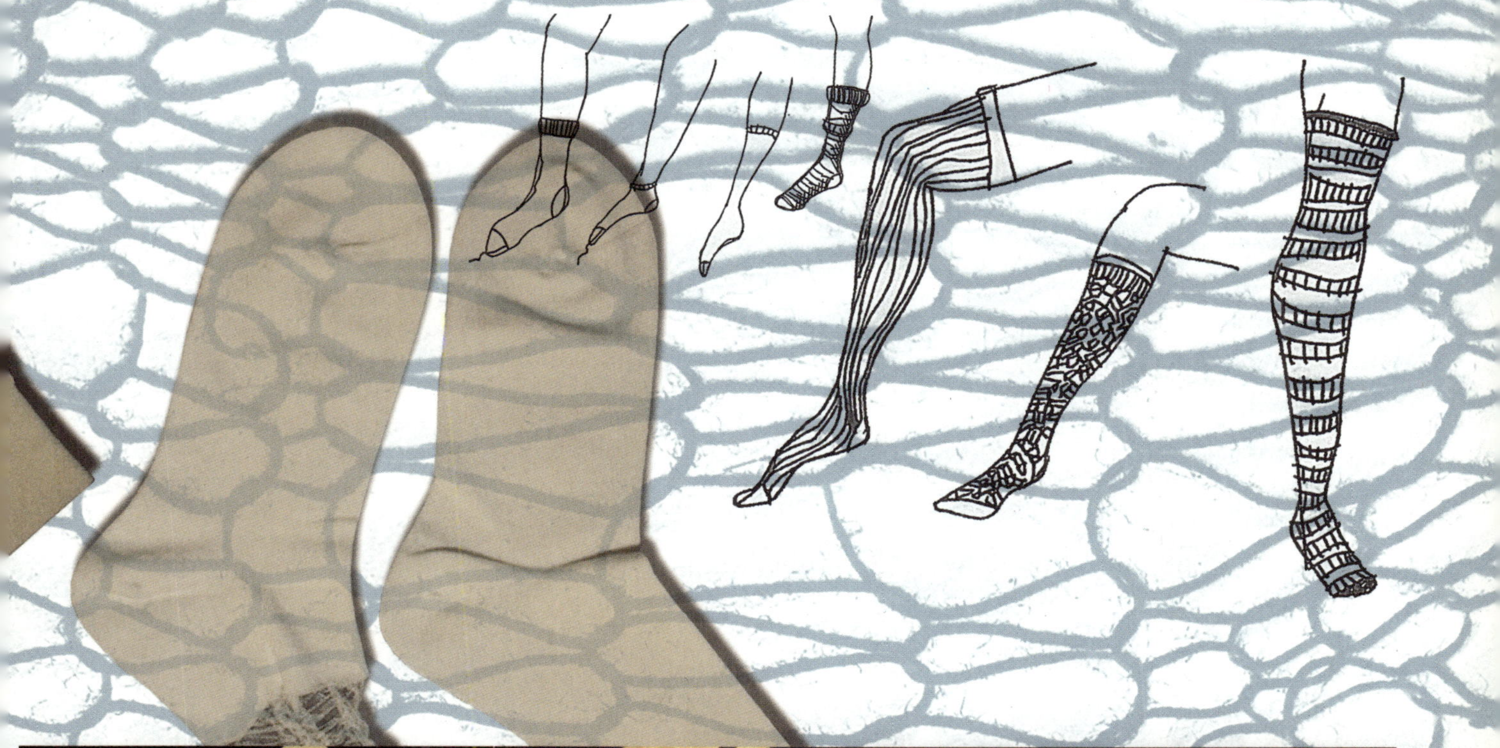

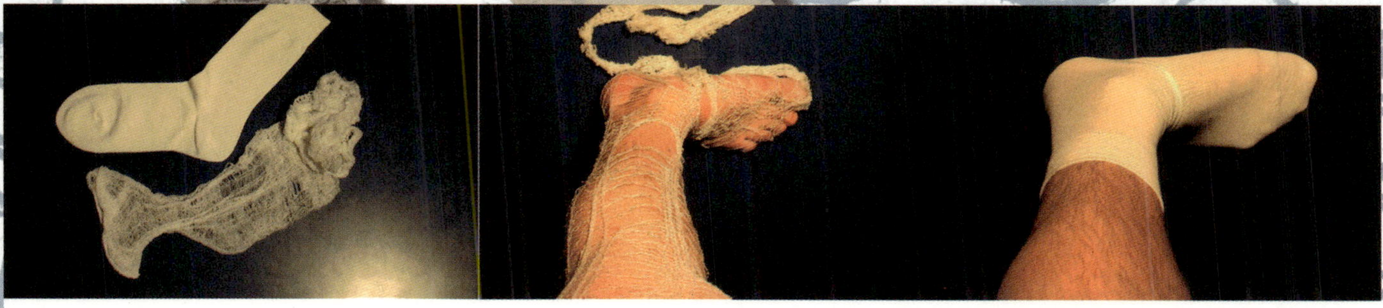

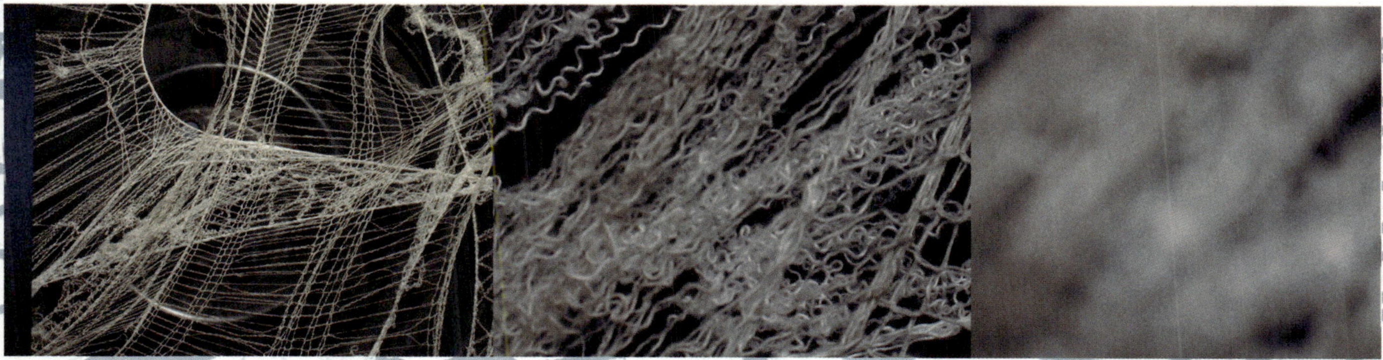

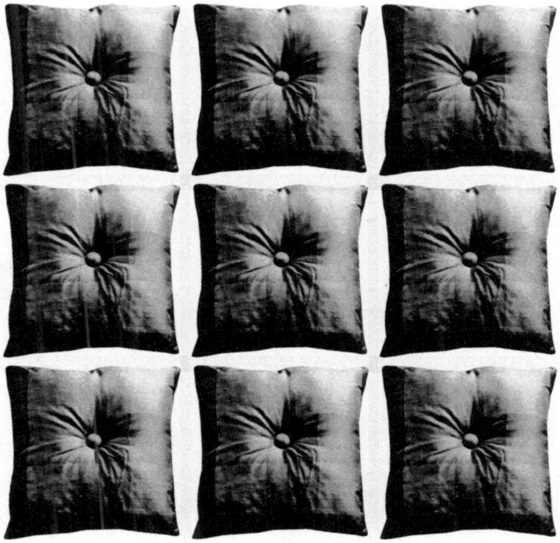

wettbewerb / competition 2002
betriebswerkstätte land oberösterreich
workshop premises upper austria
ansfelden 2006 1. preis / 1st prize

betriebswerkstätte

ein bequemer arbeitsbereich /// a comfortable workspace

erfolg des unerwarteten: entgegen der vom bauherrn angedachten linearen anordnung gruppierte caramel sämtliche hauptfunktionen u-förmig um einen transparent überdachten innenhof; dieser dient als zusätzliche manipulationsfläche. im westlichen trakt befindet sich die zweigeschossig angeordnete verwaltung mit den sozial-, umkleide- und sanitärräumen. an der stirnseite liegt als verbindung zur östlichen werkstatthalle das zweigschossige magazin. transparente tore auf beiden längsseiten der 20 m tiefen hallen dienen als ein- und ausfahrten. den abschluss des werkstättenbereichs bildet der bürotrakt an der vordersten stelle des hofes.
prägendes merkmal des bauwerkes sind die unterschiedlichen, teilweise großflächig eingesetzten kunststoffe: eingehüllt mit schwarzer dachmembran aus kautschuk bilden haupt- und nebenbau eine formal geschlossene einheit. tore aus mehrschaligem, glasfaserverstärktem kunststoff sorgen gemeinsam mit polycarbonat-dachverglasungen und jeweils ca. 120 m² großen etfe-pneus für die belichtung des gebäudes.

success of the unexpected: contrary to the linear arrangement envisaged by the owner, caramel grouped all the main functions in a u-shape around a transparent, covered courtyard, which served as an additional manipulation area. the administration offices are located in the western wing, located on two storeys, together with recreation rooms, changing rooms and washrooms. the two-storey storeroom is situated on the front side, and provides a connection to the eastern workshop shed. 20 m in length, the workshop hall is accessible by vehicle from both sides, with natural light provided by gates reinforced with fibreglass. the conclusion of the workshop area is formed by the office wing at the very front of the yard.
one distinctive feature of the building is the use of different synthetic materials, some of them used to cover a large area: enveloped in black roofing membrane made of rubber, the main building and the side building constitute a formally self-enclosed unit. natural lighting for the building is provided by the gates made of multi-layered, reinforced fibreglass synthetics, in combination with polycarbonate roof glazing and c. 120 m² etfe tyres.

projectmanager alexa zahn

konstruktion: hallenkonstruktion aus vorgefertigten seriellen stahlträgern auf stahlstützen. verwaltungstrakt als selbstständiger zweigeschossiger baukörperteil, überdeckung der freiflächen durch stahl-leichtbau bzw. pneu-konstruktion

construction: the hall is constructed of a prefabricated sequence of steel girders on steel supports. the administration wing as a separate two-storey structural element open areas covered with a lightweight steel construction or a tyre construction

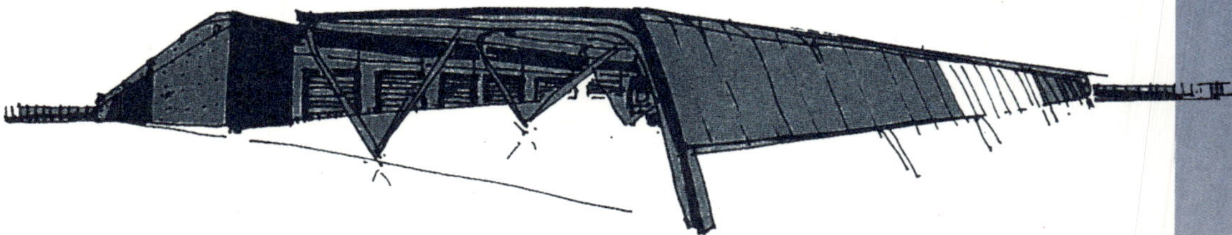

materialien: dacheindeckung/geschlossene fassaden: abdichtungsbahn eva kunststoffmembran außenwand transluzent/tore: gfk (glasfaserverstärkter kunststoff), isolierverglasung; überdeckung des hofs mit luftkissen aus zweilagiger etfe-folie in den abmessungen von ca 6 m x 20 m

materials: roof covering/closed facades: flexible waterproofing sheets of eva synthetic membrane outer wall translucent/gates: reinforced fibreglass synthetics, dual-pane glazing; courtyard covered with air pillows made of two-layered etfe sheets measuring c. 6 m x 20 m

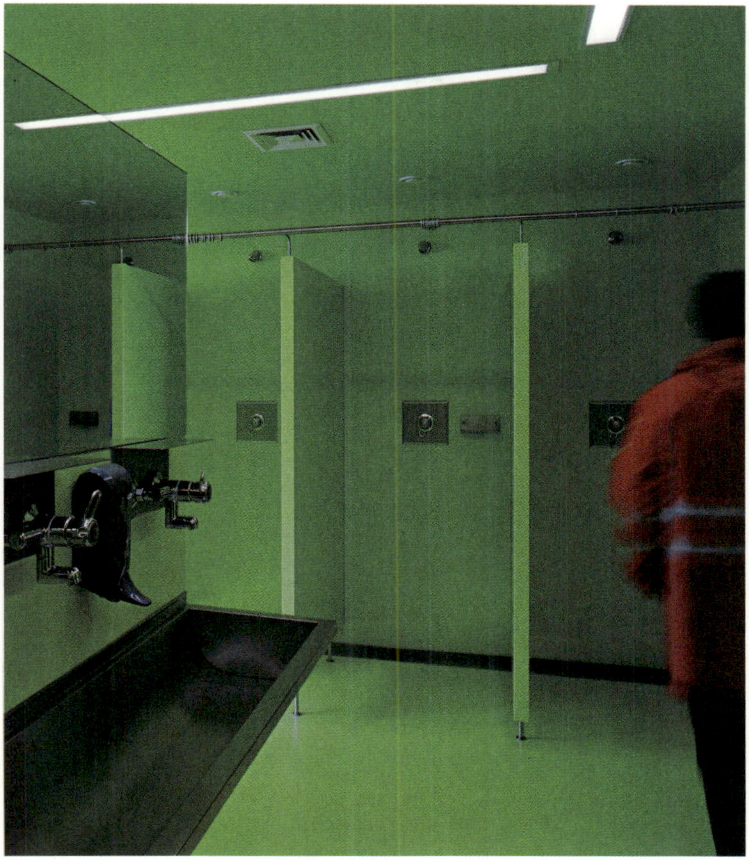

mit ausnahme der hellgrünen waschräume, tendiert das farbschema mit weiss und anthrazit zu gedämpften farben.
with the exception of the bright green washrooms, the color scheme tends to keep a low profile, sticking mainly to white and anthracite.

der sachliche und industrielle ausdruck des gebäudes ist beabsichtigt, daher die verwendung von nur wenigen materialien, z. b. stahl und glas.
the matter-of-fact and industrial vernacular of the building's interior is intentional, making use of only a few materials, e.g. steel and glass.

Caramel

architekten
www.caramel.at

seat art 08

bene 2009

bene

jeder muss muss mal sitzen // everybody has to sit down from time to time

januar / january

februar / february

märz / march

april / april

mai / may

juni / june

der büromöbelhersteller bene lud eine reihe von architekturbüros ein, einen gestaltungsvorschlag zur neu auf dem markt erscheinenden sitzschale »rondo« abzugeben …

… caramel interpretierte die gestaltung etwas freier und machte 12 vorschläge.

juli / july

august / august

september / september

oktober / october

november / november

dezember / december

the office furniture manufacturer bene invited a number of architectural studios to submit design proposals for the new »rondo« shell seat that was to be brought onto the market…

…caramel interpreted the design rather more freely and made 12 proposals.

caramelbüro

zugang architekturbüro // entrance architecture office // wien 2001

als sichtbaren ausdruck der bürogründung konzipierte caramel ein materialexperiment als neuen büroeingang: eine semitransparente kunststoffröhre ist beleuchtungskörper, logoträger und eingangsschleuse in einem. als corpus dient eine vorgefertigte tonne, die im ganzen eingebaut wurde.
den thermischen abschluss zum öffentlichen gang bildet die leider nicht patentierte erfindung einer »glasschiebetür mit anschlag«.

as a visible expression of the founding of its office, caramel devised a material experiment for a new office entrance: a semi-transparent grp tube is a lighting fixture, logo bearer and entrance turnstile all in one. a prefabricated barrel serves as the corpus, which was installed as a whole.
the thermal conclusion of the public corridor is formed by the invention of a »sliding glass door with impact«, which is unfortunately unpatented.

eingangsröhre aus semitransparentem glasfaserverstärktem kunststoff in ovaler form, ca. 1,2 x 2,3 m, abschluss zum gang mit schräg aufgehängter, rahmenloser glasschiebetür, schmutzläufer in der röhre aus kunstrasen, beleuchtung durch hinterleuchtung der gfk-röhre.

entrance tube made of oval-shaped semi-transparent glass-reinforced plastic, c. 1.2 x 2.3 m, concluding towards the corridor with an obliquely hung, frameless sliding glass door, dirt carpets in the tube made of artificial grass, illuminated by means of backlighting in the grp tubes.

wettbewerb / competition
kindergarten tisis
preis, feldkirch, 2000

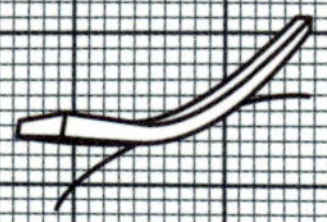

kindergarten tisis

freiraumtheater spielrampe schwebend // open-air theatre with a suspended stage ramp

aufgabenstellung: errichtung eines kindergartens und eines bewegungsraumes für drei spielgruppen. konzept: ausnutzung des hanggrundstückes für die errichtung einer zweigeschossigen spielrampe. der bewegungsraum wird als freie raumrampe mit mehrfachen nutzungsmöglichkeiten und als erlebniswelt für die kinder ausgeformt. unter dem freischwebenden oberen rampenteil wird der außenraum als überdachtes freilufttheater und eingangsbereich bis ins zentrum der gruppenräume verlängert.

brief: construction of a nursery school and a playground for three playgroups. concept: utilisation of the sloping property for the construction of a two-storey play ramp. the area for the playground was developed as a separate spatial ramp with the possibility of multiple utilization and as an adventure world for the children. beneath the free-floating upper part of the ramp, the exterior space is extended in the form of a covered open-air theatre and entrance area, reaching as far as the centre of the group rooms.

schindlberg

mit minimalen mitteln in einen bestehenden heustadel implantiert: das mühlviertler loft! // implanted in an existing hay barn using a minimum of means: the mühlviertel loft!

klo brille // loo seat

dieses wortmonster, dieses wortungeheuer ist eine unverschämtheit, eine maßlose übertreibung und eine fälschung sowieso, kurz, eine dumme affirmative übertreibung durch verdoppelung als anmaßung. das ist schön gesagt. wenn überhaupt, könnte man höchstens von einem monokel sprechen, einem riesenmonokel aus holz, blech oder plastik mit scharnier, ohne glas. ein monokel zum drauf sitzen oder hindurch schauen, in umgekehrter richtung. eine fehlkonstruktion, eine beleidigung des auges und der logik sowieso. ein gerahmtes nichts mit kanalanschluss. ein loch für ein loch. eine verhöhnung der edlen dingwelt, ja unserer abendländischen werte. der erfinder dieses monsters muss ein zyklop gewesen sein, selbst ein archaisches ungeheuer, sicher kein engländer, schon gar nicht einer der industriellen revolution. das wort gehört einfach abgeschafft, wie hosentürl oder blutschande.

this monstrous word, this word-monster, it is a disgrace, an immeasurable exaggeration and a counterfeit naturally, in short, a cockeyed affirmative exaggeration doubling as presumption. that is well-spoken. if at all, one might at best speak of a monocle, of a huge monocle made of wood, metal or plastic, hinged, without glass. a monocle to sit on or see through, in the opposite direction. a faulty design, an insult to the eye and to logic, of course. a framed void connected to the sewer. a hole for a hole. a mockery of the noble world of things, indeed of our western values. the inventor of this monster must have been a cyclops, even an archaic monster, certainly no englishman, nor anyone from the industrial revolution. the word deserves to be simply abolished, like trouser flies or inbreeding.

friedrich achleitner

die einraumwohnung auf rund 100 m² hat ein paar flexible wände und einen fixen sanitärkern; darin findet auch kleinformatiges platz
the one-room apartment of about 100 m² has a couple of flexible walls and a fixed washroom core; there is also room for small-scale objects.

die balken des dachstuhles bleiben sichtbar; aber nicht aus architektonischen gründen: die waren einfach da.
the beams of the roof structure remain visible; but not for architectural reasons: they were simply there.

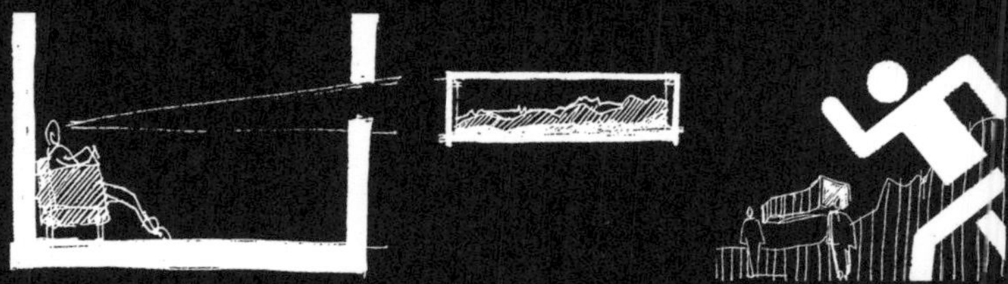

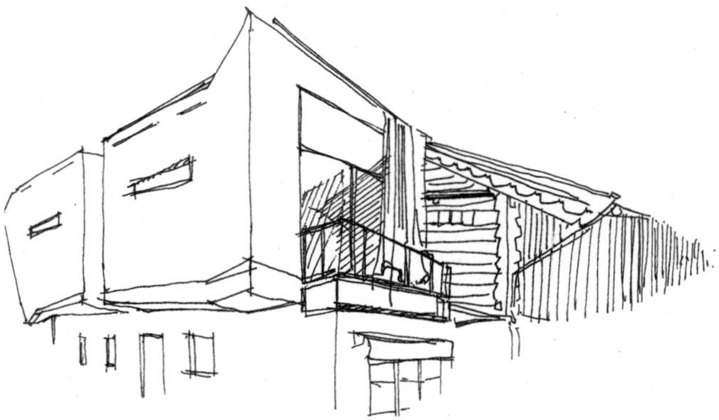

projekt / project
haus_kaps
saalfelden 2004

haus kaps

erweiterung und sanierung eines bauernhofes aus dem 13. jahrhundert // extension and renovation of a farmerhouse of the 13th century

ein rucksack gehört in den alpen zur grundausstattung. das macht dort durchaus sinn, hat tradition – und nicht alles, was tradition hat, muss automatisch von gestern sein...
die ältesten bereiche des historischen, beinahe bilderbuchartigen bauernhauses in ramseiden, direkt über dem ortszentrum von saalfelden in salzburg, stammen aus dem 13. jahrhundert. zwecks wohnraumerweiterung haben die attraktiven gemäuer 2005 zuwachs bekommen. einen an der nordseite angedockten, aus holzfertigteilen gefertigten baukörper – genau, einen echten rucksack eben. er besteht aus zwei gleichgroßen raumelementen, die durch einen achsialen, rundum verglasten freiraum voneinander getrennt sind. das dach der erweiterung dient als terrasse für die darüberliegende wohneinheit. die zwischen neu- und altbau angeordnete treppe ermöglicht den direkten gartenbezug und könnte im falle der ausgliederung der neuen einheit auch als zugang dienen. die ostseitige raumkapsel beherbergt schlaf- und badezimmer und lässt ihre großflächige verglasung schräg nach außen kippen, während die fensterfläche des westseitigen wohnraumes richtung himmel schaut.

a rucksack is part of one's basic equipment in the alps. it makes sense there, and has tradition – not everything that has tradition has to be automatically outdated...
the oldest part of the historical and almost picture-book farmer's house in ramseiden, situated right above the town centre of saalfelden in salzburg, goes back to the 13th century. for the purposes of extending the living space, the attractive walls received an addition in 2005, with a structure adjoining the north side, made of prefabricated timber – and looking exactly like a real rucksack! it consists of two spatial elements of equal size, separated from each other by an open axial space that is glazed all round. the roof of the extension serves as a terrace for the living unit above it. the staircase located between the new building and old building provides direct access to the garden and in the event of a separation of the new unit could even serve as its entrance. the space capsule on the east side houses the bedrooms and bathrooms and its large-scale glazing leans outwards obliquely, whereas the window area of the living spaces on the west side look towards the sky.

projectmanager: clemens kirsch

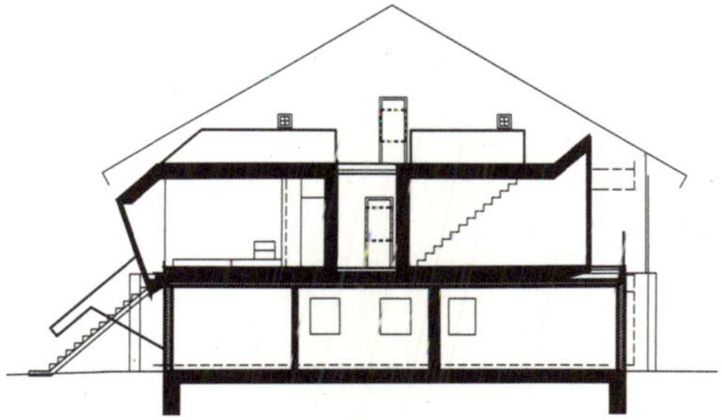

aufgesetzt wurde das ganze auf eine in den 1960er-jahren angebaute garage; dieser bereits vorhandene »fremdkörper« machte es den architekten leichter dem eigentlich perfekten historischen gebäude eine selbstbewusste, eigenständige erweiterung »anzuhängen«.

the whole structure was placed on top of a garage that had been added in the 1960s; this already existing »foreign body« made it easier for the architects to »hang« a intentionally independent extension on to the actually perfect historical buildings.

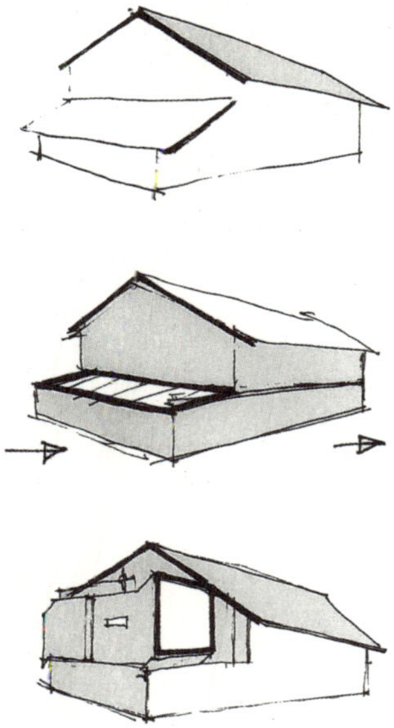

der grundriss des schlichten bestandhauses wurde dahingehend modifiziert, dass zwei unabhängige wohneinheiten mit getrennten erschließungen koexistieren und somit zwei familien heim und hof finden.

the ground plan of the already existing simple house was modified with the aim of making it possible for two independent housing units with separate entrances to coexist, and thereby become house and farm for two families.

das defizit an licht und ausblick wird durch den zubau kompensiert; auch in den sanitärräumen ist das atemberaubende umfeld allgegenwärtig

the deficit of light and views is compensated for in the extension; the breathtaking surroundings are also omnipresent in the washrooms.

zugangsfuge zwischen alt und neu
access joint between old and new

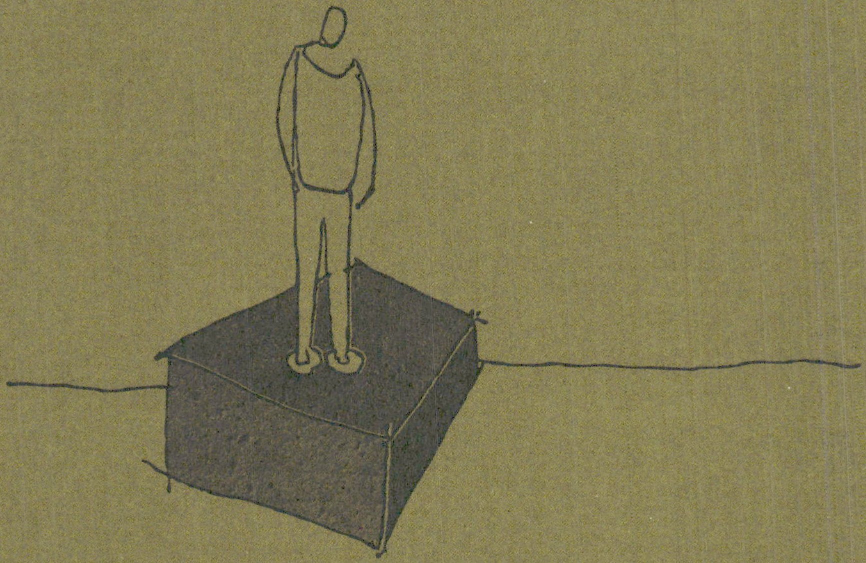

bodenständig

down-to-earth

don't ever forget bodenständiges, schätzchen

»ohne doch is a heisl nur a küwi«, markus binder (attwenger)

ohne doch is a heisl nur a küwi ¶ ohne haubm geh ned aussi und vakü di ¶ ohne wossa is da see a laare gruam ¶ ohne züpfi stengans deppad do de buam ¶ ohne belog is a pizza nur a möbab ¶ ohne salod is a ned so guad da kebab ¶ ohne grund füan die leid si auf wia trottln ¶ ohne ihr do darad er scho laung valottan ¶ ohne flughofm kaus flugzeig nirgends laundn ¶ ohne doimetscha hed i des ned vaschtaundn ¶ ohne schienen foad da zug nur mehr aum schoda ¶ ohne bebies ged nix weida oida voda ¶ ohne wind kumt so schnö ka aundas weda ¶ ohne di warad vielleicht ois nu vü bleda ¶ ohne wiesn dad die kua si schwa midn grosn ¶ ohne tuba iss ned leicht des tubablosn ¶ ohne bam is da woid a laare gstettn ¶ ohne sun do drahns sie durch unsre planetn ¶ ohne moskitos hed da vogl nix zum faunga ¶ ohne eich wa mia die lust scho laung vagaunga ¶ ohne kopf san die leid a wengal kopflos ¶ ohne plan waas kana wos is jetzt los ¶ ohne zweufi is des lebm efta stressig ¶ ohne stress is owa daun a wieder lässig ¶ ohne liacht kaust nix seng ¶ ohne woikn gibz kan reng ¶ ohne topf kaust ned kochn ¶ ohne schmäh kaust ned lochn ¶ ohne feichtichkeit is trockn ¶ ohne strom kaust ned rockn ¶ ohne lift nimm die schtiang ¶ ohne flügl kaust ned fliang ¶ ohne gwaund bist du nokad ¶ ohne pflug wird ned gockad ¶ ohne berg is ois ebm ¶ ohne herz kaust ned lebm

amoi des und amoi dos ¶ wos föd da jetzt nu wos ¶ damit da nix oged ¶ föd da nu wos bled ¶ und waun du ois beinaund host ¶ vo dem du glaubst dass du des nu brauchst ¶ hostu olles wos nur ged ¶ bis auf des wos da föd

wivou' a roof an ouse is bu' a bucket ¶ wivou' a willie boys can't fuck it ¶ wivou' a cap yu'll catch a def o' cold ¶ wivou' any wa'er a lake's an empty 'ole ¶ wivou' th topping pizza's just a mess o dough ¶ wivou' th salad there's no kebab to go ¶ wivou' reason people dunno wot they'r doin ¶ wivou' 'er e'd long ave gone to rack n ruin ¶ wivou' airports there's nowhere for planes to land ¶ wivou' transla'ors even this you wudn't understand ¶ wivou' rails the trains wud only run on gravel ¶ wivou' babies there's no fuchur, me ol devil ¶ wivou' the wind, there'd be no change in th wever ¶ wivou' you fings migh' be much worse, not be'er ¶ wivou' a meadow a cow can 'ardly graze ¶ wivou' a tube a tuba player never plays ¶ wivou' any trees th wood's an empty barren pad ¶ wivou' th sun our planets'd all go mad ¶ wivou' mosqui'os there'd be nufin for the birds ¶ wivou' you lot i'd long 'ave lost me verve ¶ wivou' an 'ead people ain' got a clue ¶ wivou' a plan they dunno wo' a do ¶ wivou' a dou' this life is of'en stressful ¶ wivou' a stress it then becomes righ' blissful ¶ wivou' th ligh' you cannot see ¶ wivou' th clouds no rain falls on me ¶ wivou' a po' you cannot cook a lo' ¶ wivou' any umur yer can't larf a jo' ¶ wivou' th damp it's all dry ¶ wivou' electrics no rock n roll 'igh ¶ wivou' th lift you climb th stair ¶ wivou' any wings yer can't fly through th air ¶ wivou' yer cloves yer naked as adam ¶ wivou' th plow th earf lies barren ¶ wivou' th moun'ins th plains never end ¶ wivou' yer 'eart yer can't live, me friend

one time it's this, one time it's that ¶ wo' is it now that yer still lack? ¶ jus so there's nufin else yer missin ¶ i's daft to be lef' standin there still wishin ¶ and when yer've go' it all togever ¶ all yer believe yer need, for ever ¶ as far as poss, yer've go' the lo' ¶ except for wo' yer've still not go'.

»due to the unique complexity, elegance and beauty of the upper austrian dialect, one should, as a matter of principle, refrain from translating upper austrian texts into high german, or any other foreign language. however, the essential message of this poem seems to be too important not to at least attempt to do so, after all one should take it to heart – in any language: without a roof, a house is just a bucket!«

translated from the upper austrian, via austro-german, into cockney © by peter waugh

wettbewerb / competition
science park linz
1. preis / 1st prize linz 2005

science park

johannes kepler universität linz

es galt mehrere einzelne gebäude zu entwerfen, die in einem zusammenhang zueinander und zum bestehenden campus der linzer universität stehen. die nachbarlichen wohnbauten mussten berücksichtigt werden, die natürliche form des hanges und die zur kühlung der stadt wichtigen fallwinde. nicht zu vergessen: der schlechte baugrund.

durch den bau des »science parks« in unmittelbarer nähe zum campus der johannes kepler universität möchte man wirtschaft und forschung näher zusammenrücken und forschungskapazitäten nach linz ziehen. im sinne eines modernen science-arbeitsklimas wurde daher besonders darauf geachtet, zwischen den einheitlichen strukturen offene bereiche zu schaffen, die einen austausch und lebendigkeit fördern.

um einer starren rasterstruktur zu entgehen, wurden durch knickungen die möglichkeiten des freiraums des grundstückes ausgereizt. dadurch entstanden eine lockerere struktur und eine bessere streuung der verschiedenen raumsituationen. um jene raumsituationen, die als treffpunkte genutzt werden können, nicht nur im außenbereich, sondern auch im inneren fortzuführen, wurden die einzelnen riegel als zweihüftige bauwerke konzipiert. der verglaste mittelbereich lässt über eine innen liegende halle nicht nur das licht bis in die unteren geschosse fallen, sondern schafft auch kommunikative flächen.

the program involved designing several individual buildings which would be interwoven as well as tied to the existing university of linz campus. the plan was to take into consideration the neighboring residential buildings as well as the natural form of the slope and the katabatic winds, which play an important role in keeping the city cool, and the poor condition of the building lot was not to be overlooked either.

with the erection of the »science park« in the immediate vicinity of the johannes kepler university the objective was to bring together economy and research and draw research expertise to linz. in keeping with the standards of a modern scientific working climate, particular attention was paid to creating open areas between the uniform structures, thus creating spaces to encourage exchange and activity.

in order to avoid an inflexible grid structure, straight lines were bent, thus also making full use of the grounds. in this way a more relaxed structure and a better distribution of the different spatial situations were created. to plan both outdoor and indoor spatial situations that could potentially serve as meeting points the individual elongated blocks were conceived as two-part buildings. the glazed central area not only allows daylight to enter the lower levels via a large indoor hall but also creates communicative zones.

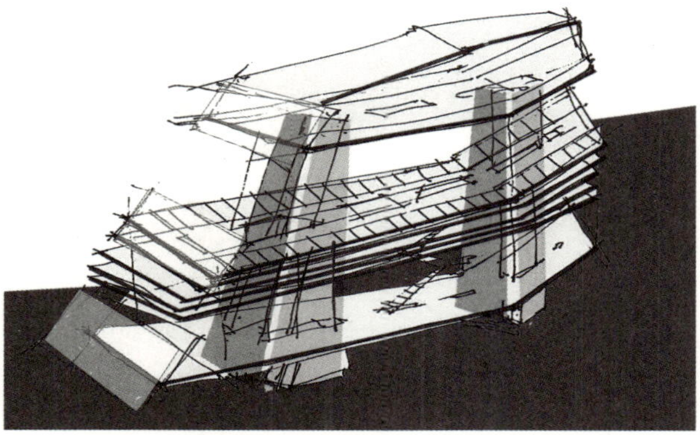

park-/leitsystem //
parking and
direction system

lage/topographie //
location/topography

bauteil 1 mechatronik	construction unit 1 mechatronik
ngf 18.521 m²	nua 18,521 m²
bgf 20.094 m²	gfs 20,094 m²

bauteile 2-4 gesamt	building units 2-4 total
ngf 48.810 m²	nua 48,810 m²
bgf 52.218 m²	gfs 52,218 m²

projectmanagers
markus bösch (2005-2008)
gisela mayr (scp1)
julia stoffregen (scp2)
matthias bresseleers, claudia rockstroh (scp3)

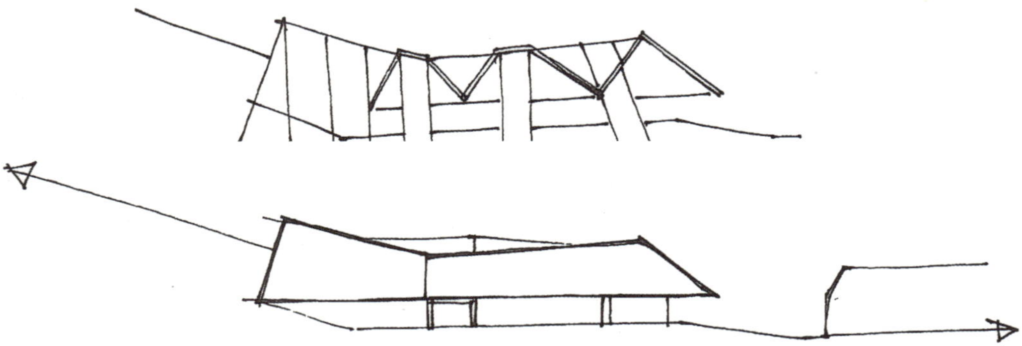

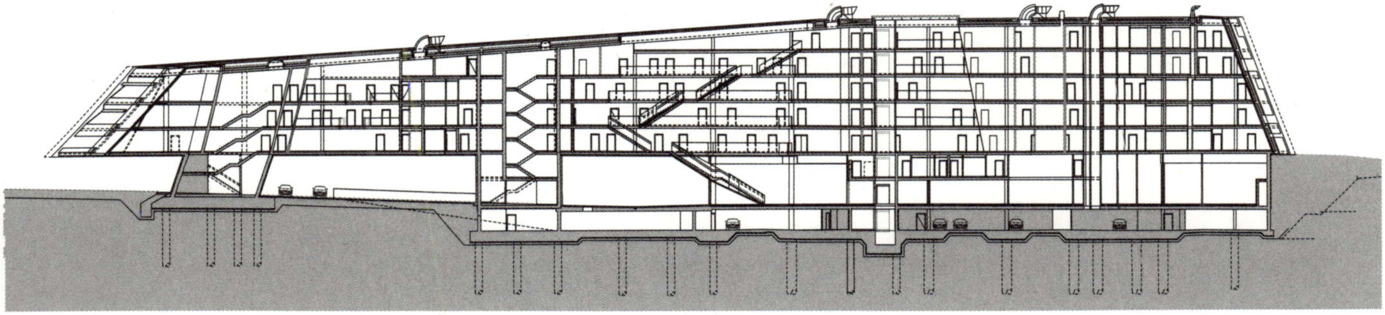

die horizontale verknickung ergibt sich aus der rücksichtnahme gegenüber den bestehenden bebauungen. so übernimmt die höhenentwicklung des gebäudes einerseits die hangoberkante im norden, und andererseits die traufenkante der südlichen wohnbauten. dass die südseite nochmals nach hinten knickt, ist aber nicht nur ein entgegenkommen den nachbarn gegenüber, sondern teil eines spiels mit der vorderkante, die in der summe der bauetappen letztendlich zur modulierten form wird. insgesamt war es wichtig, dass sich das projekt in das gelände »duckt«. deshalb wurde der hang abgegraben und an der hangseite ein sockelgeschoss errichtet, das die sonderräume wie werkstätten beinhaltet und die einzelnen bauetappen miteinander verbindet. darüber schweben die bürotrakte, zwischen denen die landschaft in das areal fließt. eine maßnahme, mit der auch die schwierige anbindung an den bestehenden campus gelöst wurde, trennt doch die stark befahrene altenbergerstraße beiden areale.

the horizontal bending of the elongated blocks arose out of consideration for the existing structures. moreover, the height of the building corresponds to the upper edge of the slope to the north and at the same time the eaves of the residential buildings to the south. the subsequent bend in the buildings on the south side, however, results not only out of consideration for the neighbors but plays with the front edge, which, as seen along with all the building sections as a whole, ultimately modulates the overall form. all in all, it was essential for the project to »crouch« into the landscape. this is why part of the slope was removed to make way for the basement, which houses the special rooms like laboratories and workshops and connects the individual building sections. above this, hover the office wings between which the landscape flows into the grounds – a measure which was used to overcome the difficult task of tying the new structures to the existing campus, although these two areas are separated by a heavily used road (altenbergerstraße).

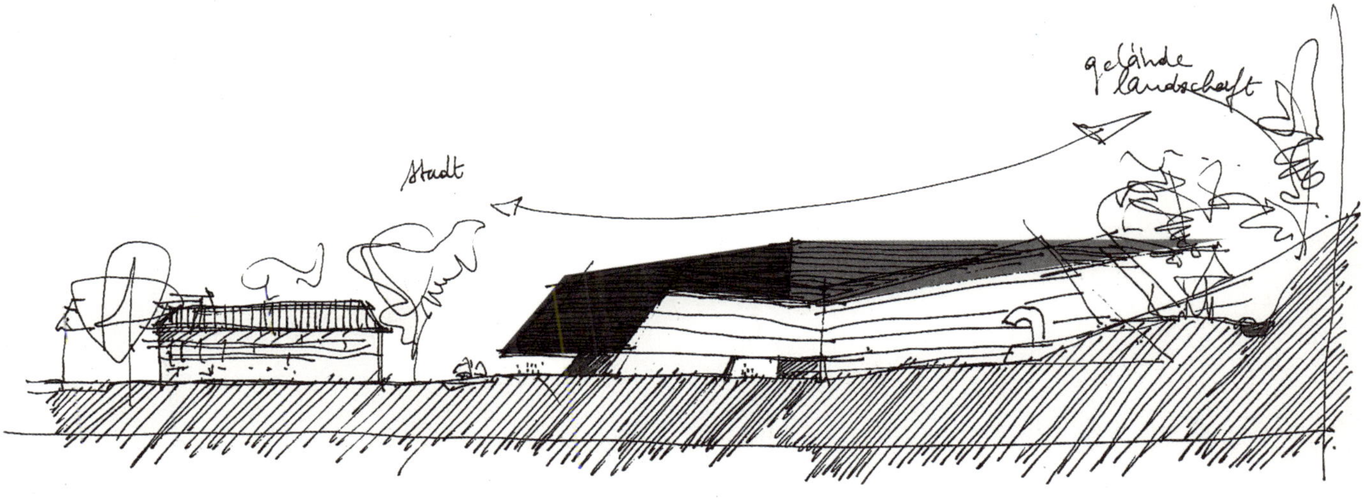

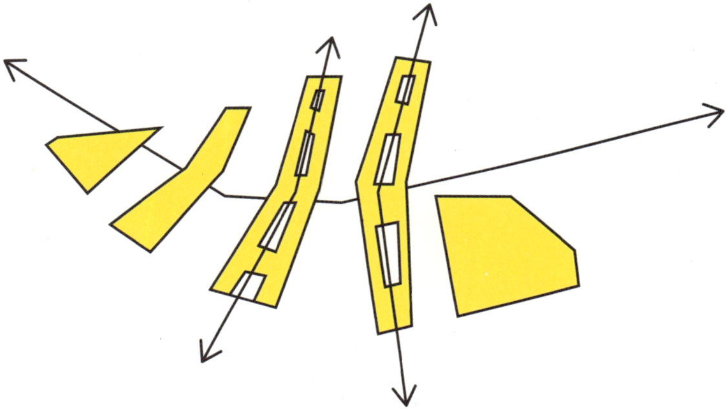

durchgang / wegeverkehr / netz //
passage / footpath traffic / network

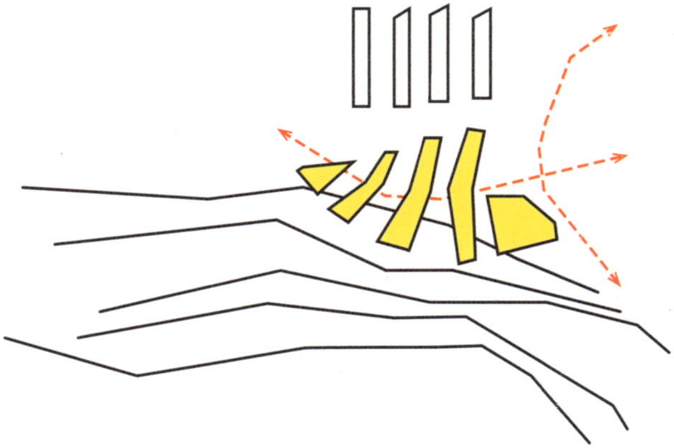

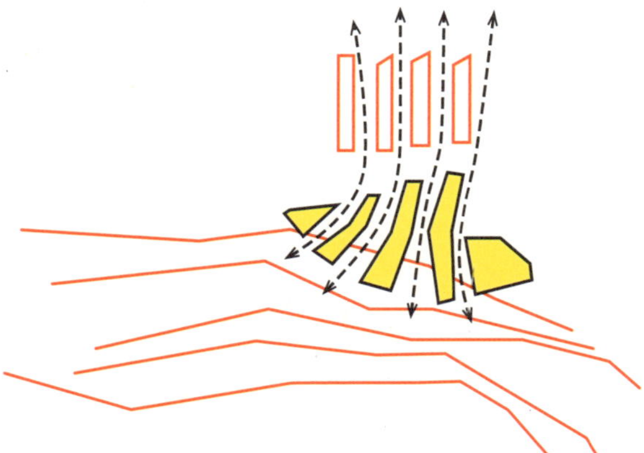

das gelände wurde so weit abgesenkt, dass man auf der seite des science parks zu ebener erde in eine unterführung kommt, die auf der seite des uni-campus mit einer langen rampe langsam durch den park bis unmittelbar vor die gebäude führt. damit ist die anbindung zumindest annähernd ebenerdig.

on the science park side, the grounds have been recessed enough so that one enters the underpass at ground level, following along a gradually sloping ramp that leads through the park straight up to the buildings on the university campus side. in this way, the connection is at least in part at ground level.

innen / außen // inside / outside

wegen der großen spannweite und der durchbiegung ist das tragwerk als brückenkonstruktion konzipiert. zwei massive kerne tragen ein stahl-hängewerk von 160 m länge.
dem statischen system des hängewerks ordnet sich auch die gestaltung der fassade unter. nicht zufällig sind die parapete angeordnet, sondern genau an den punkten der größten durchbiegung platziert. dadurch entsteht eine diversifizierende wirkung nach außen und mehr individualität im inneren. ein spiel, das durch lamellen verschiedener tiefen und abstände verstärkt wird.

due to its enormous span and the deflection, the unit has been designed as a bridge structure, in which two massive cores support a 160 m long steel truss frame. the design of the façade also conforms to the structural system of the truss frame. the parapets are not arranged randomly but have been placed to coincide with the points of greatest deflection. in this way, the outward impression is diversified, while the interior is marked by greater individuality. a fascinating tension, the effect of which is intensified by the arrangement of the lamellae at different levels and intervals.

quartett

der erste geiger hatte einen unaussprechbaren namen. der zweite geiger war linkshänder. der name des bratschisten war aussprechbar, trieb aber den meisten leuten schamröte ins gesicht. der cellist hatte behaarte unterarme, der arme, war aber rechtshänder und von tadellosem leumund. obwohl das quartett schon ein dreißigjähriges jubiläum feierte, siezten sich die mitglieder beharrlich. außerdem stritten sie unentwegt, schenkten einander nichts im zuteilen von ordinären, ja schweinischen schimpfwörtern, zitterten aber, wenn einer einen husten bekam. in diesem moment hatte ich meinen täglichen niesanfall, so dass ich die geschichte nicht mehr fortsetzen konnte, schade.

friedrich achleitner

the first violin had an unpronounceable name. the second violin was left-handed. the name of the violist was pronounceable, but made most people blush terribly. the cellist had hair on his lower arms, poor thing, but was right-handed and had an immaculate reputation. although the quartet was already celebrating its thirtieth anniversary, the members persisted in addressing one another formally. moreover they were always quarrelling, with each as bad as the next when it came to dishing out rude, even swinish four-letter words, yet they trembled if one got a cough. at that moment i had my daily attack of sneezing, so that i could no longer continue the story, a pity.

wettbewerb / competition
musikschule / music school
2. preis / 2nd prize niederwaldkirchen 2010

musikschule

ein dach für alle fälle! // a roof for all events!

schutz, ganz klar, dafür ist ein dach in erster linie da. neben dieser funktion für die musikschule und den probenbetrieb der örtlichen blasmusik übernimmt das großflächige gründach noch weitere wichtige aufgaben: - integration der bushaltestelle/ankommen zubringer - geschützter, öffentlicher freibereich mit arena (sitzstufen) - überdachung des barrierefreien zugangs zum altbau - außenliegender sonnenschutz - freiraumschaffung in unmittelbarer zuordenbarkeit zur angrenzenden volksschule

it is clear that a roof is primarily there for protection. apart from fulfilling this function for the music school and the rehearsal room of the local brass band, the large-scale roof with greenery also has other important functions to fulfill: - integration of the bus stop/arrival of delivering vehicles - protected outdoor public area with an arena (seating terrace) - covering for barrier-free access to the old building - outdoor sun protection - creation of free space in the immediate vicinity of the adjacent primary school

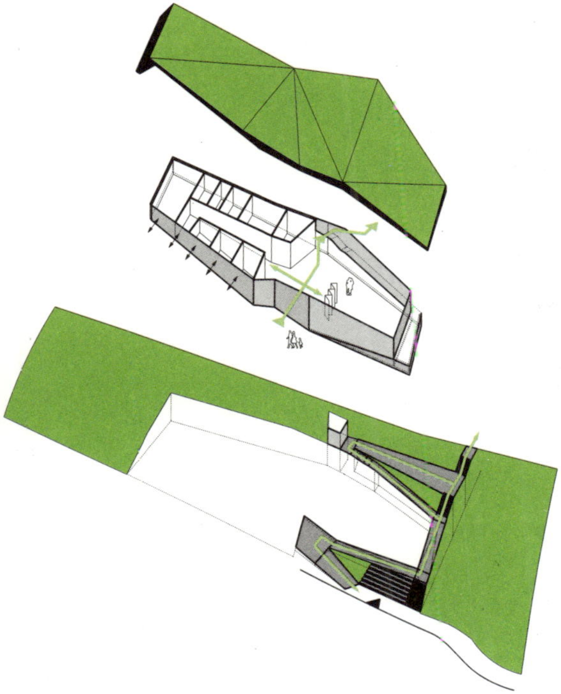

sämtliche funktionen der musikschule (südlicher bereich) und der musikprobe (nördicher bereich) sind auf einem niveau angeordnet. die allgemeinen bereiche, wie foyer, sind beiden funktionen zugeordnet. ein konstenintensiver lift kann entfallen. es ist jedoch – falls gewünscht – möglich, den zukünftig für die volksschule nötigen lift bis in den foyerbereich zu führen.
das gebäude entwickelt sich vom süden bzw. westen »aus dem hang« und bildet richtung ortszentrum hin den eingang aus.

all the functions of the music school (southern area) and of music rehearsals (northern area) are arranged on one level. apart from the attribution cf general areas, such as the foyer, to both functions, this also makes it possible to dispense with a cost-intensive lift. however, it would be possible – if so desired – to have any lift that might be necessary for the primary school in the future, going up to the foyer area.
the building emerges »out of the slope« from the south and the west, and has its entrance facing in the direction of the centre of the village.

wettbewerb / competition
sonderschule / special needs school
2. preis / 2nd prize schwechat 2001

sonderschule

mitten im nirgendwo … // in the middle of nowhere …

schön wäre es, so dachte caramel, eine grüne oase für alle schüler zu schaffen. eine besondere schule im industriegebiet. das raumprogramm sieht neun klassen, einen hort und eine turnhalle vor. durch eine raumschleife um und in den grünbereich hinein haben alle klassen einen ebenerdigen, direkten zugang zum außenbereich. der auf diese art zu einem »grünen klassenzimmer« unter freiem himmel wird.

wouldn't it be nice, caramel thought, to create a green oasis for all the pupils. a special school in an industrial area. the room plan envisages nine classes, an after-school care club, and a gymnasium. a loop of rooms leading round and into the green area ensures that all the classrooms have direct ground-floor access to the outside, which, in this way itself becomes a »green classroom« outdoors.

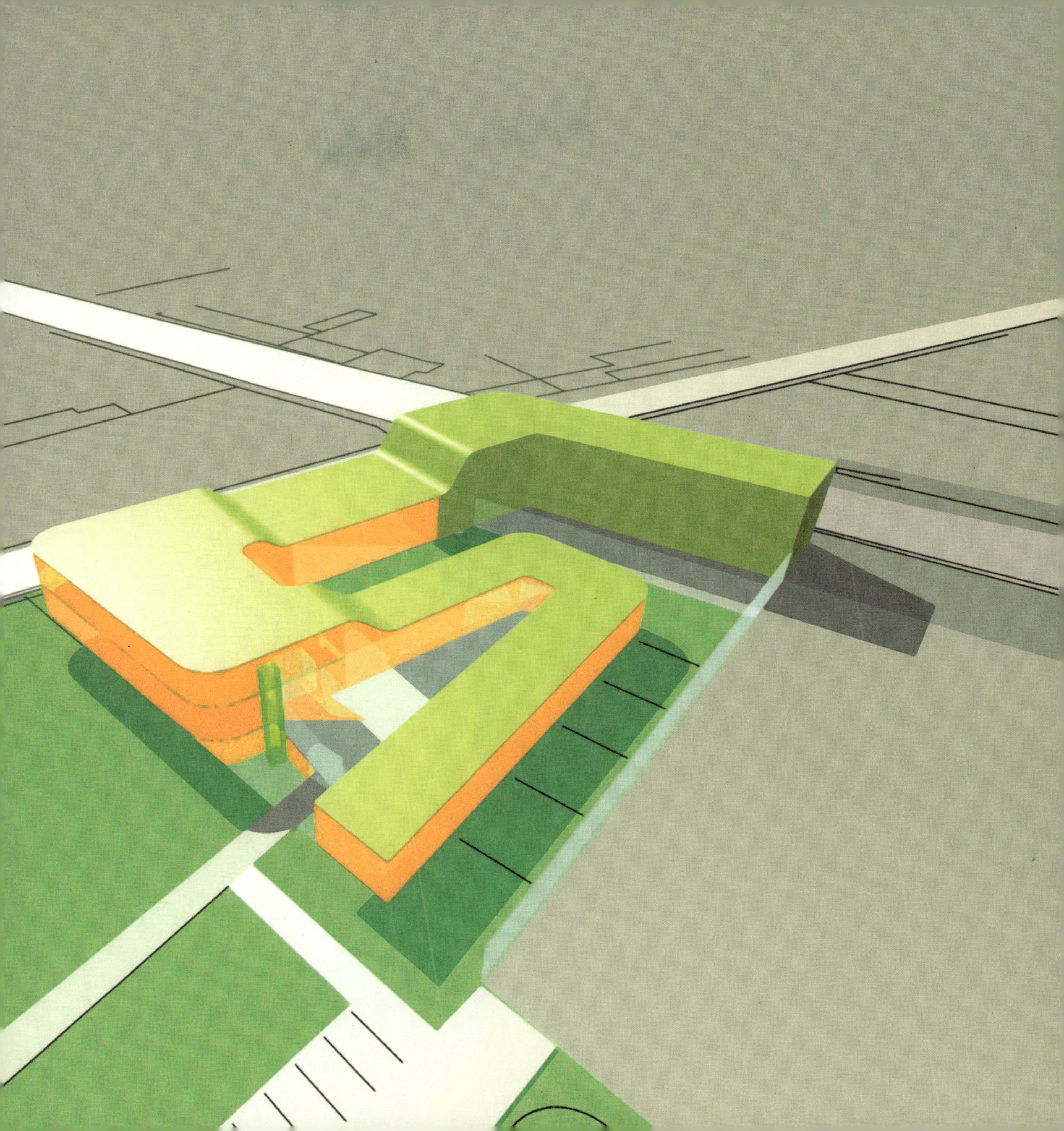

LAGE- und HÖHENPLAN
1:250
0 2,5 5 7,5 10 12,5 15 17,5 20 m
EZ 472, Bfl.(begr.)
Kögler Maria (2/3)
Untinger Ingrid (1/3)
Neudauerstr. 13, 3420
EZ 1773, Bfl. (Geb., begr.)
Neumüller Brigitte (1/2)
Springerg. 14, Wien 1020
Paar Walter (1/2)
Neudauerstr. 13, Kritzendorf 3420
800
9
Apfel
Sichtschutz

haus s

ein wirklich schönes gartengrundstück am wiesenhang mit zwei aufgabenstellungen: die bauherrin will zwar bauen, aber keinen quadratmeter ihres geliebten gartenparadieses verlieren – schöner hang, aber leider nach norden orientiert.
lösungsvorschlag: abheben, der sonne entgegen.

a really beautiful garden property on sloping fields with two briefs: although the owner wanted to build on the property, she did not want to lose even one single square metre of her beloved garden paradise – a beautiful slope, but unfortunately not north-facing.
proposed solution: raise it towards the sun.

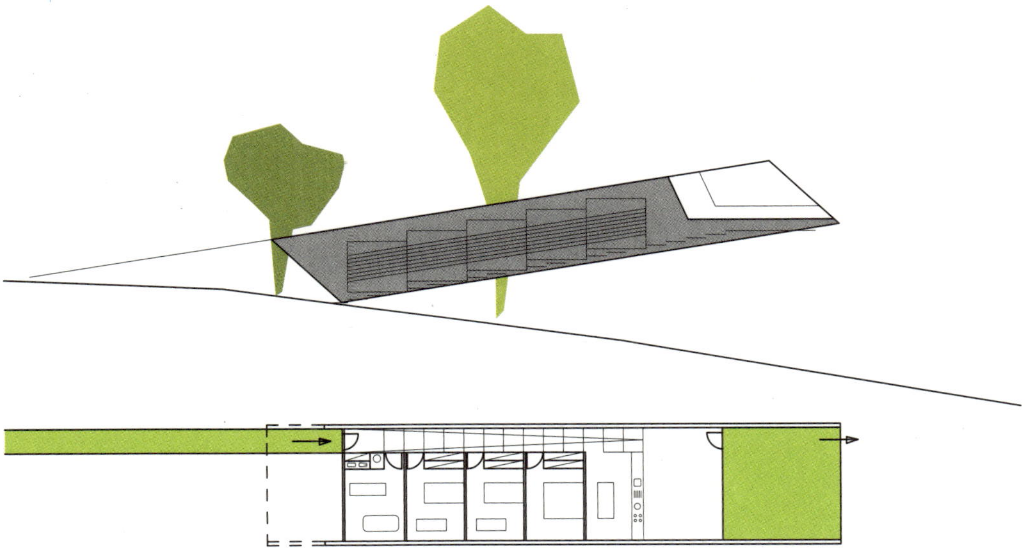

wettbewerb / competition
tunnel lüftungszentrale / tunnel ventilation center
wien 2008

landscape-house-hybrid

das konzept für die tunnellüftungszentrale ist eine hybride struktur aus landschaft und gebäude. aufwölbungen aus verdichtetem aushubmaterial und begrünte landschaftsbildende dächer, die sich zu einzelnen gebäudeteilen aufrichten.

the concept for the tunnel ventilation headquarters is a hybrid structure comprising landscape and building. vaulting composed of compressed excavation material and roofs with landscaped greenery rises to form the individual parts of the building.

nur wir und die frei fließende landschaft, oder ist da noch wer?
only us and the freely flowing landscape – or is there anyone else here?

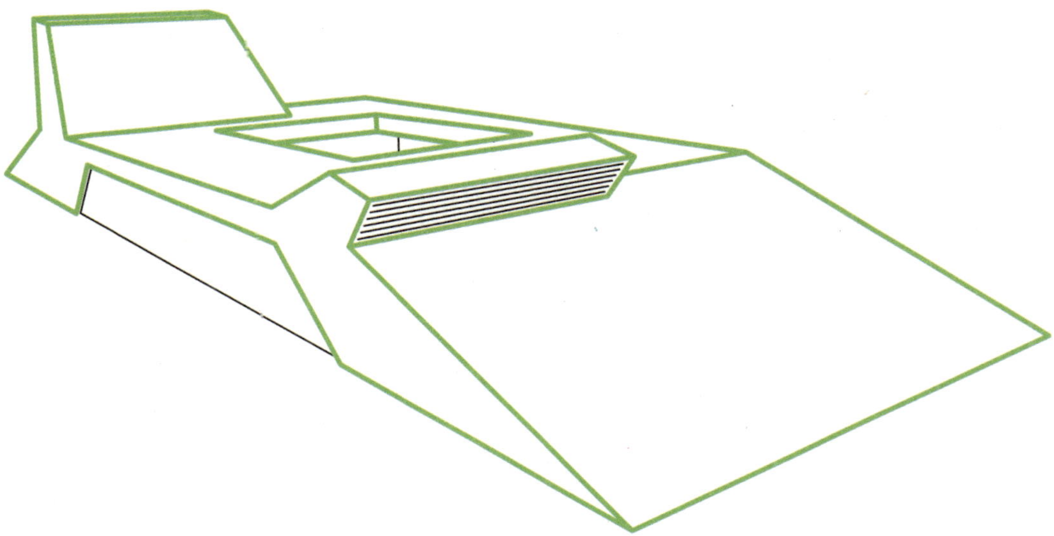

wettbewerb / competition
erweiterung stadthalle / extension to the town hall
heidelberg 2009

erweiterung stadthalle heidelberg

die stadt wächst zum fluss // the city grows towards the river

stadthallenerweiterung als verbindende landschaftsgestaltung zwischen altstadt und neckarufer. das dach, eine öffentliche tribüne zum neckar, dient als großes freilufttheater und aussichtsplattform in die altstadt heidelbergs.

an extension to the stadthalle as a piece of connecting landscape design between the old town and the banks of the neckar. the roof: bleachers looking towards the neckar. they also serve as a large open-air theatre and as a panorama platform for viewing the old town of heidelberg.

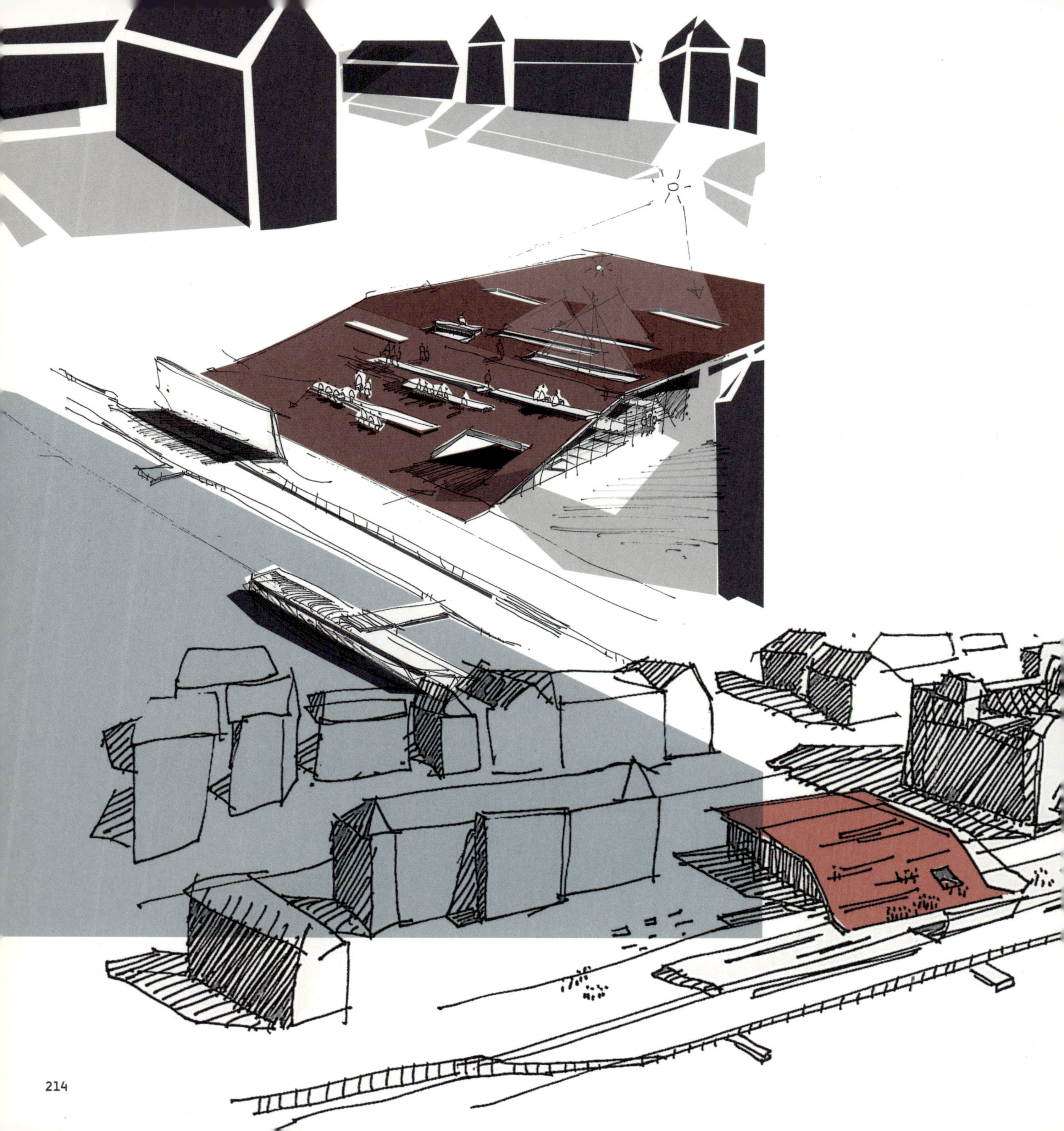

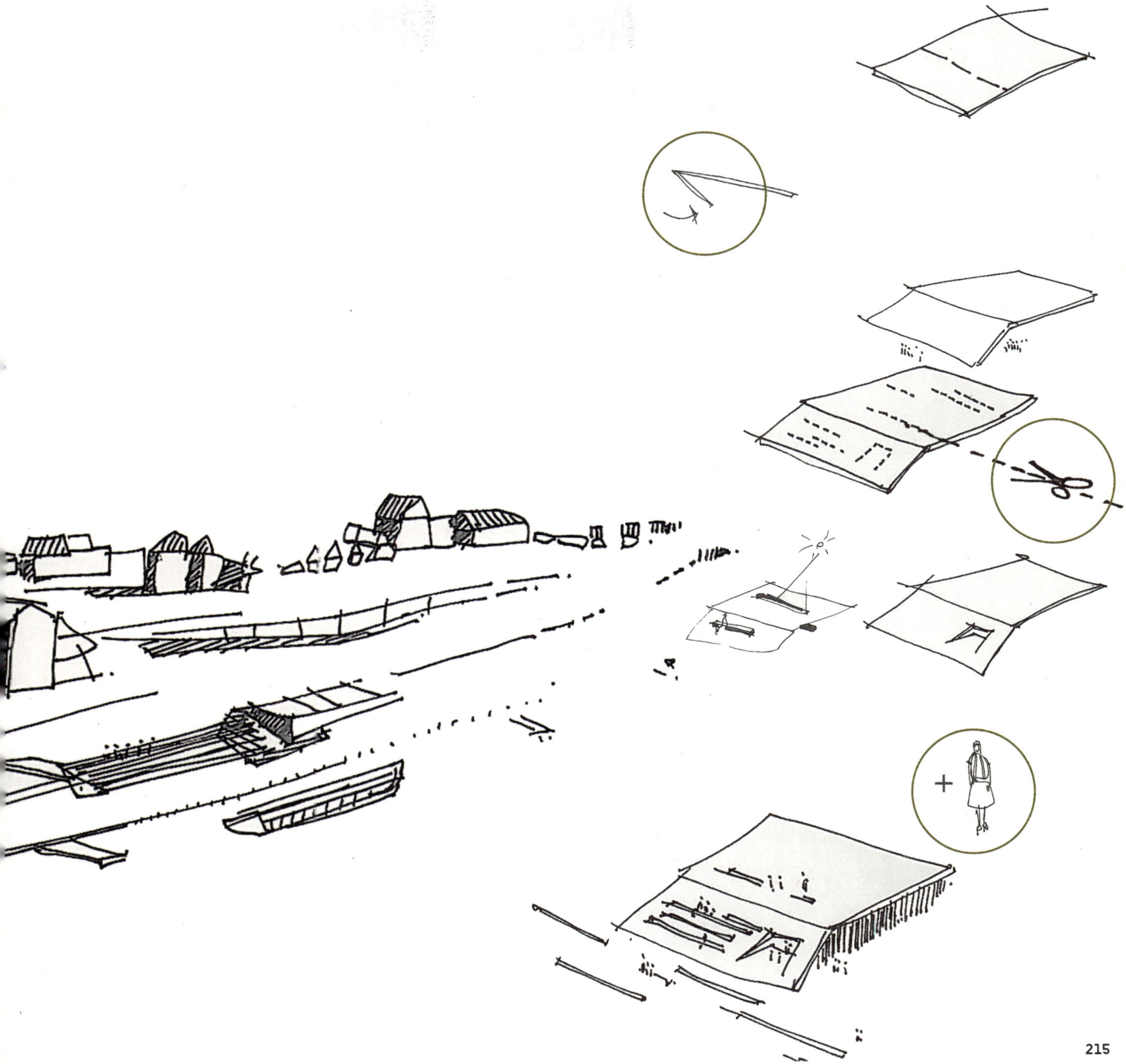

wettbewerb / competition
erweiterung verwaltungsbau / office building extension
preis prize wien 2004

arbeiterkammer wien

schad' um den park // pity about the park

zu schad', um das grün der erweiterung zu opfern;
die erweiterung ist der park ...
der verwaltungsbau aus den 1950er-jahren platzt aus allen nähten. ein zeitgemäßer servicebereich ist nicht vorhanden. durchgrünt und lichtdurchflutet präsentiert sich der erweiterte verwaltungstrakt. der park wölbt sich als dach über die neuen funktionen der arbeiterkammer.

too much of a pity to sacrifice the green to an extension;
the extension is the park ...
the administration building, which dates from the 1950s, is bursting at the seams. a contemporary service area is non-existent. full of greenery and flooded with light is how the extended administration section appears. the park bulges as a roof above the new functions of the chamber of labour.

wettbewerb / competition
stadthalle / town hall
neunburg 2008

stadthalle neunburg

gleichung ohne unbekannte: 70 satteldächer + 7 satteldächer = altstadt + stadthalle. // equation without unknowns: 70 gable roofs + 7 gable roofs = old town + civic centre.

die lange reihe von satteldachhäusern bestimmt das bild der altstadt entlang der hauptstraße. als verlängerung davon entwickelt sich die angrenzende neue stadthalle als neuinterpretation dieser archetypischen gebäudeform.

the long row of buildings with gable roofs dominates the image of the old town along the main street. as a prolongation of it, the adjacent new civic centre is developed as a reinterpretation of this archetypal form of building.

die dachabwicklung an der hauptfassade bildet den grundlayer für die gebäudeform. differenzierte faltungsmaßstäbe vereinen die funktionen veranstaltungssaal, cafe, verwaltung und fremdmieter unter einem dach.

the roof development on the main facade provides the first layer of the building's form. the various ways in which it is folded combine the different functions of the events hall, cafe, administration and external tenants under one roof.

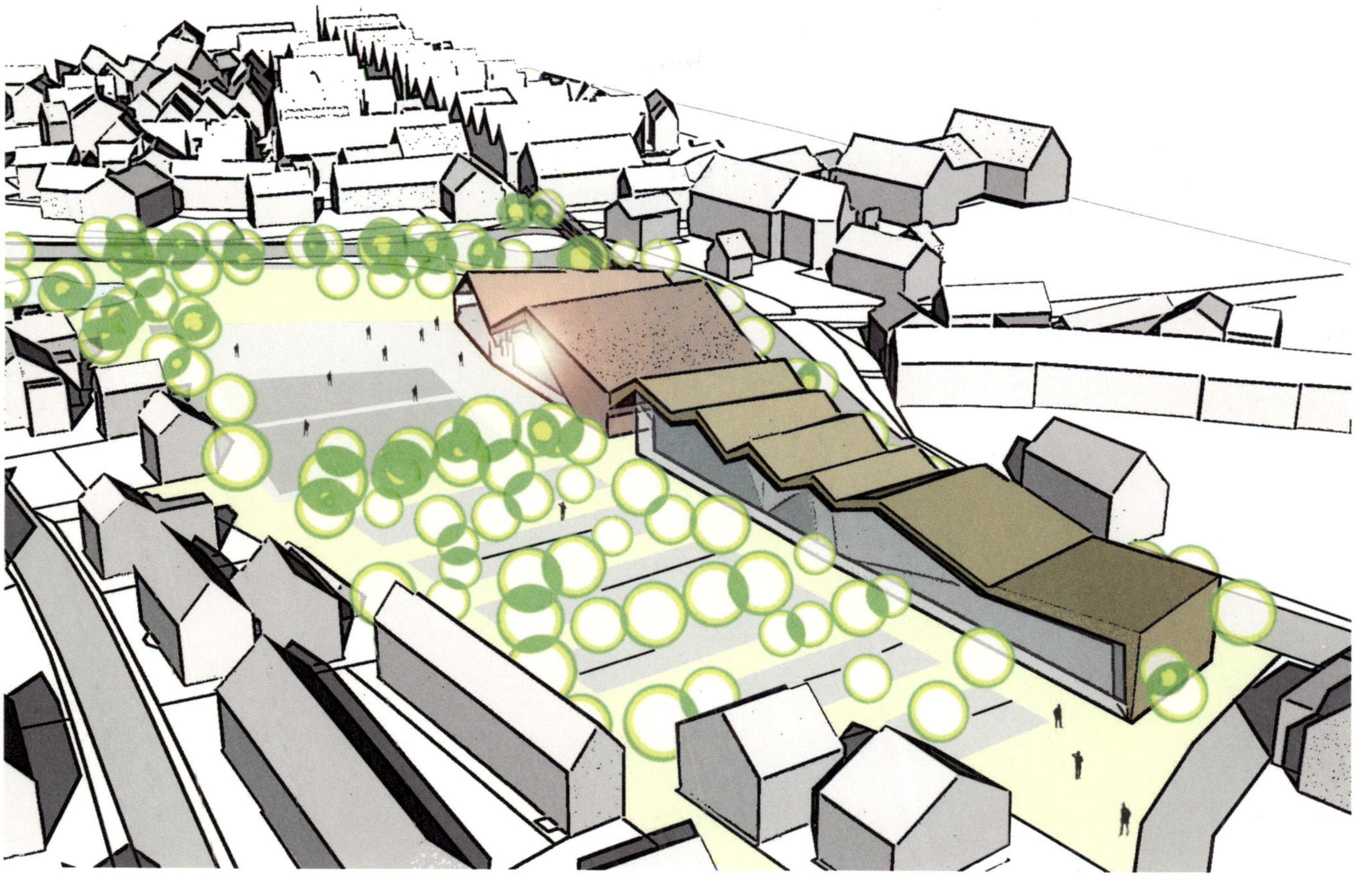

wettbewerb / competition
neubau fachhochschule / new building university of applied sciences
ankauf / award wels 2002

fachhochschule wels

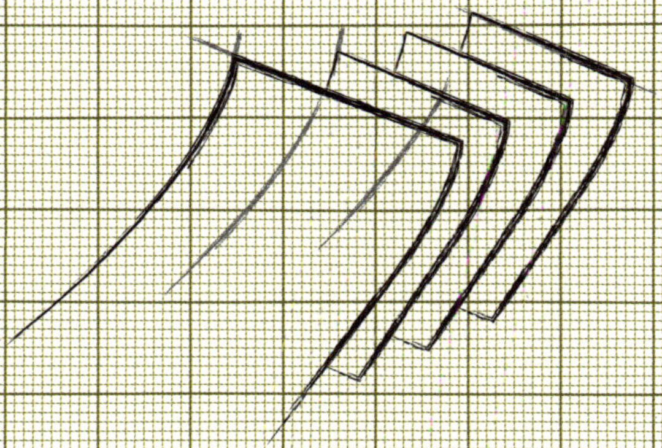

der neubau der fh wels wird – den beiden grundfunktionen lehre und werkstatt folgend – in zwei baukörper aufgeteilt. im höheren der beiden zeichnet sich die ausformung der hörsäle nach außen ab; die aufständerung des baukörpers »lehre« bildet gleichzeitig den großzügigen eingang der fh aus; das ansteigende dach des werkstättengebäudes ist die fortführung des vorplatzes und wird zur tribüne.

the new building of the university of applied sciences in wels is divided into two architectural structures – according to its two basic areas of instruction: theory and workshop practice. in the higher of the two, the shape of the lecture theatres can be seen from the outside; at the same time, the elevation of the architectural volume for »theory« constitutes a spacious entrance to the college of higher education; the inclined roof of the workshop building is a continuation of the forecourt and becomes the theatre stands.

zwei schwünge fassen das quartier – und alle sitzen gerne in österreichs größtem freiluftkino.
two curves frame the quarter – and everybody likes to sit in austria's biggest open-air cinema.

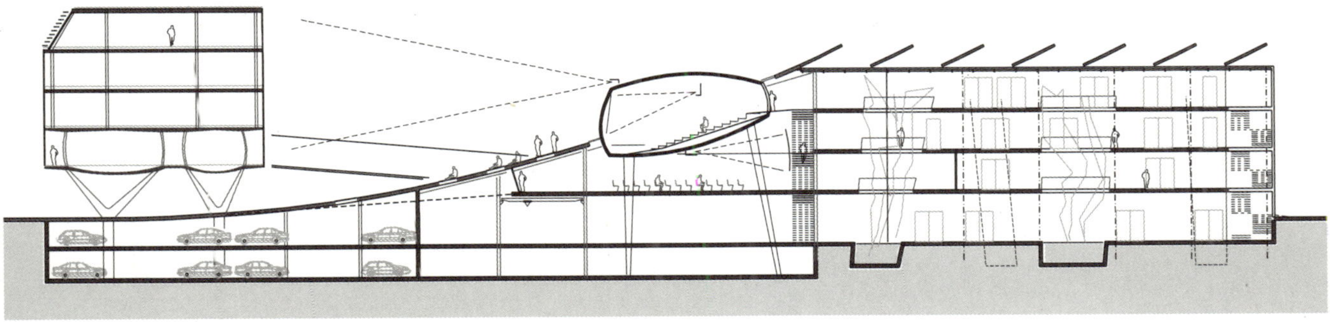

2. pause, you don't have to do it now...

kopf-rumpf // head-rump

der kopf ist eine mehrzweckkugel, sagte der funktionalist, man kann damit schauen, riechen, hören, nahrung aufnehmen, notfalls auch abgeben, einen schnupfen austragen, reden, singen, husten. die haare waren einmal notwendig, solange es noch keine kopfbedeckungen gab, später hat man sie zur schönheit verwendet, locken gebrannt, zöpfe geflochten, neuzeitlich schneidet man sie auch weg. die augen stehen mit dem riechen in verbindung, das riechen mit dem schmecken. weil der kopf so wertvoll ist, muss er sanft getragen werden, vorzugsweise in gehrichtung. er ruht auf einem drehbaren stativ, in das auch die leitungen zum körper eingebaut sind. der kugelkopf ist die leitzentrale für den körper. will man diese zerstören, muss man sie vom rumpf trennen. man nennt dies köpfen, nicht rumpfen, womit sich auch der stellenwert beider ausdrückt. man könnte ohne kopf auch so einen text schreiben.

the head is a multipurpose ball, said the functionalist, one can see, smell and hear with it, take in food, if needs be even pass it on, slug out a cold with it, talk, sing, cough. the hair used to be necessary, as long as there was no headgear, later one used it for beauty, curls burnt, braids plaited, in modern times one also cuts them off. the eyes are linked to the sense of smell, and smell to taste. because the head is so valuable, it has to be carried gently, preferably in the direction of walking. it rests on a pivoted tripod, with built-in connections to the body. the ballhead is the body's headquarters. if one wishes to destroy it, one has to dissever it from the rump, known as beheading, not rumping, which expresses the status of each. one could even write such a text without a head.

friedrich achleitner

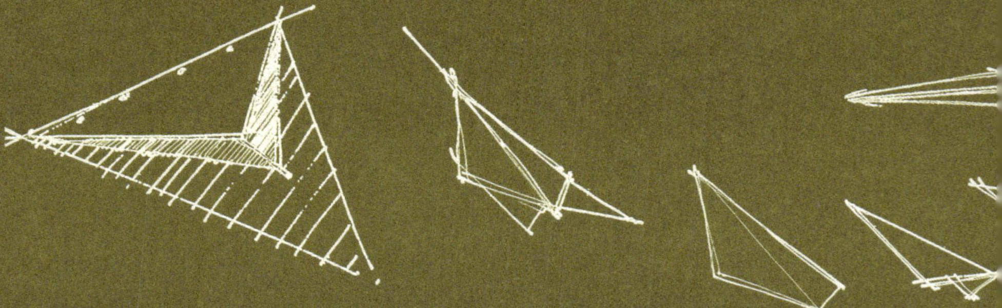

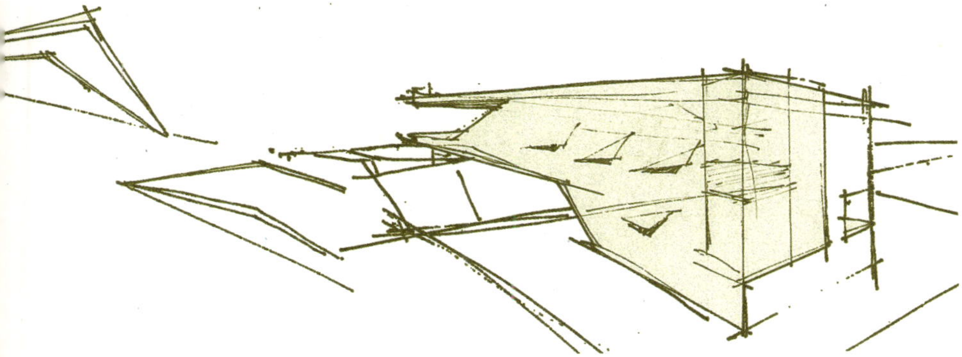

haus p

wie ein unbekanntes tier aus einer welt der tetrisformen // like a unknown animal from a world of tetris forms

wie ein unbekanntes tier aus einer welt der tetrisformen sitzt haus p auf dem hanggrundstück in klosterneuburg und scheint ins tal zu blicken. die skulpturale, homogene form wird durch die ausführung der fassade aus betonfertigteilen noch zusätzlich verstärkt.

like an unknown animal from a world of tetris forms, house p is situated on a sloping property in klosterneuburg and seems to look down into the valley. its sculptural, homogeneous form is further emphasised by the fact that the facade has been executed in prefabricated concrete parts.

projectmanager: sabine bovelino

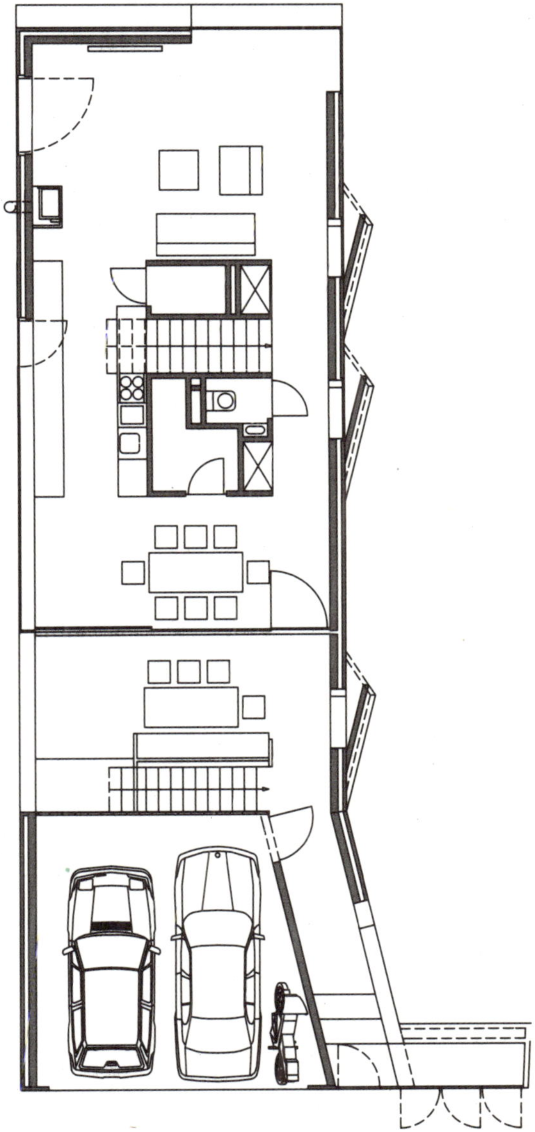

die fassade wirkt, je nach ausrichtung, offen oder geschlossen. während sie sich auf der westseite, bei wohnküche und terrasse, komplett in richtung pool und garten öffnet, verschließt sie sich zur ostseite nahezu vor dem nahe gelegenen nachbarhaus. hier lenken kiemenklappen die sicht in richtung tal und schaffen privatsphäre im wohnbereich. im kontrast dazu steht die öffnung der halben fassade auf der nordseite dieses bereichs. sie bietet einen traumblick bis zur donau. verstärkt wird der eindruck der kompletten öffnung noch durch die profillose verglasung, die sich als überkopfverglasung in einem teil des daches fortsetzt.

depending on one's position, the façade seems either open or closed. on the west side, where the kitchen-cum-living room and the terrace are situated, it opens up completely in the direction of the pool and the garden, on the eastern side it is practically closed off from the nearby neighbouring house. here, gill-like shutters direct one's gaze to the valley and create a private sphere in the living area. this is in contrast to the opening of half of the facade on the north side of the living area. this presents an unobstructed view down to the danube. the impression of complete openness is accentuated still further by the unprofilated glazing, which continues as overhead glazing in one part of the roof.

der straßenseitige zugang führt entlang der rückgradartigen längsachse an garage und terrasse vorbei ins hausinnere, wo sie sich, entlang der wohnküche, garderobe und dem treppenabgang, bis zur glasfront des wohnzimmers verliert. mit atemberaubendem blick in die donauniederungen…
einzig die ausrichtung des pools, der als optische fortsetzung der unteren überdachten terrasse eine querrichtung aufnimmt, unterbricht die langgestreckte form des wohnhauses.
in der unteren gartenzugangsebene befinden sich zwei schlafräume, zwei bäder, eine sauna und ein kleines atelier, das sich zum garten und zur unteren überdachten terrasse hin öffnet. gegenüber dem atelier, auf der anderen seite der terrasse, schiebt sich der keller in den hang unter der garage.

the street-side entrance leads one along a spine-like longitudinal axis, past the garage and the terrace, into the interior of the house, along by the kitchen-cum-living room, cloakroom and the top of the staircase, to the glass facade of the living room, with its breathtaking view of the danube lowlands…
solely the orientation of the pool, which as an optical continuation of the lower covered terrace adopts a transverse direction, interrupts the elongated form of the residential house.
on the lower level of the garden entrance there are two bedrooms, two bathrooms, a sauna and a small studio, which open onto the garden and the lower covered terrace. opposite the studio, on the other side of the terrace, the cellar is squeezed into the slope beneath the garage.

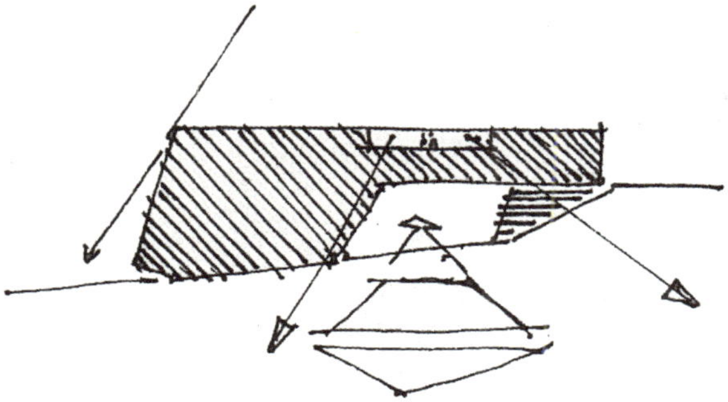

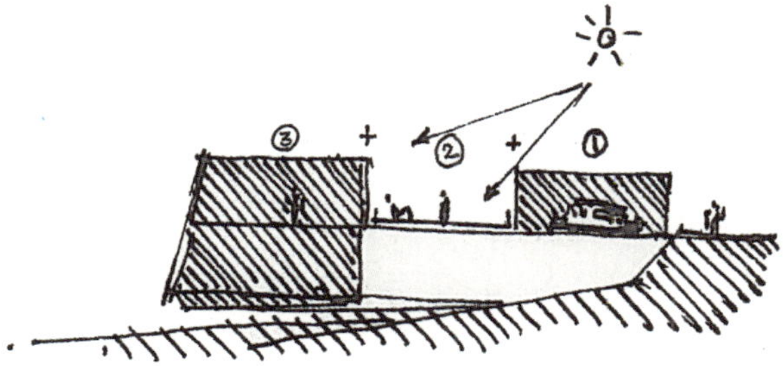

konstruktion: sichtbeton-fertigteil-sandwich-elemente
fußboden: estrich versiegelt

construction: prefabricated fair-faced-concrete-sandwich-elements
floors: sealed floor screed

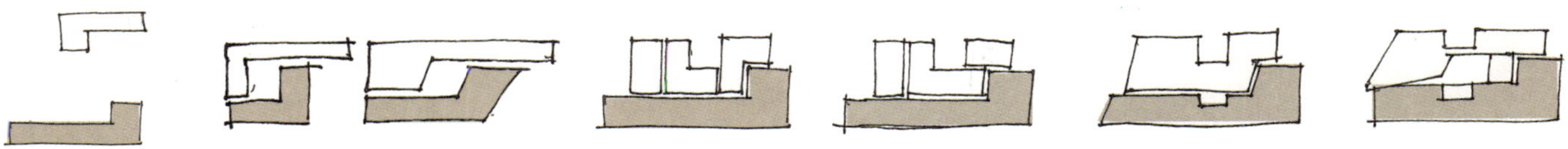

wettbewerb / competition
öbb konzernzentrale /
company headquarters of austrian railways
wien, 2009

öbb konzernzentrale

hier überall ist die österreichische bundesbahn. // austrian railways is everywhere here.

neben dem neuen wiener zentralbahnhof soll mit der errichtung der neuen öbb konzernzentrale der öffentliche platz räumlich definiert werden. wie? durch eine raumscheibe, die sich vom boden in die senkrechte aufknickt. die öffnung zwischen knickung und platz ist ein klar ausgebildeter eingang, die senkrechte scheibenfront zum vorplatz schließt diesen deutlich ab. die schräg abgestufte rückseite richtung süden wird als »hängende gärten« für die mitarbeiter ausgeführt.

together with the new vienna central station, the construction of a new company headquarters for austrian railways is intended to provide a spatial definition of the public space. how? by means of a spatial plate that bends up vertically from the ground. the open space between the kink and the square forms a clearly developed entrance, and this is distinctly concluded by the front of the vertical plate that overlooks the forecourt. the obliquely gradated rear part facing south is executed as a »hanging gardens« for the employees.

das foyer öffnet sich zum platz, kundenbereich und restaurant sind ebenerdig angeordnet.

the foyer opens up on to the square, with a customer area and restaurant arranged on the ground floor.

kunstuni linz

der kunstvirus breitet sich über eine verschlafene stadt aus. // an art virus infects a sleepy town.

virus-membran

zwischen virusstruktur und den umgebenden bestandsflächen befindet sich eine membran als kommunikationsoberfläche. sie ermöglicht direkte und indirekte blickbeziehungen und dient als trägeroberfläche für ausstellungsobjekte der studentischen arbeit. die membran besteht in den obergeschossen aus einer tragenden formrohrkonstruktion mit beidseitig angeschraubten lichtdurchlässigen gfk-paneelen und transparenter hohlraumdämmung. in den untergeschossen wird die gleiche membran mittels unterkonstruktion direkt am bestand befestigt. die anschließenden bodenflächen übernehmen die gfk-oberfläche als beschichtung auf trockenestrichplatten. im hohlraum zwischen bestand und membran befindet sich die infrastruktur haustechnik.

virus-membrane

between the virus structure and the surfaces surrounding the volume, there is a membrane that serves as a communication surface. this makes it possible to have direct and indirect eye contact and serves as the supporting surface for exhibiting examples of the students' work. on the upper storeys, the membrane consists of a shaped load-bearing tube construction with double-sided translucent fbe panels screwed on to it and transparent cavity insulation. on the lower storeys, the same membrane is directly attached to the volume by means of a substructure. the adjoining floor surfaces adopt the fbe surface as a coating on dry screed slabs. in the cavity between the structure and the membrane is to be found the infrastructure for the in-house technology.

virus-infektion

das historisch belastete brückenkopfgebäude am linzer hauptplatz – der beginn von hitlers »achse« durch die heimatstadt - wird von einem kommunikationsvirus infiziert. der virus erobert sich in dieser alten struktur neuen raum für positive kommunikationsaktivitäten.
den infektionsherd bildet die neue zentrale aula mit direktzugang vom hauptplatz. von hier aus wächst die raumstruktur in alle teilbereiche der alten gebäudehülle. raumerweiterungen zu den flächen des hauptplatzareals vernetzen die struktur mehrfach mit dem öffentlichen raum.

virus-struktur

die virusbereiche dienen als horizontale und vertikale erschließungsflächen für alle funktionsbereiche der beiden ehemals getrennten gebäudeteile. an den knotenpunkten erweitert sich die struktur zu kommunikations- und ausstellungsflächen. im zentrum befinden sich die neue aula und die cafeteria mit zugang vom hauptplatz und von der donaubrücke. daran angeschlossen sind die funktionen mensa, ausstellungshalle, werkstätten und bibliothek. der luftraum der aula erweitert sich vertikal in das bestandsgebäude und bildet mit liften und kommunikationsinseln eine neue raumeinheit durch alle geschosse. mehrere oberlichten und die vertikale raumskulptur berühren und durchdringen den öffentlichen raum des freigespielten gewölbedurchgangs im erdgeschoss und kommunizieren so mit der stadt.

virus-infection

the historically incriminating bridge head building on the main square of linz – the start of hitler's »axis« through his home town – is infected with a communication virus. in this old structure, the virus takes over new spaces for positive communication activities.
the source of the infection is the new central assembly hall, with its direct access from the main square. proceeding from here, the spatial structure grows in all the subzones of the building's old shell. spatial extensions to the areas of the main site connect the structure in multiple ways with the public space.

virus-structure

the viral areas serve as horizontal and vertical access areas for all the functional areas of the two formerly separate parts of the building. at the points of intersection, the structure extends to the communication and exhibition areas. in the centre are to be found the new assembly hall and the cafeteria, with access from the main square and from the danube bridge. adjoining it are the mensa, an exhibition hall, workshops and the library. the empty space of the assembly hall is extended vertically into the existing building to form a new spatial unit with lifts and communication islands on all floors. several skylights and the vertical spatial sculpture come into contact with and interact with the public space of the released arched passageway on ground floor, in this way communicating with the city.

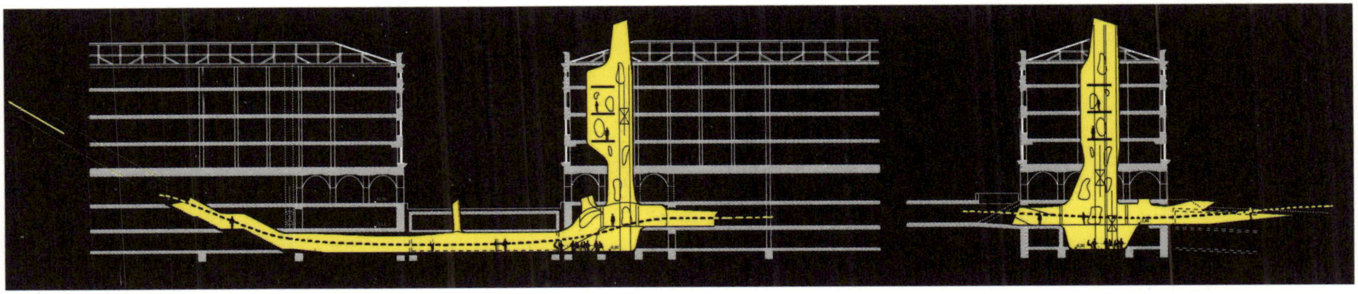

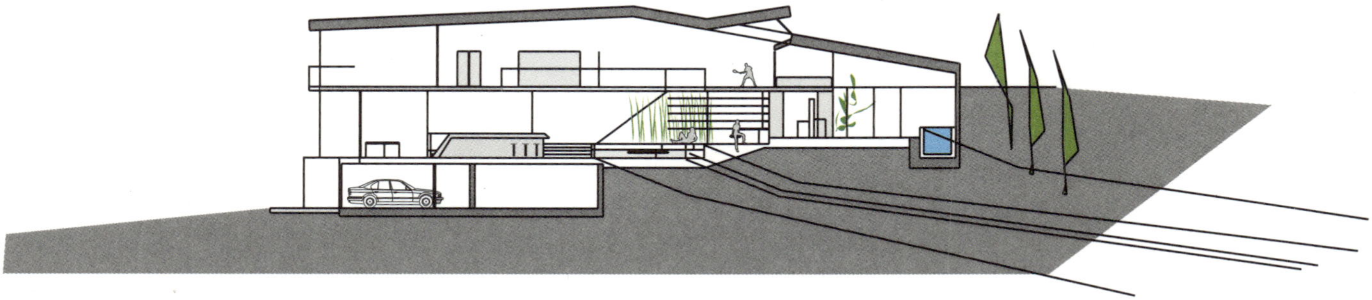

haus r: räumliche bewegungen am hang – geländestufe > mauer > wand > raumeinhüllung > dachauskragung > mauer > geländestufe
house r: spatial movements on the slope – terrace > outside wall > house wall > spatial envelope > roof projection > outside wall > terrace

haus r

räumliche bewegungen am hang // spatial movements on the slope

aus dem hanggelände erwächst eine grundstücksmauer, sie wird zur hausbegrenzenden wand, zur gebäudehülle, zur dachauskragung, und kehrt als brüstungsmauer wieder ins gelände zurück. dieser fließbewegung folgend entwickeln sich auch die innenräume als rythmische abfolge über drei geschosse.
innen und außen verschlingen sich zu einem dynamischen gesamterlebnis.

out of the sloping terrain emerges a property wall, which becomes the wall that forms the boundary of the house, the shell of the building, the roof projection, and then retires back into the terrain again as a parapet wall. the development of the space inside traces this flowing spatial movement, as a sequence of rooms over three storeys.
the interior and the exterior interlock to produce a dynamic total experience.

wettbewerb / competition
infobox hauptbahnhof öbb
infobox at the main station of austrian railways (öbb)
wien 2008

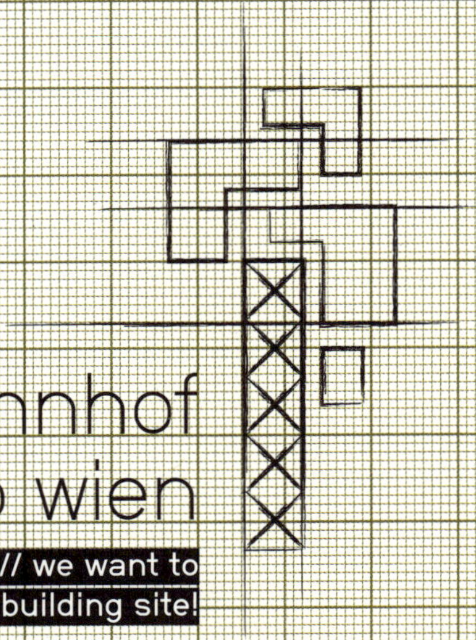

infobox hauptbahnhof öbb wien

wir wollen baustelle bahnhof schaun! // we want to see the station building site!

bahnmitarbeiter und neugierige sitzen in luftiger höhe in bahncontaineren und schauen zu, wie bahncontainer per bahn antransportiert und zu ihnen hochgehoben werden um bahnmitarbeitern und neugierigen einen platz zu geben, wo sie in luftiger höhe in bahncontainern zuschauen, wie bahncontainer antransportiert und zu ihnen hochgehoben werden, um…

railway employees and inquisitive people sit high up in the air in rail containers and watch how rail containers arrive by rail and are hoisted up towards them in order to give railway employees and inquisitive people a place from which they can watch, high up in the air in rail containers, how rail containers arrive and are hoisted up towards them in order to…

art.
bits.

projekt / project
temporerer eingang galerie
temporary entrance to a gallery
wien 2005

the infinite oasis

ein projekt mit isomax individualdekorplatten für »salon iris« / »galerie artbits« von caramel architekten // a project with individual decorative isomax panels for salon iris/galerie artbits

eine künstlich geschaffene oase im stadtraum, ein begehbares und begreifbares objekt – die eingangsschleuse aus bedruckten maxplatten im dschungeldesign. nicht wahrnehmbare dünne hpl-trägerplatten stellen allein die künstlichkeit der oberfläche in den vordergrund.

durch gegenüberliegende spiegel multipliziert sich die oase in die unendlichkeit. durch die ausführung der glaseingangstüre als einwegspiegel ist sie vom straßenraum beobachtbar, ohne selbst akteur zu sein.
die benützung des objektes erzeugt eine abfolge unterschiedlichster raumeindrücke beim weg in die galerie.

an artificially created oasis in urban space, a walk-in object that is also comprehensible – with entrance turnstiles made of printed maxplates in jungle design. imperceptibly thin hpl mounting panels place only the artificiality of the surface at the forefront.

by placing mirrors opposite each other, the oasis is multiplied to infinity. by executing the glass entrance door as a one-way mirror, it can be observed from street outside, without being a protagonist itself.
the use of the object produces a series of very varied spatial impressions on the way into the gallery.

in der röhre bei geschlossener türe: aufgelöst in der unendlichkeit
eintritt in die röhre: gegenüberliegender spiegel reflektiert den zugangsraum

inside the tube with the doors closed
vanished into infinity
entrance into the tube
the mirror opposite reflects the access space

austritt in die galerie: klar abgegrenzter innenraum mit dem von außen begreifbaren unendlichkeitsraum der eingangsröhre.

exit into the gallery: clearly delimited interior with the space of infinity of the entrance tube comprehensible from the outside.

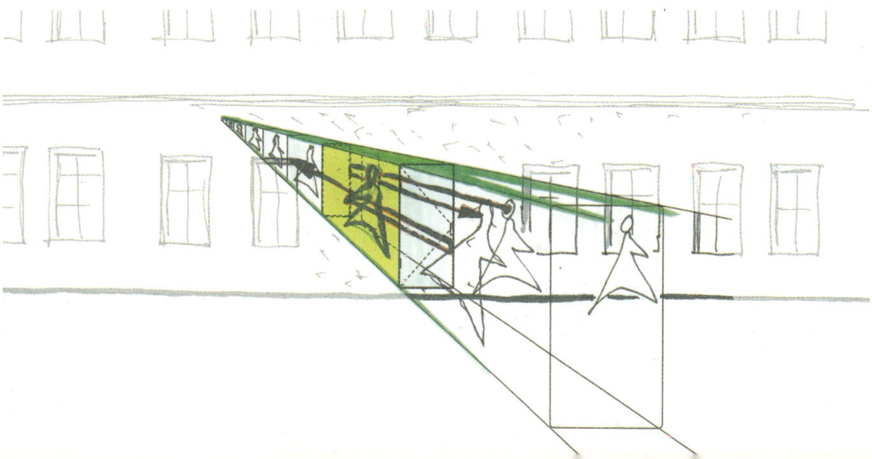

wettbewerb / competition
simmeringer markt / simmering market
preis / prize wien 2006

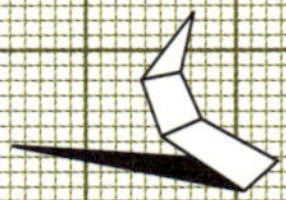

simmeringer markt

neues schulzentrum und alter grätzelmarkt – der spagat zwischen großzügiger urbanität und traditioneller maßstäblichkeit. bestehende gebäudefluchten und wege werden analysiert und interpretiert, um sich dann mit rücksicht auf die angrenzende städtebauliche situation freizuspielen: durch ergänzung und komplette neuinterpretation der heterogenen, lockeren bebauungsstruktur der bestehenden marktpavillons; die beiden schulen werden als groß dimensionierte pavillions eigenständig ausgebildet.

new school centre and an old local market – the balancing act between spacious urban life and traditional standards. the existing lines of the buildings and pathways were analysed and interpreted, in order to break away from them, while still taking the neighbouring urban development situation into consideration, namely by supplementing and completely reinterpreting the loose heterogeneous development structure of the existing market pavilion; the two schools are developed independently as large-scale pavilions.

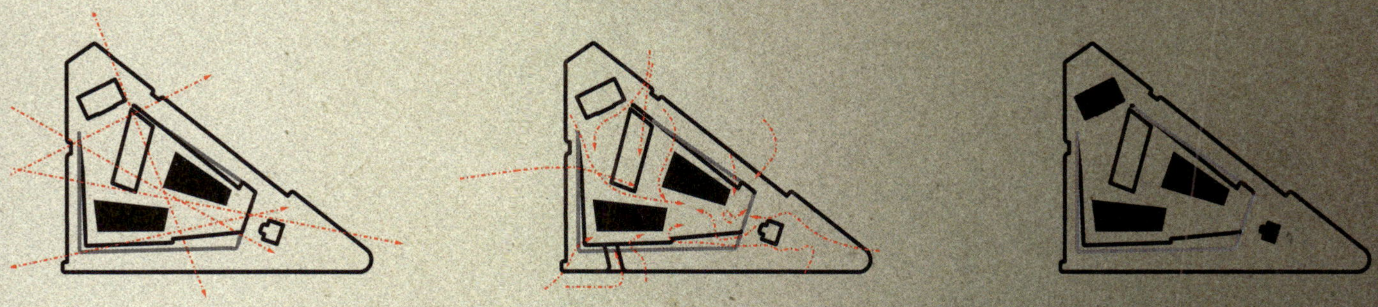

der grünraum des benachbarten parks wird erweitert und fließt in die neu geschaffene struktur.
der markt wird durch den neubau urbanisiert und so dem gedanken eines zusätzlichen »lokalzentrums« gerecht. die traditionelle kleinteiligkeit bleibt erhalten.

the green area of the neighbouring park is expanded and integrated into the newly created structure.
the market becomes urbanised through the new building, and in this way justice is done to the idea of a additional »local centre«. the traditional fragmented character of the area is retained.

2

wettbewerb / competition
neubau molekulare biowissenschaften
new building institute for molecular bioscience
2. preis / 2nd prize graz 2003

molekulare biowissenschaften

ganz schön große löcher im käse // great big holes in the cheese

in ein städtebaulich sehr undefiniertes umfeld setzt caramel einen markanten, selbstbewussten baukörper. eine funktionsmaschine mit horizontal wie vertikal gesetzen höfen. ganz schön böse! die dichte bebauung der grazer innenstadt geht in diesem bereich in etwas lockerere bebauung über, der baukörper markiert diesen übergang, wobei das quartier großzügige grünflächen und auch öffentliche durchgänge erhält. die stringente komprimierung entspricht den engen räumlich-funktionalen zusammenhängen der universitären einheiten einerseits und der gewünschten nähe der privaten forschungseinrichtungen zu den universitären andererseits. aufgelockert und belichtet wird das gebäude durch innenhöfe, die in charakteristik, größe und form unterschiedlich ausgebildet sind. die vertikalverbindungen konzentrieren sich auf ein hauptstiegenhaus pro nutzungseinheit in kombination mit fassadenprägenden umlaufenden fluchtstiegen an den gebäudeaußenseiten. die sehr kompakte lösung einer vielschichtigen bauaufgabe

in urban development surroundings that are very undefined, caramel placed a distinct and self-confident building structure. a functional machine with horizontally and vertically placed courtyards. really wicked! in this area, the dense development of the inner city of graz changes to a rather looser development, and the building structure marks this transition, with spacious areas receiving greenery and also public thoroughfares. the stringent compactness corresponds to the spatial and functional connections of the university units on the one hand, and the desired proximity of private research institutions to the universities on the other. the building is varied and lit by means of inner courtyards which, in their characteristics, size and form, are variously formed. the vertical connections are concentrated on one main staircase per utilization unit, in combination with continuous escape stairs that dominate the facade on the outside of the building. a very compact solution for a many-layered construction brief.

KFUG

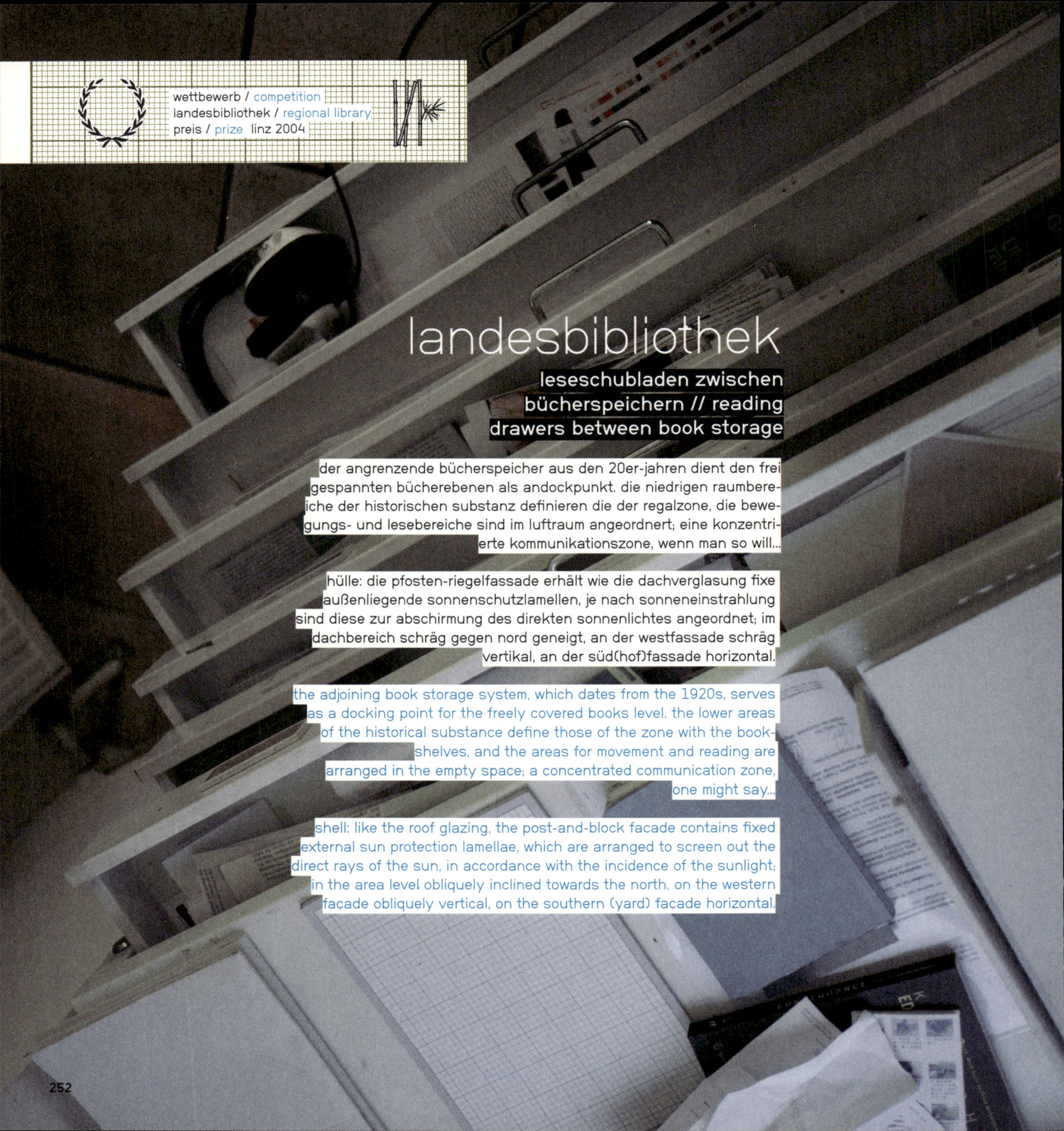

wettbewerb / competition
landesbibliothek / regional library
preis / prize linz 2004

landesbibliothek

leseschubladen zwischen bücherspeichern // reading drawers between book storage

der angrenzende bücherspeicher aus den 20er-jahren dient den frei gespannten bücherebenen als andockpunkt. die niedrigen raumbereiche der historischen substanz definieren die der regalzone, die bewegungs- und lesebereiche sind im luftraum angeordnert; eine konzentrierte kommunikationszone, wenn man so will...

hülle: die pfosten-riegelfassade erhält wie die dachverglasung fixe außenliegende sonnenschutzlamellen, je nach sonneneinstrahlung sind diese zur abschirmung des direkten sonnenlichtes angeordnet; im dachbereich schräg gegen nord geneigt, an der westfassade schräg vertikal, an der süd(hof)fassade horizontal.

the adjoining book storage system, which dates from the 1920s, serves as a docking point for the freely covered books level. the lower areas of the historical substance define those of the zone with the bookshelves, and the areas for movement and reading are arranged in the empty space; a concentrated communication zone, one might say...

shell: like the roof glazing, the post-and-block facade contains fixed external sun protection lamellae, which are arranged to screen out the direct rays of the sun, in accordance with the incidence of the sunlight; in the area level obliquely inclined towards the north, on the western façade obliquely vertical, on the southern (yard) facade horizontal.

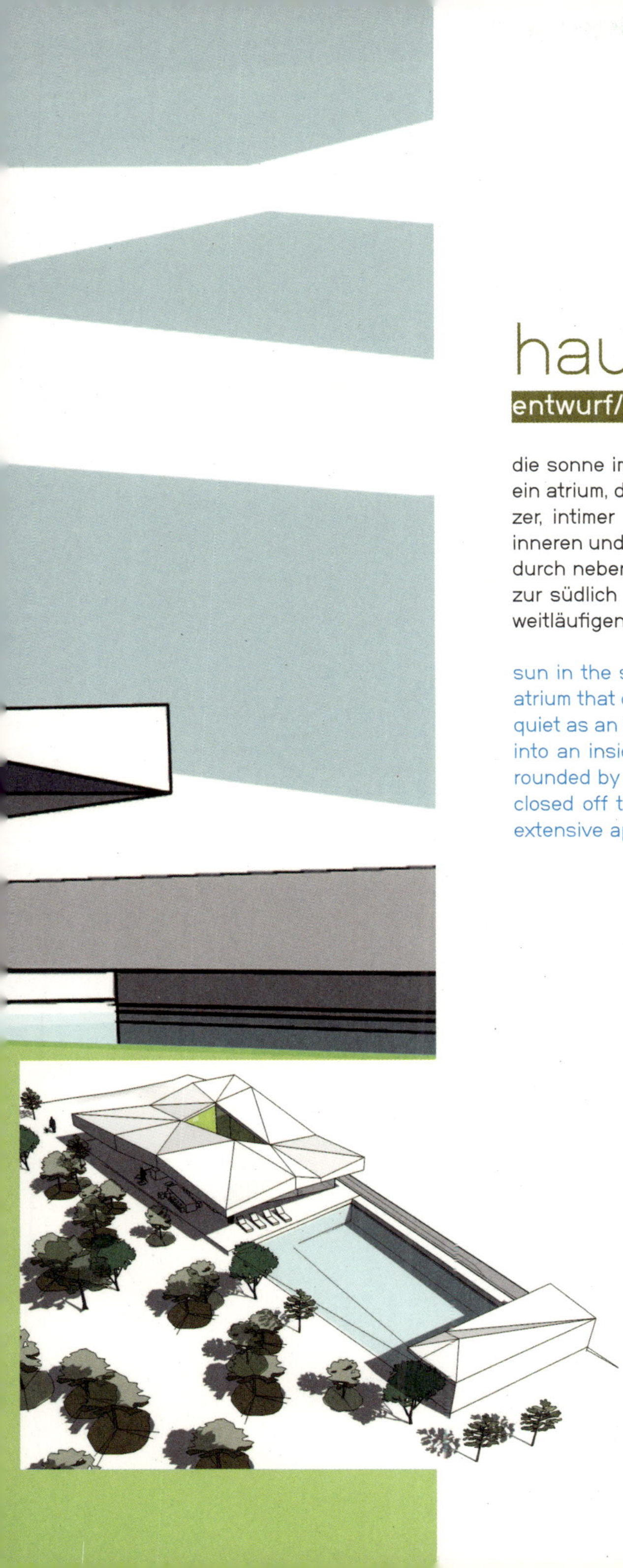

haus in der wachau

entwurf/sketch wohnhaus // design for residential house

die sonne im süden, die aussicht im norden. das weit ausladende dach faltet sich um ein atrium, das die sonne in den großzügigen wohnbereich lenkt. und als windgeschützer, intimer garten eine ruheoase bildet. der wohnbereich wird wie zufällig in einen inneren und einen äußeren getrennt; im westen anschließend eine große wasserfläche, durch nebengebäude eingefasst.
zur südlich angrenzenden nachbarschaft geschlossen, öffnet sich das bauwerk zum weitläufigen apfelhain im norden.

sun in the south, view in the north. the roof protrudes a long way, folding around an atrium that draws the sun into a spacious living area. and forms an oasis of peace and quiet as an intimate, wind-protected garden. the living area is divided, as if accidentally, into an inside and an outside; finally, in the west, there is a large area of water surrounded by auxiliary buildings.
closed off towards its neighbours on the southern side, the building opens onto an extensive apple grove in the north.

3

wettbewerb / competition
amtsgebäude / federal government building
3. platz / 3rd prize graz 2001

körösistraße 17

ein monolithischer block definiert seine form durch die weiterführung der umliegenden bestandsbebauung. im süden hebt er vom boden ab und lädt die besucher über die fuge zur erforschung der offenen innenwelt ein.

a monolithic block that defines its form by constituting a continuation of the surrounding architectural development. towards the south, it rises from the ground and invites the visitor to pass through a gap and explore the open interior.

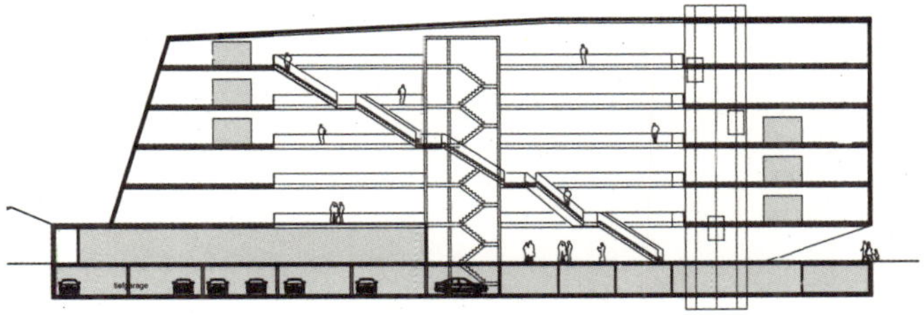

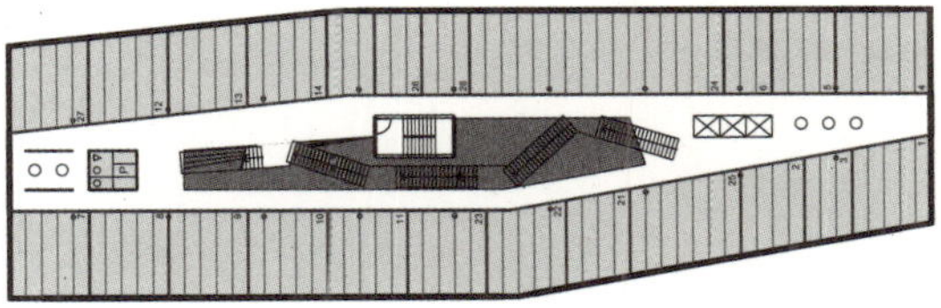

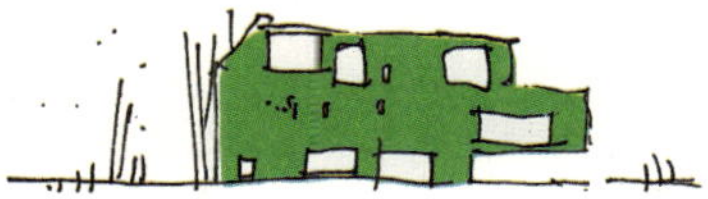 

wohnbau am krautgarten

die häuser im haus // houses in the house

wohnen am stadtrand – man verbindet den standort atmosphärisch mit »wohnen im grünen«. nicht jeder muss dafür zum »häuslbauer« werden. caramel stapelt häuser zu einem wohnbauprojekt, der »nichthäuslbauer« braucht bloß die terrasse zu möblieren.
die einzelnen wohnungen werden wie eigene häuser ausgeformt, mehrgeschossig, mit unterschiedlichen ausblicken in die umgebung, und dann zu einem gesamtbau ineinandergeschachtelt. jede wohnung hat einen individuellen grundriss, der durch unterschiedliche loggien und balkonen auch von außen als das jeweilige »haus« erkennbar ist.

eigengärten, dachgärten, loggien und balkone geben jeder wohnung auf verschiedenen ebenen direkten kontakt zur grünraumumgebung – wie bei einem einfamilienhaus im grünen. durch die individuelle innere struktur des gebäudes entsteht nach außen hin ein spielerischer charakter der gebäudehülle als positive atmosphäre zur nutzung »wohnen«. dies wird durch das haptische erlebnis des sehr groben außenputzes und durch die fröhliche farbgebung unterstützt.

living on the edge of the city – one atmospherically associates the location with »living in leafy surroundings«. yet not everyone has to become a »house builder« to do so. caramel stacks houses to make a housing project, and »non-builders« simply need to furnish the terraces.
the individual apartments are designed like separate houses, multi-storied, with a variety of views of the surroundings and then interlaced into a whole building. every apartment has its own individual ground plan which, among all the variety of loggias and balconies, is recognizable as belonging to that particular »house« even from the outside.
having one's own garden, roof garden, loggia and balcony ensures that all the apartments on the different levels have direct contact to the surrounding greenery – as in the case of a single-family home in a green setting. through the individual inner structure, the shell of the building acquires a playful exterior character, thereby creating a positive atmosphere that is advantageous to »living«. this is reinforced by the haptic experience of the very rough external plastering and the cheerful colours in which it is painted.

das gebäude ist als niedrigenergiehaus nach den kriterien klimaaktivhaus errichtet.

wohnungseinheiten 17
TG plätze 17
gärten/terrassen 500 m²
BGF 2705 m²
NF (ohne loggien) 1590 m²

the building is built as a low-energy house, in accordance with the criteria for a thermally active house.

apartment units: 17
TG places 17
gardens/terraces 500 m²
GBA 2705 m²
BA (without loggias) 1590 m²

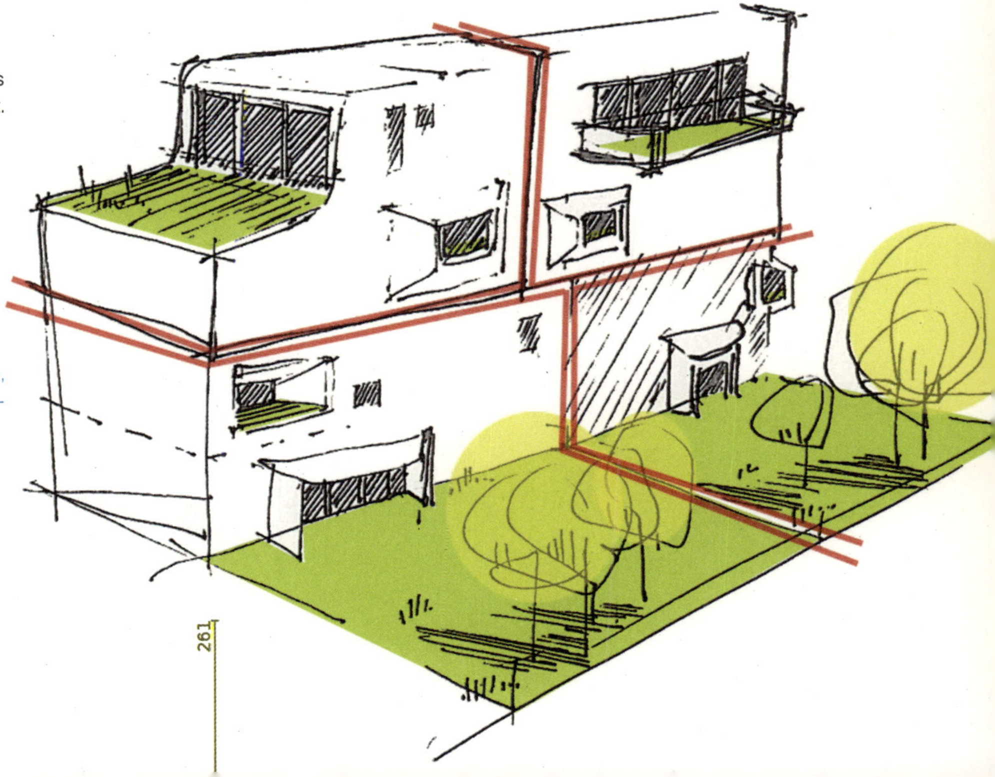

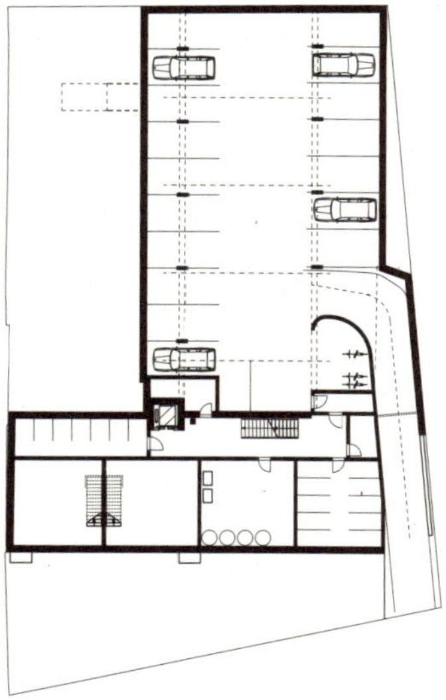

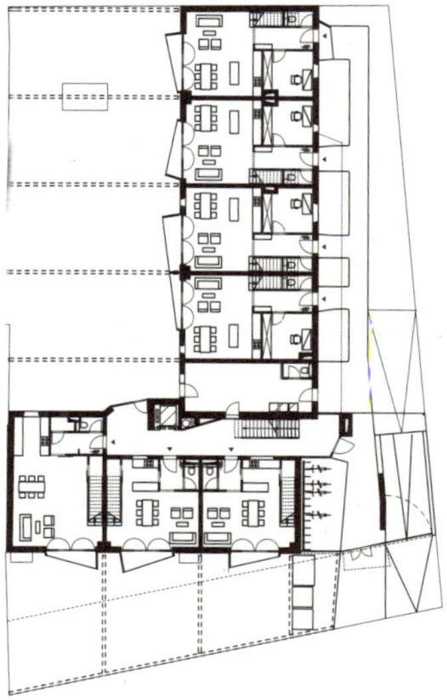

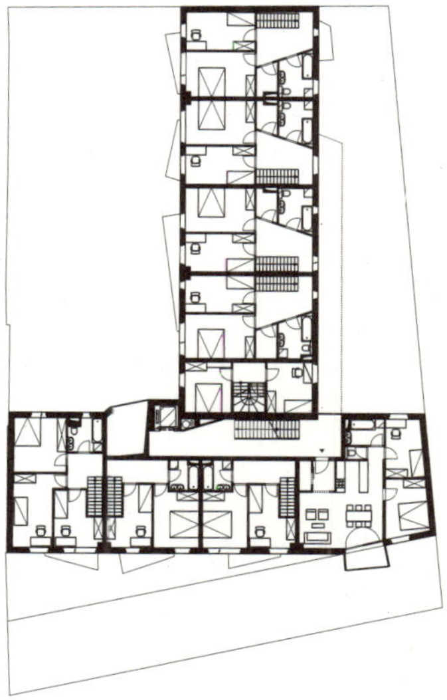

städtebaulich befindet sich das grundstück in sehr heterogenem umfeld. der baukörper nimmt die hauptrichtungen der angrenzenden bebauung in seiner der öffentlichen verkehrsfläche zugewandten bebauungskante auf.
entlang der straße entsteht so ein grünraumzwickel als pufferraum zwischen öffentlich und privat.

stadtrandwohnungen mit »grünem« umfeld sollen vor allem jungfamilien ansprechen. sämtliche wohnungen sind mit mietergärten, terrassen oder loggien ausgestattet.
zudem verfügen die wohnungen – größtenteils als reihenhausartige maisonettetypen ausgebildet – über ein höchstmaß an individualität; diese unterschiedlichkeit der wohnungen ist auch an der außengestaltung bzw. dem fassadenbild abzulesen. die loggien (»augen«) markieren die wohnzimmer, die in unterschiedlicher geometrie angeordneten kleineren fenster die schlafräume.

gewissermaßen im »herzen« des hauses, im geometrischen mittel des erdgeschosses, an das stiegenhaus angeschlossen, befindet sich ein allgemein/kinderspielraum inklusive zugeordnetem (kinderspiel)garten mit sandspiel- und klettermöglichkeit.

from the urban development point of view, the property is located in very heterogeneous surroundings. the building structure adopts the principal orientation of the adjacent building in its development edge, which is turned towards the public traffic area.
in this way, there arises along the street a triangle of greenery that forms a buffer zone between the public and the private worlds.

apartments on the edge of the city in »green« surroundings should appeal above all to young families. all the apartments have tenants' garden, terraces or loggias.
in addition, the apartments – most of which are designed as terraced maisonette-type of buildings – are highly individual; this variety of the apartments can also be seen from the design of the exterior of the buildings, or from the facades. the loggias (»eyes«) mark the living-rooms, while the smaller windows, which are arranged in varying geometrical patterns, mark the bedrooms.
to a certain extent, in the »heart« of the house, the geometrical centre of the ground floor, and connected to the building's staircase, is to be found a general/children's playroom with allocated garden (children's playground), including possibilities for playing in the sand and climbing.

wettbewerb / competition
schule / school langobardenstraße
preis / prize wien 2003

schule langobardenstraße

in der peripherie ist noch platz genug; so sind hier nicht nur sämtliche schulklassen ebenerdig um eine lichtdurchflutete halle angeordnet, jede klasse hat auch noch einen eigenen garten, die freiklasse. der verwaltungsteil und die sonderunterrichtsräume heben dann vom boden ab und setzen sich quasi aufs eigene dach; und natürlich bekommen auch sie ihren freiraum – in form von vorgelagerten terrassen.

there is still enough space on the periphery; that is why not only are all the rooms arranged around a light-flooded hall on the ground floor, but every class also has its own garden, an open-air classroom. the administrative section and the rooms for special education are raised above ground level and placed on their own roof as it were; and of course they too also have their own open-air spaces – in the form of terraces outside the rooms.

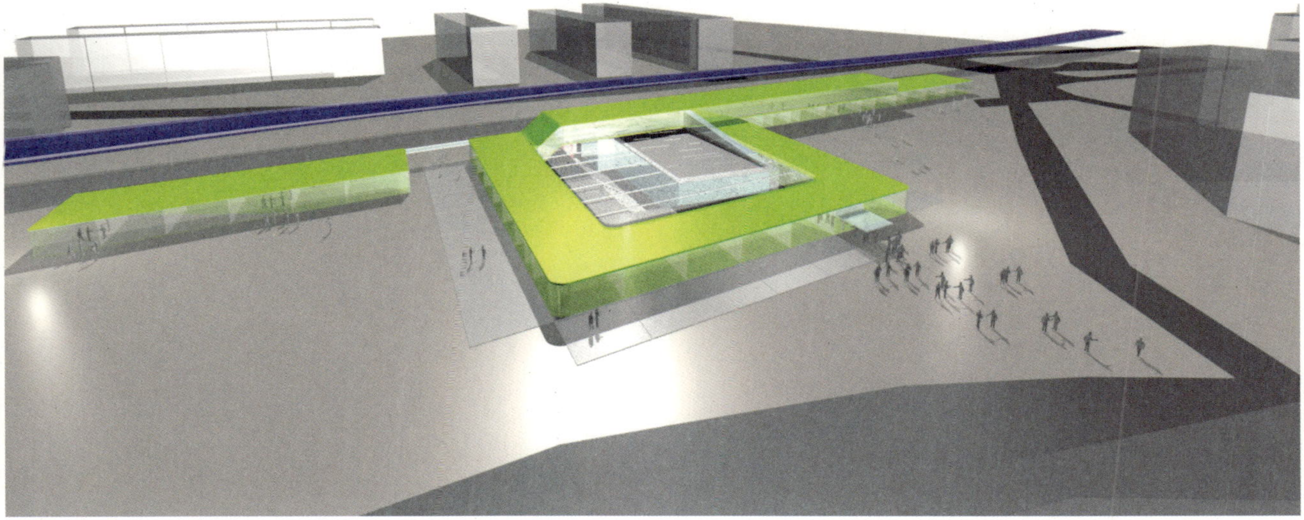

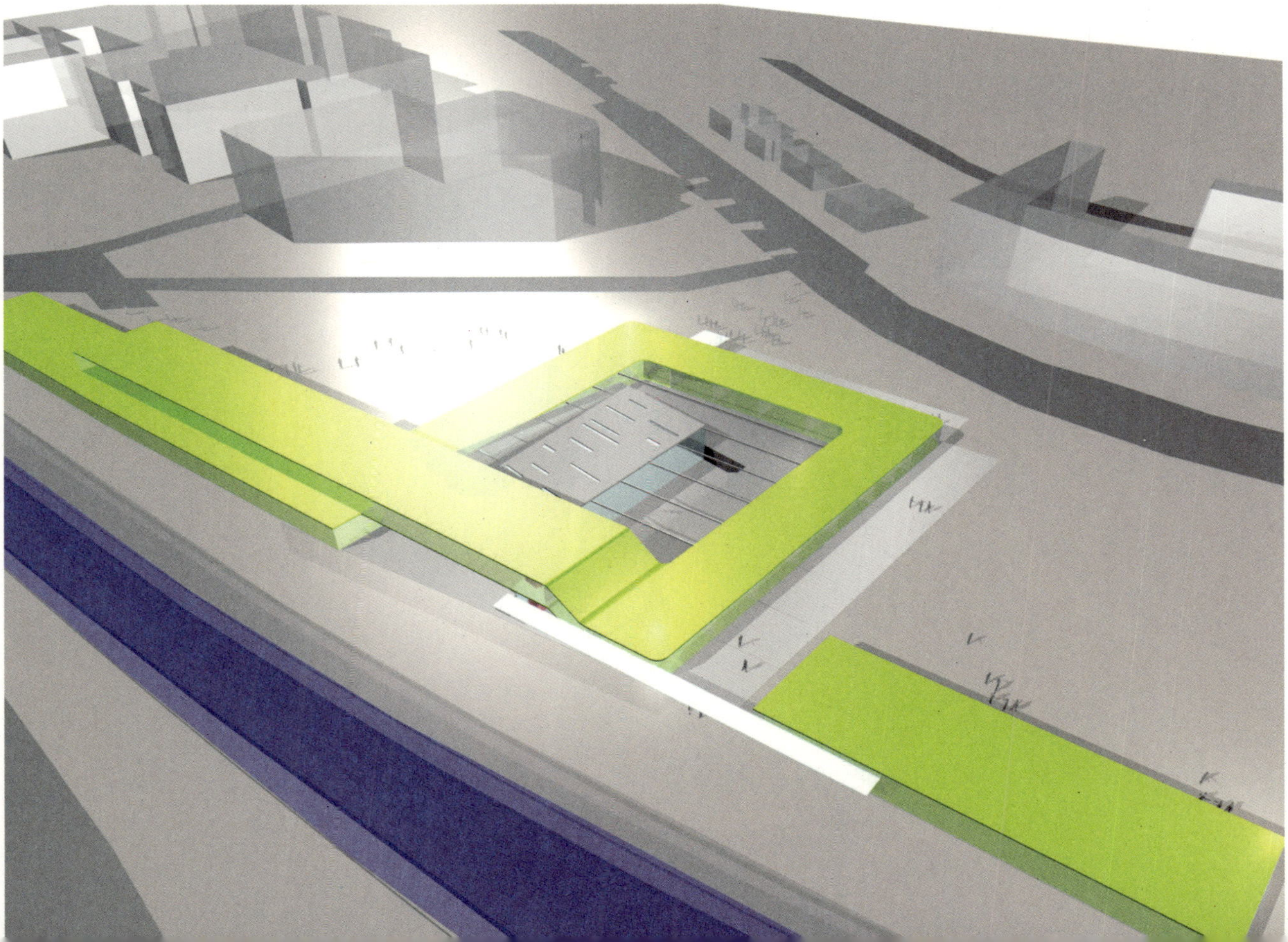

L´idylle Autrichienne

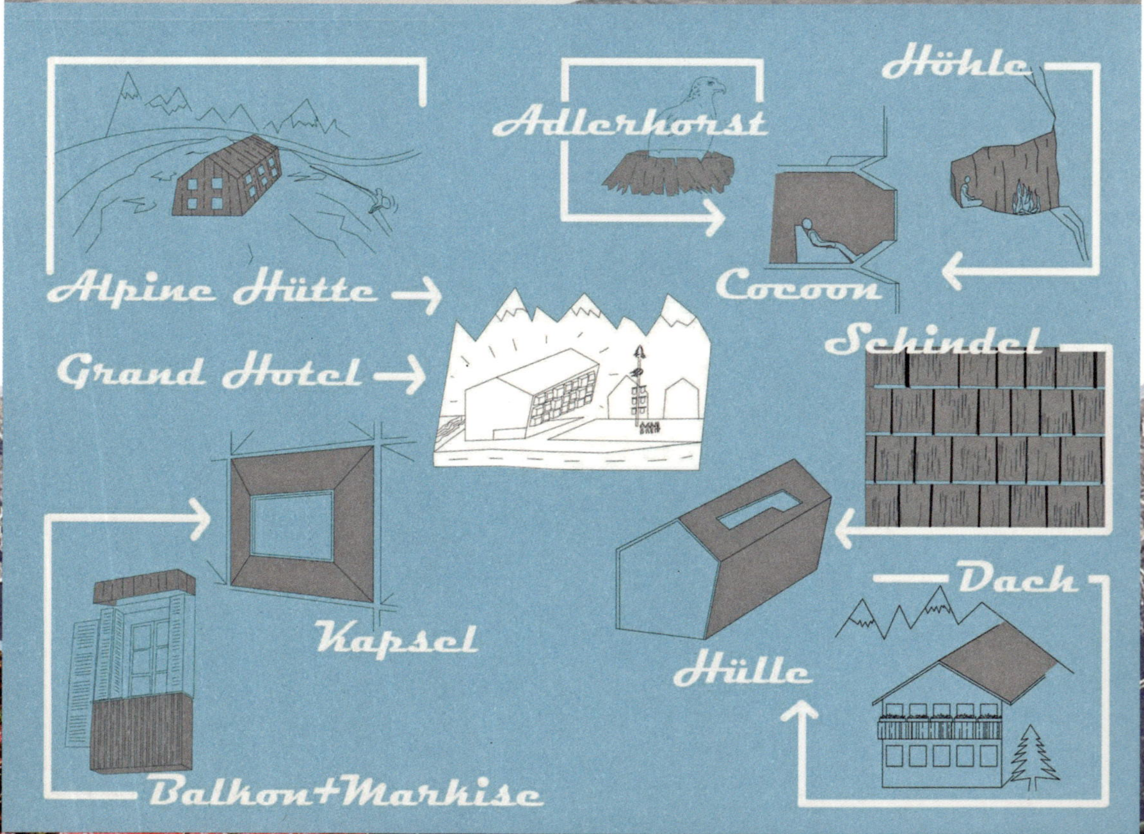

hotel kaprun

gibt es so was wie alpine architektur? // is there such a thing as alpine architecture?

nein vergiss es, architektur gibt's nicht aber alpines: höhle, adlerhorst, hütte aus eigenen bäumen, schindeln aus uralten lärchen, alpenrosen, und aus all dem kann natürlich auch ein haus oder gar ein hotel werden, das »idylle autrichienne«.

no, forget it, architecture doesn't exist. but there are alpine features: caves, eyries, huts made from one's own trees, roof tiles from ancient larches, rhododendrons, and from all of these there might emerge a house or even a hotel, the »austrian idyll«.

wettbewerb / competition
wirtschaftsuniversität / university of economics
wien 2008

wirtschafts-universität wien

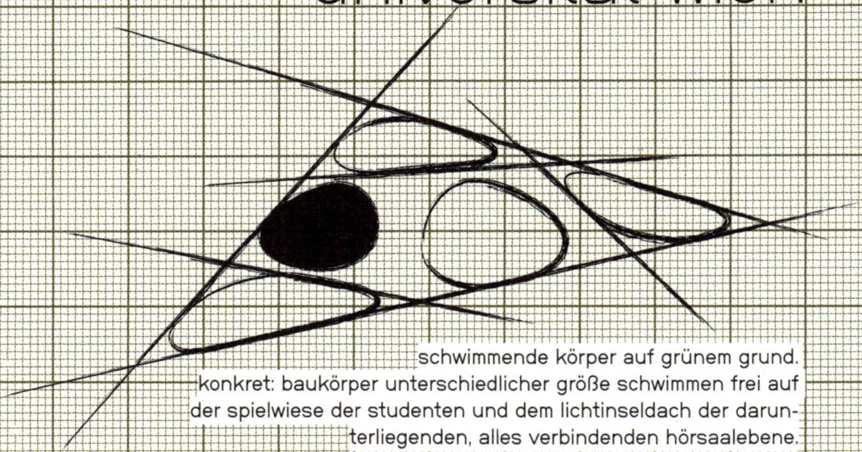

schwimmende körper auf grünem grund.
konkret: baukörper unterschiedlicher größe schwimmen frei auf der spielwiese der studenten und dem lichtinseldach der darunterliegenden, alles verbindenden hörsaalebene.

swimming body on green background.
concretely: architectural volumes of different sizes swim freely on the students' playing field and on the lighting-island roof of the all-connecting level of the lecture halls below.

das geheimnisvolle licht aus dem seerosenteich. the mysterious light from the water lily pond.

zwei alles verbindende ebenen. oben die campuslandschaft, unten die lernlandschaft.
two levels that connect everything. above the campus landscape, below the study landscape. and the library and so on…

luftschlösser

castles in the air

and never ever fucking forget luftschlösser, schätzchen

»der sohn des schriftstellers«, roberto yañez honecker

ein hochhaus am rande der stadt war mein zuhause. unten an meiner straße boten prostituierte ihre dienste an. in einem kleinen cafe unterhielten sich intellektuelle. ich hatte eine große wohnung. meine bücher waren bereits in vielen auflagen erschienen und ich war nicht mehr arm.

vor einem jahr war in chile ein erdbeben und im süden hatte das land sehr gelitten. in santiago war es nicht so schlimm gewesen. trotzdem hatte ein hochhaus gegenüber schaden erlitten und das rathaus hatte es als unbewohnbar erklärt. das hochhaus hatte fünfundzwanzig etagen.

niemand wusste, was mit dem gebäude geschehen wird.

in der nacht träumte ich, dass sich mein sohn in diesem gebäude verirrt hatte und dass ich ihn retten musste. ich ging durch lange korridore und leere wohnungen. einige lichter gingen an und dann wurde es wieder dunkel. geräusche und echos bedrängten mich. ich erinnerte mich an die geburt meines sohnes und an seine kindheit.

ich wusste, dass er sich gerne verlor und wenn ich ihn suchte, machte er sich über mich lustig. manchmal verließ er unsere wohnung um mich zu provozieren. er sagte immer: »ich habe ein labyrinth in meinem kopf.« seine klugheit brachte mich durcheinander. ich wusste, er war intelligenter als ich.

in meinen träumen sah ich einige ausgestoßene, die in diesem hochhaus wohnten, menschen, die von der gesellschaft misshandelt worden waren. sie wechselten schnell den ort, hatten bärtige gesichter, saßen an feuern und unterhielten sich in toten sprachen. war mein sohn mitglied einer sekte, die sich im dunklen hochhaus versammelte? hatte er die kunst der telepathie erlernt und die wissenschaft der schwarzen magie?

am anfang steht für mich das bild eines niedlichen kindes. ich erinnere mich noch immer an unsere ausflüge an die küste, als er die ersten wörter lernte. doch dann fühlte ich, dass etwas schwarzes in ihm heranwuchs. ein geist drang in ihn ein und führte ihn in psychische und physische labyrinthe. davor war für mich die welt klar und offen, aber während mein sohn heranwuchs, bekam ich ein bewusstsein für die geografie der hindernisse. ich war mir sicher, dass das leere hochhaus etwas mit ihm zu tun hatte.

besuchte er das hochhaus regelmäßig?

ich musste die angst bezwingen und so entschloss ich mich, das hochhaus zu betreten. ein großes schild hing dort und verbot mir hineinzugehen. es war ein uhr nachts. eine fensterscheibe war gesprungen und ich hatte keine mühe sie endgültig zu zerbrechen. langsam ging ich eine treppe hinauf. ich hatte das gefühl, ich würde etwas schrecklichem begegnen. ich war im sechsten stock. am ende eines korridors sah ich ein helles licht und hörte ein nasses langgezogenes geräusch und ging näher zu einer offenen tür und sah das folgende szenario: in einem großen raum waren tausende schwarze schmetterlinge an den wänden und flatterten durch die luft. gegenüber saß ein mönch in einer schwarzen kutte und hatte ein messer in der hand. ein totes kalb lag vor ihm auf dem boden und war entstellt durch schnitte und stiche. der mönch schmiss rohes fleisch auf den boden, wo hunderte von schmetterlingen saßen und sich daran labten. das geräusch, das dadurch entstand, war ekelhaft. der mönch sprach also: »wenn du den horror suchst, hast du ihn gefunden. ich warte schon lange zeit auf dich. ein zauberer aus alten zeiten hat all diese geschehnisse vorbereitet. hier kommst du in die unterwelt, wo dein sohn ein imperium gegründet hat.« dann zeigte er auf eine tür und sagte: »du kommst auf jener treppe in die verbotene stadt und wirst dort den könig kennenlernen.«

der psychiater sagte zu mir: »warum sind sie stumm geworden?« ich antwortete ihm: »ich glaube, dass die menschen mit denen ich verkehre nicht ganz normal sind. mein sohn, zum beispiel, malt mit spraydosen graffitis an die wände hoher gebäude: schwarze schmetterlinge. er hat ein terrarium mit hunderten von schmetterlingen. er züchtet sie.« der psychiater sagte: »nehmen sie das alles nicht so ernst. ich kann ihnen ein beruhigungsmittel verschreiben.«

ich war die treppe hinuntergegangen und durch eine tür und kam in eine große wüste. und es war ein heißer wind dort, der den sand vor sich hertrieb. ich sah kein zeichen von leben. ein gelbgrünes licht stand über dem weiten horizont der unterwelt. auf einmal sah ich eine lange mauer, vielleicht tausende kilometer lang. in der wand waren hunderte von roten türen, die halb geöffnet waren. ich brauchte stunden, bis ich an der wand angelangt war. ich ging, ohne nachzudenken, durch die erste tür. ich bemerkte, dass ich zurück im verlassenen hochhaus war. die luft wurde auf einmal rot wie die türen. große insekten mit roten flügeln summten umher und dieses geräusch wurde stärker, während ich die treppen hinaufging. tausende insekteneier klebten an den wänden. kalter schweiß trat mir aus den poren und ich wollte so schnell wie möglich den ausgang finden.
der psychiater sagte zu mir: »mein lieber herr, ich sehe sie sind unruhig und sie zittern. an was denken sie? warum stellen sie sich nicht die farbe blau vor? kennen sie die moderne blau-therapie?«
die insekten änderten auf einmal die farbe, von rot zu orange, von orange zu gelb, von gelb zu grün und von grün zu blau. ich fühlte mich erleichtert. das blau war überall. ich hörte, wie ein reiner blauer bach mit blauen steinen und fischen aus dunkelblauem gold durch das hochhaus floss. ich fühlte mein herz klopfen und schaute auf meine brust und sah hinter meinen rippen ein großes und fleischiges blaues herz. mein sohn kam schwimmend im bach auf mich zu, der mund blau wie eine pflaume, blau seine beine, blau sein körper. er streckte mir seine zarten hände entgegen und schwamm vorbei. »hier bin ich!«, schrie ich, »ich hol dich aus dem wasser! ich werde dich retten!« aber er schwamm weg und verlor sich in der dunkelheit des hochhauses.
»warum sind sie so aufgeregt?«, fragte mich der psychiater. »ich habe meinen sohn wieder verloren«, antwortete ich. »aber sie haben doch gesagt, dass ihr sohn bei ihnen lebt und schmetterlinge sammelt?« – »ja, aber ich hatte das gefühl, dass ein blauer bach ihn weggetrieben hat und das war ihre schuld, da sie die blau-therapie erwähnt hatten.« der psychiater sagte: »ich habe jetzt noch einmal nachgedacht und denke, dass es gut ist, dass sie ihren sohn eine weile nicht sehen. sie sind zu besessen. sie sollten das problem besser aus der ferne beobachten.«
und auf einmal wuchs der abstand. ledersessel und psychiater entfernten sich, erst fünf meter, dann zehn meter. alles wurde kleiner und kleiner, die lampe aus bronze und die gardinen, der blaue mond im fenster. dann das gebäude, die straßenlichter. ich entfernte mich von meinem sohn, meiner wohnung, meinen büchern und ich schwebte weiter in die unendlichkeit. ich entfernte mich endgültig von mir selber.

roberto yañez honecker
berlin 1974, schriftsteller, liedermacher und maler.
lebt in santiago de chile. gibt mit der surrealistischen gruppe »derrame« eine zeitschfrift des gleichen namens heraus. beteiligt sich an internationalen surrealistischen ausstellungen und lesungen.

gedichtbände:
gedichte gefunden in san pedro de atacam
(editorial magica de chile)
der spiegel des tiefen schattens
(libros la calabaza del diablo)
der gegenstand der schwindlichkeit
(brazo de cervantes editores)

»the writer's son«, roberto yañez honecker

a high-rise building on the edge of the city was where i lived. on the street below, prostitutes used to offer their services. in a small café, intellectuals would engage in discussions. i had a big flat. many editions of my books had already been published and i was no longer poor.

a year before, there had been an earthquake in chile and the south of the country had suffered a lot. in santiago it had not been so bad. nevertheless, a high-rise opposite had suffered some damage and the city hall had declared it uninhabitable. the high-rise had twenty-five floors.

no-one knew what would happen to the building.

in the night i dreamed that my son had got lost in this building and that i had to rescue him. i walked down long corridors and through empty apartments. some lights went on and then it became dark again. sounds and echoes tormented me. i remembered the birth of my son and his childhood.

i knew that he used to like to get lost and when i looked for him, he would make fun of me. sometimes he left our flat in order to provoke me. he would always say: »i have a labyrinth in my head.« his cleverness confused me. i knew that he was more intelligent than me.

in my dreams i saw several outcasts, who lived in this apartment building, people who had been mistreated by society. they changed locations quickly, had bearded faces, sat around fires and talked in dead languages. was my son a member of a sect that held their gatherings in the dark high-rise building? had he learned the art of telepathy and the knowledge of black magic? the first image i have is that of a cute little child. i still remember our excursions to the coast, when he was learning his first words. yet then i began to feel that something black was growing within him. a spirit entered into him and led him into mental and physical labyrinths. prior to that, the world had been clear and open for me, but while my son was growing up i acquired an awareness of the geography of obstacles. i was certain that the empty high-rise had something to do with him.

did he visit the high-rise regularly?

i had to overcome the fear, and so i decided to enter the high-rise. there was a large sign hanging there, forbidding me to enter. it was one in the morning. one of the windows was cracked and i had no trouble in smashing it completely. slowly i went up the stairs. i had the feeling that i would encounter something dreadful. i was on the sixth floor. at the end of the corridor i saw a bright light, heard a loud long and wet sound, went nearer to an open door, and saw the following scene: in a large room there were thousands of black butterflies on the walls and fluttering through the air. on the other side of the room sat a monk in a black frock who had a knife in his hand. a dead calf lay on the floor in front of him, disfigured by cuts and stabs. the monk was throwing raw meat onto the floor, where hundreds of butterflies had settled and were feasting on it. the sound that arose from this was nauseous. the monk spoke thus: »if you are looking for horror, then you have found it. i have been waiting for you for a long time. a sorcerer from ancient times has prepared all these events. here you have entered the underworld, where your son has founded an empire.« then he pointed to a door and said: »up those steps you will enter the forbidden city, where you will become acquainted with the king.«

the psychiatrist asked me: »why have you become so silent?« i told him: »i believe that the people with whom i am involved are not quite normal. my son, for example, uses spray cans to paint graffiti of black butterflies on the walls of high buildings. he has a terrarium with hundreds of butterflies. he breeds them.« the psychiatrist said: »don't take everything so seriously. i can write you a prescription for some tranquillisers.«

i had gone down the stairs and through a door and come out in a huge desert. and there was a hot wind there, which blew the sand ahead of it. i saw no signs of life. a yellowish-green light hung over the distant horizon of the underworld. all of a sudden, i saw a long wall, perhaps a thousand kilometers long. in the wall there were hundreds of red doors, all of them half-open. i needed hours before i arrived at the wall. without thinking, i went through the first door. i noticed that i was back in the deserted high-rise. suddenly the air became red like the doors. huge insects with red wings were buzzing around and the sound became louder as i walked up the steps. thousands of insect eggs were stuck on the walls. cold sweat was exuding from my pores and i wanted to find the exit as fast as possible. the psychiatrist said to me: »my dear sir, i see that you are ill-at-ease and are trembling. what are you thinking about? why don't you just imagine the colour blue? do you know the modern blue therapy?«

all at once, the insects changed colour, from red to orange, from orange to yellow, from yellow to green and from green to blue. i felt a sense of relief. the blue was everywhere. i heard a pure blue stream with blue stones and fishes of dark-blue gold flowing through the high-rise. i felt my heart beating fast, looked down at my breast and saw behind my ribs a big and fleshy blue heart. my son came swimming up the stream to me, his mouth blue as a plum, his legs blue, his body blue. he reached out his delicate hands to me and swam on by. »here i am!« i shouted, »i'll get you out of the water! i'll save you!« yet he swam away and disappeared in the darkness of the high-rise.

»why are you so upset?« the psychiatrist asked me. »i've lost my son again,« i replied. »but you said that your son lives with you and collects butterflies?« – »yes, but i had the feeling that a blue stream had swept him away and it was your fault, because you mentioned the blue therapy.« the psychiatrist said: »i have just been thinking about it again and in my opinion it would be good if you didn't see your son for a while. you are obsessed with him. it would be better for you to look at the problem from a distance.«

and all of a sudden, the distance grew. the leather chair and the psychiatrist became more distant, first five metres, then ten metres. everything became smaller and smaller, the lamps made of bronze and the curtains, and the blue moon in the window. then the building, and the streetlamps. i distanced myself from my son, my apartment and my books, and floated further out into infinity. finally, i distanced myself from myself.

roberto yañez honecker

berlin 1974, writer, songwriter and painter, lives in santiago de chile. in collaboration with the surrealist group »derrame«, he edits a magazine of the same name. he frequently participates at international surrealist exhibitions and readings.

poems:

poems found in san pedro de atacama
(editorial magica de chile, 1999)
the mirror of deep shadow
(libros la calabaza del diablo, 2002);
the object of vertigo
(brazo de cervantes editores, 2003).

1

wettbewerb / competition
verwaltungsbau / administration building
1. preis / 1st prize augsburg 2001

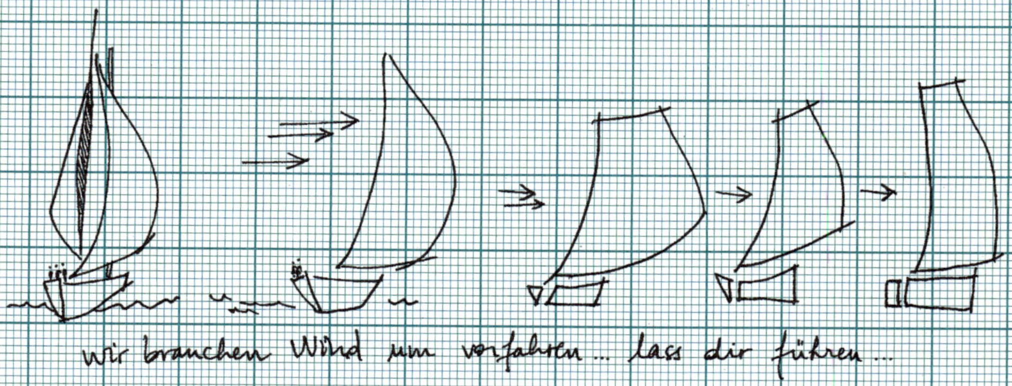

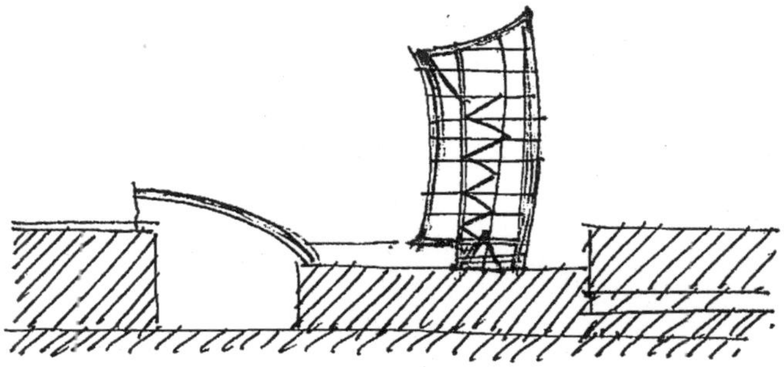

i am sailing ...

50 arbeitsplätze und eine hausmeister-wohnung // 50 jobs and a janitor's apartment.

350 architekten-teams versuchten sich an der lösung folgender bauaufgabe: errichtung eines bürohauses als neuen verwaltungstrakt zum bestehenden produktionsstandort »glasbau seele«.
das nie gebaute siegerkonzept kam von caramel: der neue verwaltungsbau ist das segel, das mit dem wind der vorhandenen produktion die firma seele in die zukunft zieht. der sechsstöckige bau öffnet sich in blickrichtung der produktionsstätten über alle geschosse und bildet so ein offenes kommunikationsregal zwischen verwaltung und produktion.

350 teams of architects attempted to find a solution for the following brief: to erect an office building to serve as the new adminstration wing at the existing production works of »glasbau seele«.
the winning concept, which was never built, was designed by caramel: the new administration building is the sail by means of which the seele company is blown into the future by the wind of the company's already existing production. the six-storey building looks out over all the storeys toward the production plant, and in doing so forms an open communication shelf between administration and production.

die nördlich gelegene rückseite wird, bis auf kleine belichtungsöffnungen, zur minimierung des energieverlustes als wärmegedämmte, geschlossene paneelfassade ausgeführt.

with the exception of small openings for natural light, the rear side, which is located in the north, is fitted with closed, thermally insulated panel facades, in order to minimise the energy loss.

wettbewerb / competition
wohnhaus und privatmuseum
private museum and residential building
1. preis / 1st prize offenhausen 2007

museum & wohnhaus

das grundstück: ein traum. am scheitel eines unbebauten hügels mit spektakulärem weitblick richtung süd wie nord; ein kunstsammler-ehepaar mit dem wunsch, gemälde halböffentlich zu machen und mit ihnen zu leben;
die rahmenbedingungen: die hausdimensionen sollen denen der in dieser region üblichen solitärbauernhäuser entsprechen. nutzungen museum und empfang, großzügig angeordnet im zugangsgeschoss; aber auch wellness und fuhrpark werden in den perforierten hügelscheitel eingebettet; die privaten räume darüber im mehrschaligen monolithen; darauf noch extrovertiert die 360° lounge.

die ausführung scheiterte letzendlich an den naturschutzbehörden.

the property: a dream. on the crown of an undeveloped hill, with a spectacular views into the distance both southwards and northwards; an art collecting married couple with the desire to make their paintings semi-public and to live with them;
the building's dimensions should correspond to those of the solitary farmhouses so typical of this region. functional designations: used for the museum and reception, spaciously arranged on the access level; however, facilities for wellness and a car fleet are also embedded in the perforated crown of the hill; the private rooms above in multi-layered monolith; on top the extroverted 360° lounge.

in the end, the execution failed because of the nature conservation authorities.

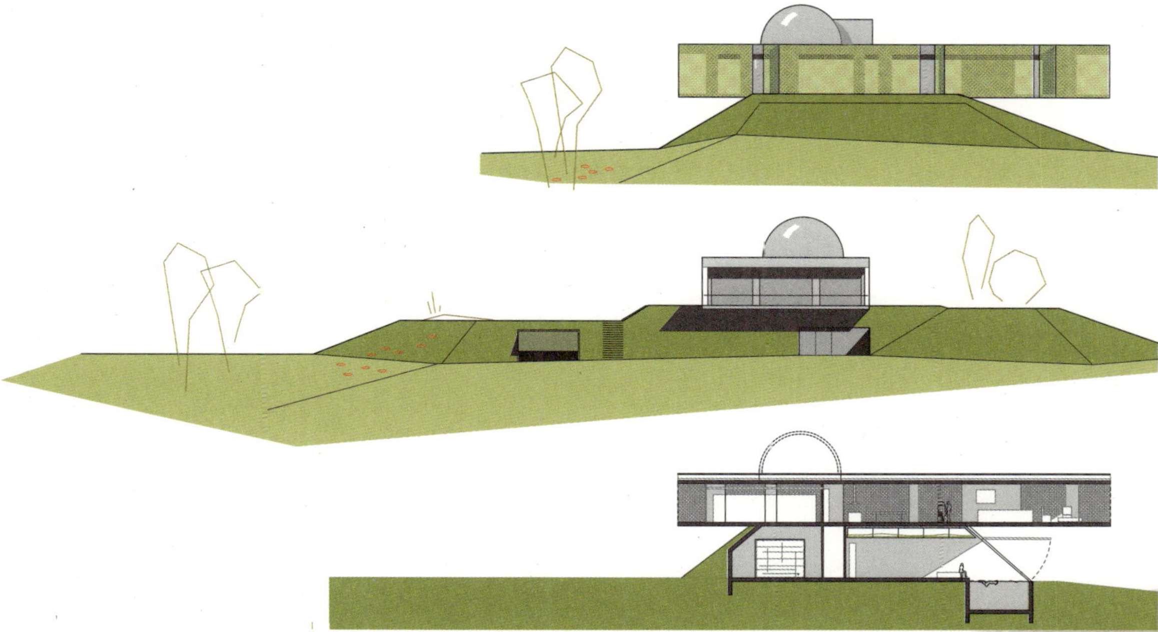

projekt / project
dachbodenausbau / roof conversion
wien, 2011/2012

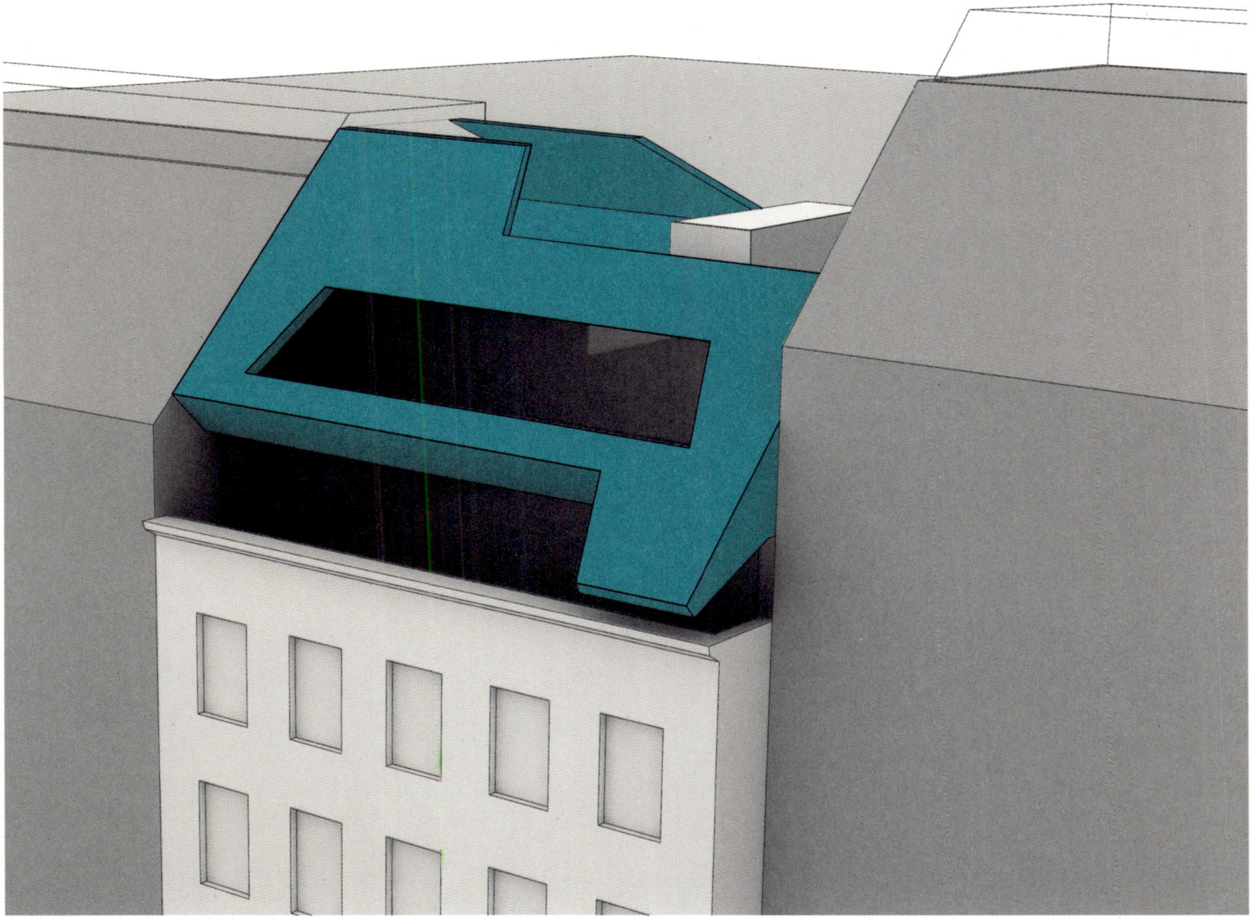

feld 11

dachbodenausbau feld 11 // roof conversion feld 11

ein kleines schloss, hoch in der luft. ein echtes luftschloss also, das derzeit mitten im 7. wiener gemeindebezirk entsteht. dementsprechend stößt man innen auch auf und an keine dachschräge. alle räume haben außenbereiche vorgelagert; und natürlich thront ganz oben noch ein großzügiger garten. weitsichtige planung nennt man das!

a small castle, high up in the air. a real »castle in the air«, at present under construction in the middle of vienna's seventh district. consequently, no sloping ceilings are to be encountered on the inside. all the rooms have external areas located outside of them; and of course, right at the top, everything is crowned by a spacious garden. now that's what one calls far-sighted planning!

2

wettbewerb / competition
haus / house in sievering
2. preis / 2nd prize wien 2010

haus sievering

projekt, wien // project, vienna

ein angebauter nachbar und zwei straßen; die grundstücksgröße sehr überschaubar ... im süden die sonne und ein bach; grün der gegenhang. daher die ausrichtung des u-förmigen grundrisses, ein atrium mit ausblick.
der kleine, wertvolle garten als das eigentliche zentrum des hauses, um den sich die funktionen gruppieren. ein amorphes zentrum, welches erst mal aus dem monolithischen ganzen rauszuschnitzen war. straßenseitig ein metallenes teil; so etwas wie ein satteldach deutet möglicherweise ein haus an ...

an attached neighbour and two streets; very easy to get an overview of the size of the property ... in the south, the sun and a stream; green the hill opposite. hence the orientation of the u-shaped ground plan, an atrium with a view.
the small, valuable garden as the actual centre of the house, around which are grouped the other functions. an amorphous centre, which first of all had to be carved out of the monolithic whole. on the road side, a metal element; something resembling a saddle roof possibly indicates a house ...

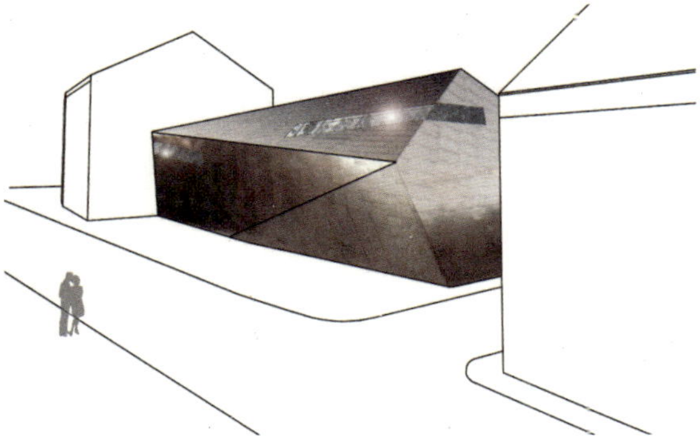
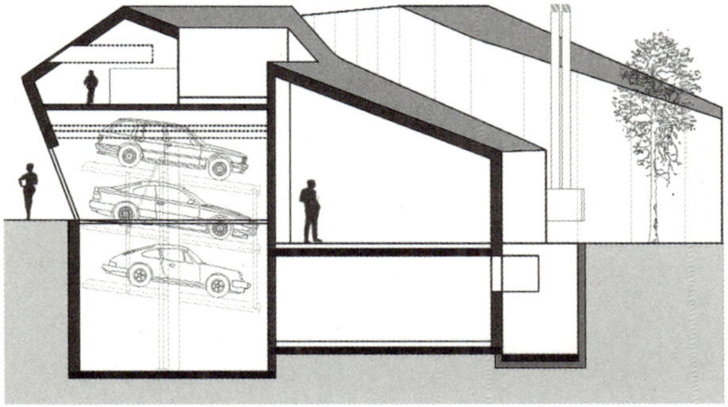

wettbewerb / competition
museums- und erlebniswelt haus des brotes
museum and theme world at the house of bread
enns 2010

haus des brotes

dort auf dem hügel ist die geschichte vom brot und der hügel bin ich und wir alle // there on the hill is the history of bread and the hill is me and us all

die ausstellungsbereiche sind nach themenschwerpunkten in sechs geschossen übereinander gestapelt. ein luftraum mit liftkörper verbindet alle ebenen mit dem brotduft der bäckerei im erdgeschoss. ausgehend vom obersten sechsten stock mit dem intro »zitatetisch« dringt man immer tiefer ins zentrum vor. dabei inszeniert sich der museumsweg durch die außenliegenden stiegen als themenweg mit ständig wechselnden ausblicken in die umgebende landschaft. im erdgeschoss liegt unter den ausstellungsbereichen das zentrale foyer, das die bereiche gastronomie, multifunktionsraum, bäckerei, shop und bibliothek miteinander verbindet. alle ebenerdigen funktionen sind unter einem begrünten hügel situiert, mit einer großzügigen eingangsöffnung, die den vorgelagerten marktplatz einrahmt.

the exhibition areas are stacked in six storeys, one on top of the other, according to the focus of the themes. an empty space with a lift connects all the storeys to the smell of bread from the bakery on the ground floor. proceeding from the topmost sixth storey with the »quotations table« as an intro, one pentrates deeper and deeper towards the centre. in doing so, the route down through the museum via the staircase, which is situated on the outside, becomes a theme route, with constantly changing views of the surrounding landscape. on the ground floor, under the exhibition areas, lies the central foyer, which interconnects the areas for gastronomy, a multi-functional room, the bakery, a shop and a library. all the ground-floor functions are situated under a hill with greenery and a spacious entrance aperture that frames the market place in front of it.

begrüntes flachdach mit oberlichten über der erdgeschosszone. der museumsturm wird von gefalteten betonwänden eingefasst, welche mit metall verkleidet sind. doppelboden zur medienverteilung in den ausstellungsbereichen. bubble- und stahlbetondecken mit bauteilaktivierung zur heizung/kühlung.

a flat roof with greenery and skylights above the ground floor zone. the museum tower is enclosed by folded concrete walls which are covered with metall. double floors for distributing media to the exhibition rooms areas bubble ceilings and reinforced concrete ceilings with activation of the heating/cooling by the building components.

krank ...
müde langweilig...
macht sport!
nein, kreativität!
Sport ist tatsächlich gesundheit!!!
Architektur ist eine frage von MAßSTAB!
Medikament im Abfall!

sporthalle krems

sport ist tatsächlich gesund // actually sport is healthy

der schulkomplex »bundesschulzentrum krems« besteht aus der hotelfachschule mit eigenem schulhotel (»europaschule krems«) und der bundeshandelsakademie/bundeshandelsschule krems. er wurde in den 1970er-jahren der zeit entsprechend funktionalistisch-modern errichtet. große flächendefizite führten 2001 zu einem eu-weit offenen 2-stufigen wettbewerb.

die jury empfahl eine zweiteilung der vergabe in aufstockung der klassentrakte und neubau der pausenhalle mit der erweiterung des turnsaalbereiches. caramel wurde als generalplaner mit der errichtung der pausenhalle und des turnsaals beauftrag.

zwei in längsrichtung nebeneinander angeordnete turnsäle über 46 m statisch auszuwechseln und zu einer vollwertig nutzbaren dreifach-turnhalle zu erweitern, verlangte dem statikbüro »werkraum wien« einiges an ingenieurskunst ab. dies gelang durch einen lediglich 1,8 m hohen vorgespannten stahlbetonträger, in den sowohl die lasten der bestandshallen, wie auch die der erweiterung einfließen.

um einerseits dem engen finanziellen korsett zu entsprechen und andererseits den neubauteil deutlich als solchen zu artikulieren, wurde der erweiterungsteil als leichtbau mit hohem vorfertigungsgrad errichtet. lediglich 16 cm schlanke stahlbetonrippen tragen holzfertigteilpaneele; für belichtung und ausblick sorgen standard-kunststofflichtkuppeln in scheinbar unregelmäßiger anordnung

the school complex that goes by the name of the »krems federal school centre« comprises the college for hotel and catering (»europaschule krems«), which even has its own school hotel, and the federal commercial academy/federal commercial school in krems. it was built in the 1970s, in the functionalist modern style of the time. in 2001, spatial deficits led to a 2-stage eu-wide open competition.
the jury recommended dividing the award of the contract in two, namely between the addition of another storey to the classroom wing, and the construction of a new building for the breaktime hall, together with an extension to the gymnasium. caramel was employed as the general planners to build the break time hall and the gymnasium.

to structurally change two gyms arranged next to each other longitudinally over 46 m and extend them into an adequately utilisable threefold gymnasium, demanded a great deal of engineering skill from the firm of structural analysts, »werkraum« wien. it was achieved by means of a pre-stressed reinforced concrete girder that was only 1.8 m high, which absorbed the load of the existing halls, as well as that of the extension.
in order, on the one hand, to keep within the financial restrictions, and on the other hand to clearly articulate the new building as such, the extension was built as a lightweight structure with a high degree of prefabrication. thin reinforced concrete ribs measuring only 16 cms bear the prefabricated wooden panels; for the purposes of lighting, and for the view, standard plastic rooflight domes were employed in an apparently irregular arrangement.

projectmanager kolja janiszewski

einer bodenaufwölbung gleich entwickelt sich der zubau schalenförmig; es wird nicht in dach und wand unterschieden; die beiden stirnseiten bleiben mit ihrer vollflächigen verglasung gewissermaßen offen. die neue pausenhalle schließt an den turnsaal an und ist mit ihm durch eine filigrane, rahmenlose glaskonstruktion optisch verbunden.

the extension develops as a saucer shape, like an arching of the floor; there is no difference between the roof and the wall; the two front parts remain to a certain extent open, being continuously glazed over the whole surface. the new breaktime hall adjoins the gym, to which it is optically connected by a filigree frameless glass construction.

kenndaten: bgf 2.790 m²; kubatur 16.714 m³
baubeginn: 01/2006
fertigstellung: 09/2007

technical data: gross floor space 2,790 m²; cubage 16,714 m³
start of construction: 01/2006
completion: 09/2007

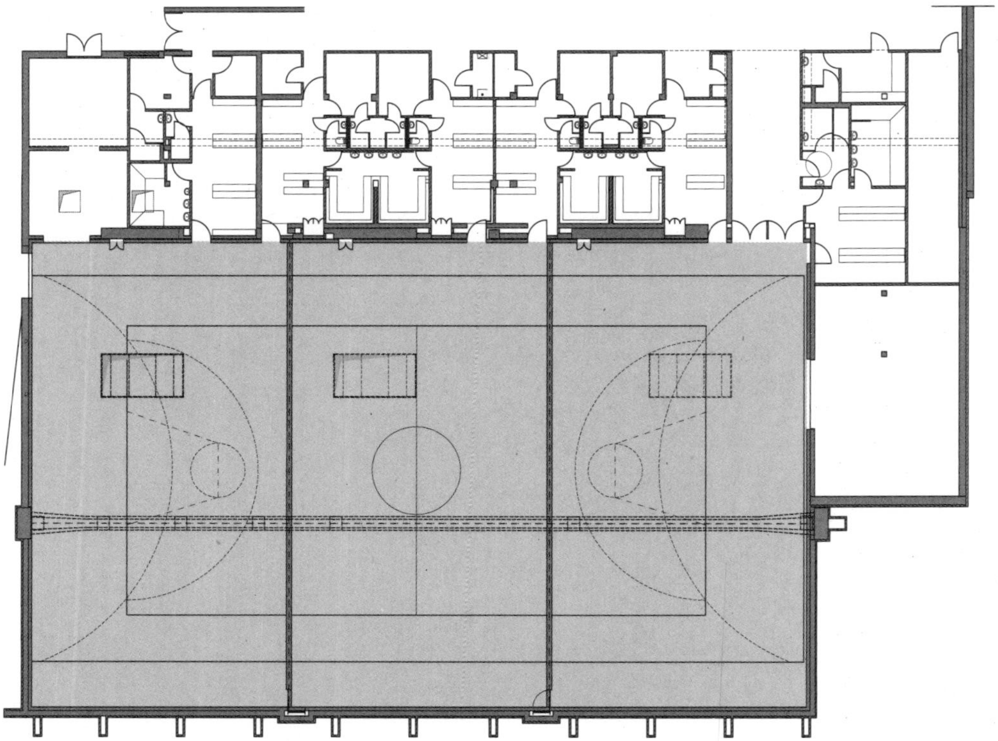

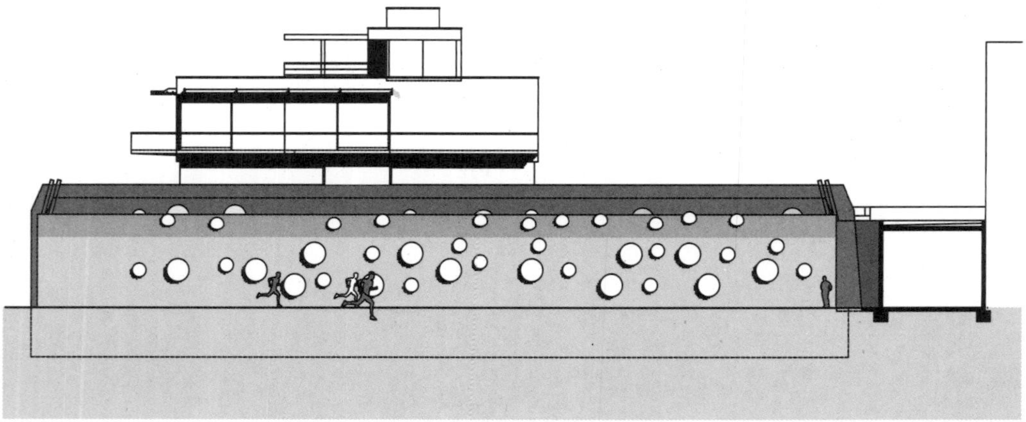

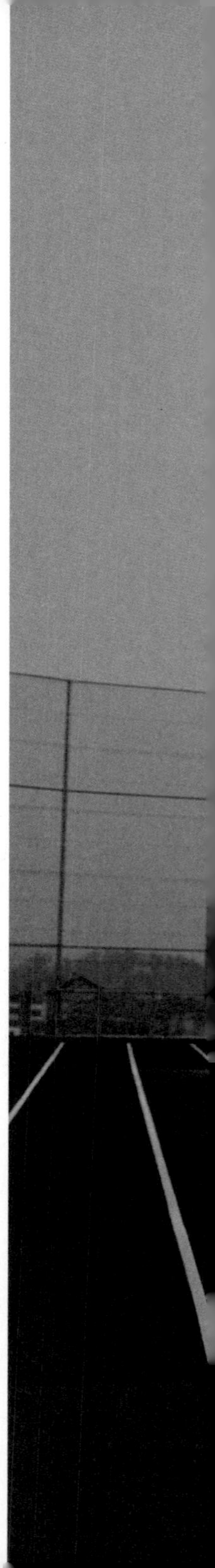

wettbewerb / competition
feuerwehr / fire brigade satteins
preis / prize vorarlberg 2003

feuerwehr satteins

eine »raumschleife« für satteins. das hält uns zusammen. wenns brenzlig wird. // a »space loop« for satteins. to keep us together. when things get hot.

feuerwehr. auch fürs feiern. und so... das mit den feuerwerhäusern ist ja so eine sache, ganz besonders in landgemeinden. einsatzzentrale, unterbringung der löscheinrichtungen und wartung sind nur ein teil der unter dem titel »feuerwehr« zusammengefassten einrichtungen. gar nicht unwichtig für den erhalt dieser so freiwilligen wie wichtigen institution sind die außerberuflichen aktivitäten der mitglieder; wollen schließlich bei laune gehalten werden. und der nachwuchs muss motiviert werden. dazu braucht es einen entsprechenden rahmen. auch fürs feiern. und so.

the fire brigade. also for partying. and so forth... fire stations are funny things, especially in rural communities. operation centres, premises for storing fire-extinguishing equipment and workshops for service and maintenance constitute only a part of the functions that are lumped together under the heading of »fire brigade«. by no means insignificant for the continuation of this voluntary and important institution are the activities engaged in by its members outside of their job; after all, they want to be kept in a good mood. and the younger generation has to be encouraged. for that, a corresponding framework is required. also for partying. and so forth.

wettbewerb / competition
sigmund freud klinik / clinic
preis / price graz 2006

sigmund freud klinik

eine klinikerweiterung für suchtkranke; und wiedermal ein schöner park, der verbaut werden soll. das gebäude orientiert sich zum park und umhüllt sich mit park.

an extension to a clinic for people with addiction disorders; a good thing. and a beautiful park. should it simply disappear? the building faces the park and is surrounded by the park. a good thing.

wettbewerb / competition
hotelroom
london 2010

room for london

bei dem wettbewerb »a room for london« geht es um ein hotelzimmer, das auf einem dach, mitten in einem sehr betriebsamen stadtviertel, gebaut wird, um einen ausblick über das treiben unten, sowie einen außergewöhnlichen stadtrundblick, zu bieten. »die grundidee bei unserem konzept ist, dass das hausdach allein nicht ausreiche… « mit diesem zimmer werden die gäste hinaufgehoben auf ein höheres niveau. um dieses ziel zu erreichen, wird ein ganzes system von hebevorrichtungen, die üblicherweise lasten, baumaterialien und menschen tragen, und die auf baustellen verwendet werden, gemietet und auf ungewöhnlichen art eingesetzt. eine moderne variante des systems soll sicher genug sein, um diesen zweck zu erfüllen, da die beständigkeit, optimale leistung und zuverlässigkeit sogar unter extremen wetter- und betriebsbedingungen schon bewiesen wurde. auf der konstruktion befinden sich ein zahnstangenaufzug sowie eine hebeplattform mit kabine und eine notausgangsstiege. alle erforderlichen einrichtungen sind vorhanden, wenn auch raumminimiert.

the competition »a room for london« is about placing a hotel room on a rooftop in the middle of a busy neighbourhood, in order to enjoy the view of the human hustle and bustle below, and to get extraordinary vistas of the city panorama. »the main idea of our design is that the rooftop is not enough … « with this room, guests will be lifted to a higher level. in order to achieve that goal, a system of hoists, commonly used for carrying loads, building materials and people on large construction sites, will be rented and then used in an unconventional way. a modern version of the system should be safe enough to serve the purpose, since it has already proved its durability, optimal performance and reliability even under extreme weather conditions and operating circumstances. the construction has a rack and pinion hoist on its mast system, a lifting platform with a cab box on it, and an additional escape staircase. all the required facilities are provided, although they are certainly not the most spacious ones.

construction steinway böcker

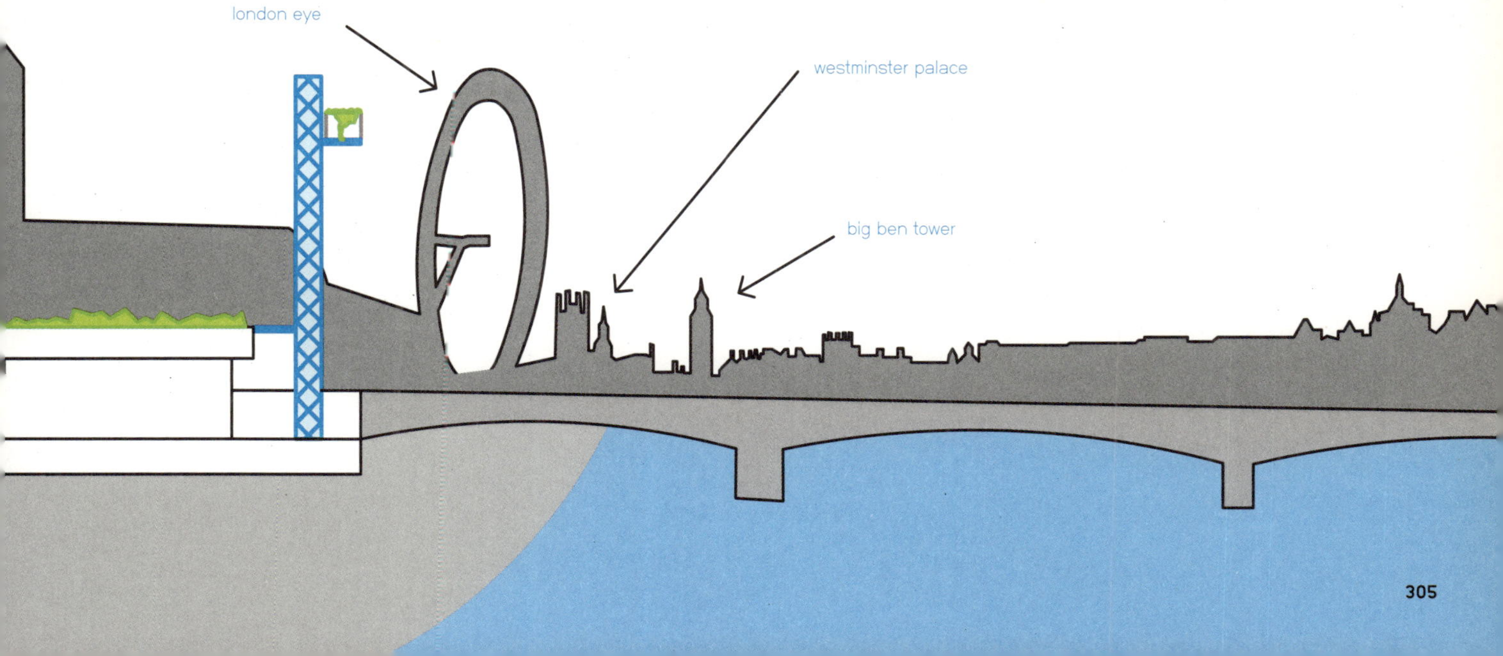

london eye
westminster palace
big ben tower

studie / study
fliegendes / flying appartement
in the air 2005

airloft

baugrund 0 m² aussicht 100 % //
0 m² building area with a 100 % view

0 m² baugrund mit 100 % aussicht – und die antwort auf die frage: kann ich mit meinem gesamten hausrat fliegen? ja ich kann. in einem autarken singlewohnhaus. ein heliumgefüllter transparenter würfel von 5 x 5 x 7 m mit einem freien innenwohnraum von 3 x 3 x 3 m hat genügend auftrieb um die 100 kg mensch und maschinen in den himmel zu heben. die zu hebende last beträgt nur 100 kg, da alle einrichtungsgegenstände aus der raumbildenden, fast gewichtslosen kunststoffhaut geformt werden. durch mehrfachnutzung des raumes eignet sich die raumkapsel fürs arbeiten, wohnen, essen, schlafen, duschen und körperentleeren. eine seilwinde stellt die verbindung zur erde fürs gelegentliche wasserauftanken dar. solarzellenbeschichtungen auf der hüllenfläche sorgen für den erforderlichen strom. also, auf in den himmel!

0 m² building area with a 100% view – and the answer to the question: can i fly with all my household and personal effects? yes I can. in a self-sustaining single dwelling. a helium-filled transparent cube measuring 5 x 5 x 7m with an open interior living space of 3 x 3 x 3 m has enough ascending force to lift 100 kgs of human being and machines into the sky. the load to be lifted only amounts to 100 kg because all the furnishing objects are made of a space-creating and almost weightless synthetic skin. through multiple use of the space, the space capsule becomes suitable for working, living, eating, sleeping, showering and bodily discharge. a cable winch provides the connection to the earth for occasionally refueling with water. layers of solar cells on the surface of the skin provide the required electricity. so, let's be off, up into the sky!

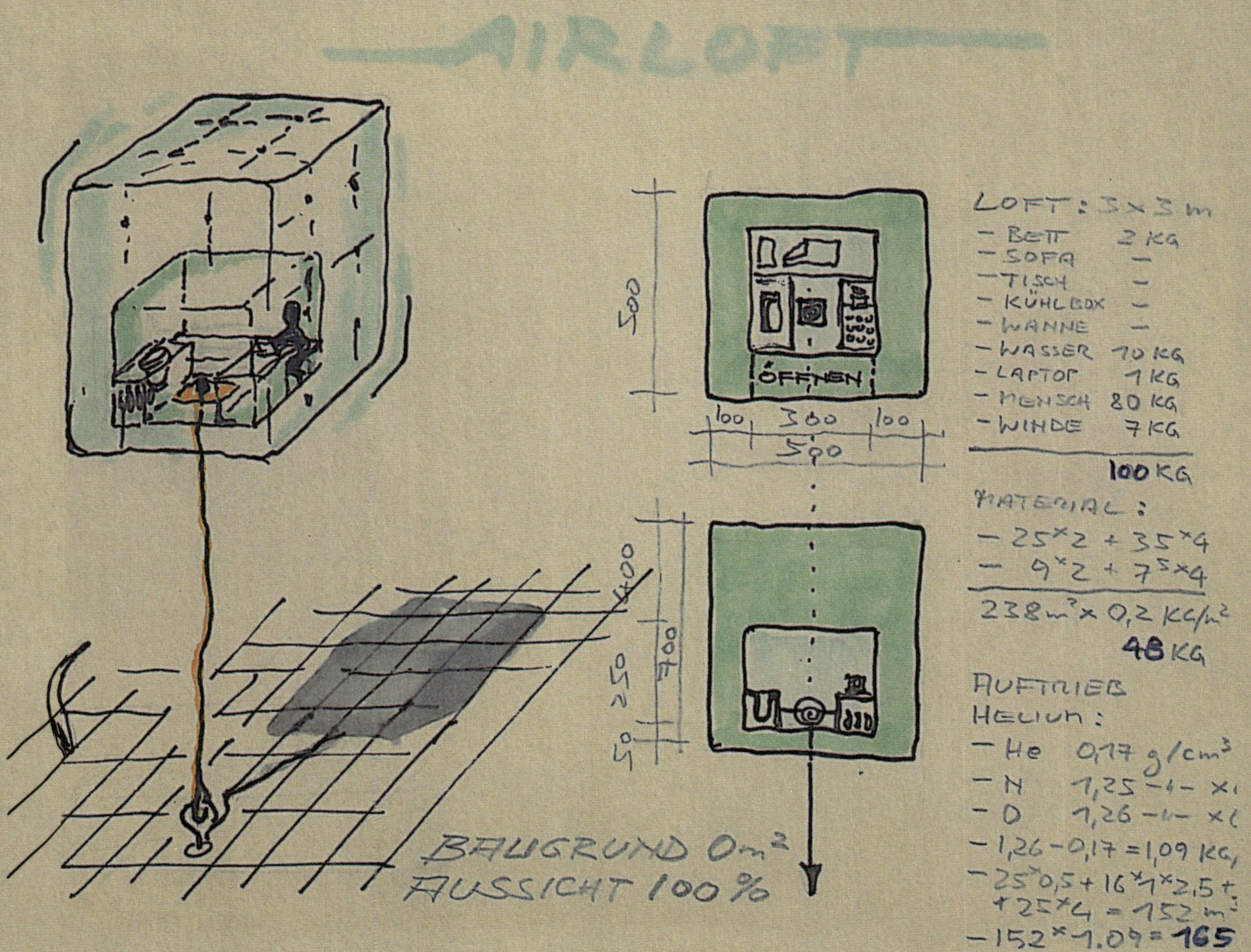

AIRLOFT
500
100 300 100
500
ÖFFNEN
LOFT: 3x3 m
– BETT 2 KG
– SOFA –
– TISCH –
– KÜHLBOX –
– WANNE –
– WASSER 10 KG
– LAPTOP 1 KG
– MENSCH 80 KG
– WINDE 7 KG
100 KG
MATERIAL:
– 25x2 + 35x4
– 9x2 + 75x4
238 m² x 0,2 KG/m²
48 KG
AUFTRIEB
HELIUM:
– He 0,17 g/cm³
– N 1,25 –"–
– O 1,26 –"–
– 1,26 – 0,17 = 1,09 KG
– 25x0,5 + 16x1x2,5 +
+ 25x4 = 152 m²
– 152x1,09 = 165
BAUGRUND 0 m²
AUSSICHT 100 %

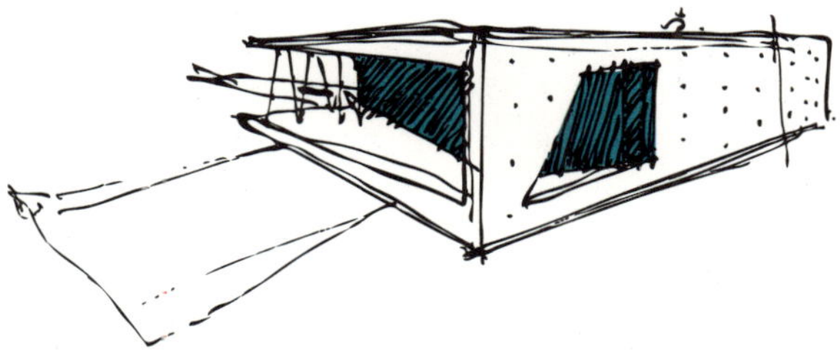

polsterartig eingehüllt wird der kubus von kunststoffmembranen: im dachbereich von weißem epdm; im fassadenbereich (unsichtbar mit der dachbahn verschweißt) von weißem, teflonbeschichtetem pvc. durch die zwischen holzkonstruktion und membrane liegende wärmedämmung wird die folie punktuell befestigt.
the cube is enveloped like a pillow in synthetic membranes. for the roof area white epdm was used; for the façade area (invisibly welded to the roof liner), white teflon-coated pvc, which was secured at intervals through the thermal insulation layer between the outer membrane and the structural panels.

haus m

am hang des linzer pöstlingberges // on the slope of pöstlingberg in linz

am hang des linzer pöstlingberges gelegen nutzt der 12x12 m große kubus das grundstück so weit als möglich aus und rückt so nah wie baurechtlich erlaubt an die nordöstliche grundstücksecke. diese beiden seiten treten sehr geschlossen in erscheinung und schützen so vor den einblicken der höher gelegenen nachbarschaft.
nach süden und westen hingegen öffnet sich das haus mit zwei nurglasfassaden. die westgerichtete gebäudefront bietet einen herrlichen ausblick über das donautal und fängt bis spät abends das sonnenlicht ein, dabei schützt ein außen liegender gewebevorhang vor zuviel einstrahlung und überhitzung. die südfassade weicht in freier form von den außenkanten des kubus zurück und bildet einen überdachten terrassenbereich. im direkten anschluss daran ist ein großzügiger schwimmteich angelegt.

sitting on the slope of pöstlingberg in linz, the 12x12 m cube takes full advantage of the lot by establishing itself as far into the north-eastern corner of the site as building codes permit. these two sides have a very hermetic appearance, thus preventing neighbors from looking in.
by contrast, the house opens itself toward the south and west with two all-glass façades. the west side of the building offers a magnificent view of the danube valley and receives sunlight until late in the evening; an externally mounted textile curtain guards against excessive sunlight and overheating. the south façade pulls away from the edge of the cube in free-form retreat, producing a covered terrace area. extending directly from the terrace is a large swimming pond.

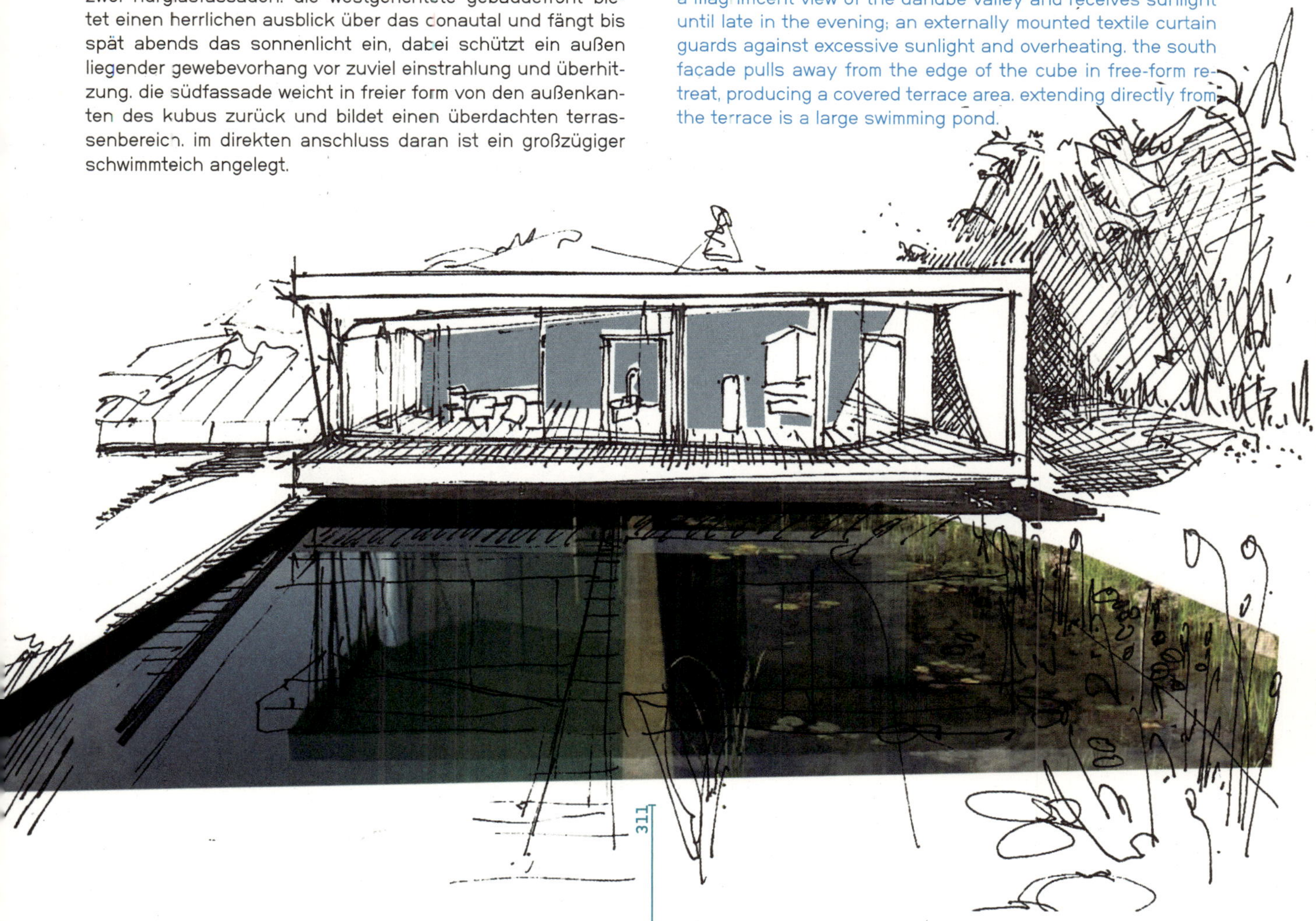

die einfache form des baukörpers und der hohe vorfertigungsgrad, sowie eine sehr gute wärmedämmung aus zellstoff, der einsatz von brennwerttechnologie und außen liegender beschattung sorgen für ein sehr ökonomisches und ökologisches gebäude.

the simple form of the building volume, the high degree of prefabrication, its excellent cellulose-fiber thermal insulation, as well as the application of calorific value technology and external shading, all contribute to making this a very economical and ecological building.

die leicht nach osten geneigte dachplatte entwässert das dach rinnenlos über die fassade in einen schottergefüllten sickerschacht an der rückseite des hauses.

slightly inclined toward the east, the roof slab provides gutterless drainage via the façade into a gravel-filled french drain at the back of the house.

wettbewerb / competition
schulzentrum / school centre
2. preis / 2nd prize bad ischl 2003

schulzentrum bad ischl

es fliegt, es fliegt, es fliegt, ein krokodil //
it flies, it flies, it flies, a crocodile

freier außenraumbezug auf allen ebenen. der schulneubau wird eingeschossig aufgeständert, um, ohne weiteren freiraum zu verbauen, die erforderlichen autostellplätzen zu ermöglichen. dadurch bleibt der gesamte bestehende freibereich für die schüler als großzügige pausenfläche erhalten. von den klassenzimmern in den oberen stockwerken schweift der blick, so er nicht auf den lehrer und die tafel gerichtet ist, zweifach ungestört über die begrünten pausenflächen: zum großen parkplatz besteht kein blickbezug – von ihm wird die aussicht also in keiner weise gestört. vom lehrer vielleicht. von der tiefer gelegenen außenfläche gibt es keine direkte einblickmöglichkeit.

open connections to the outdoor space on all levels. the new school building comprises one elevated storey, in order to create the requisite parking spaces for cars without building on further undeveloped land. in this way, the whole existing outdoor space remains as a spacious breaktime area for the school pupils. the view pans out from the classrooms of the upper storeys, insofar as all eyes are not fixed on the teacher and the board, twice undisturbed, over the greenery of the breaktime areas: the large area of the car park cannot be seen – so that the view is not obstructed in any way. perhaps by the teachers. from the external area, which is sunk lower, there is no possibility of looking directly into the classrooms.

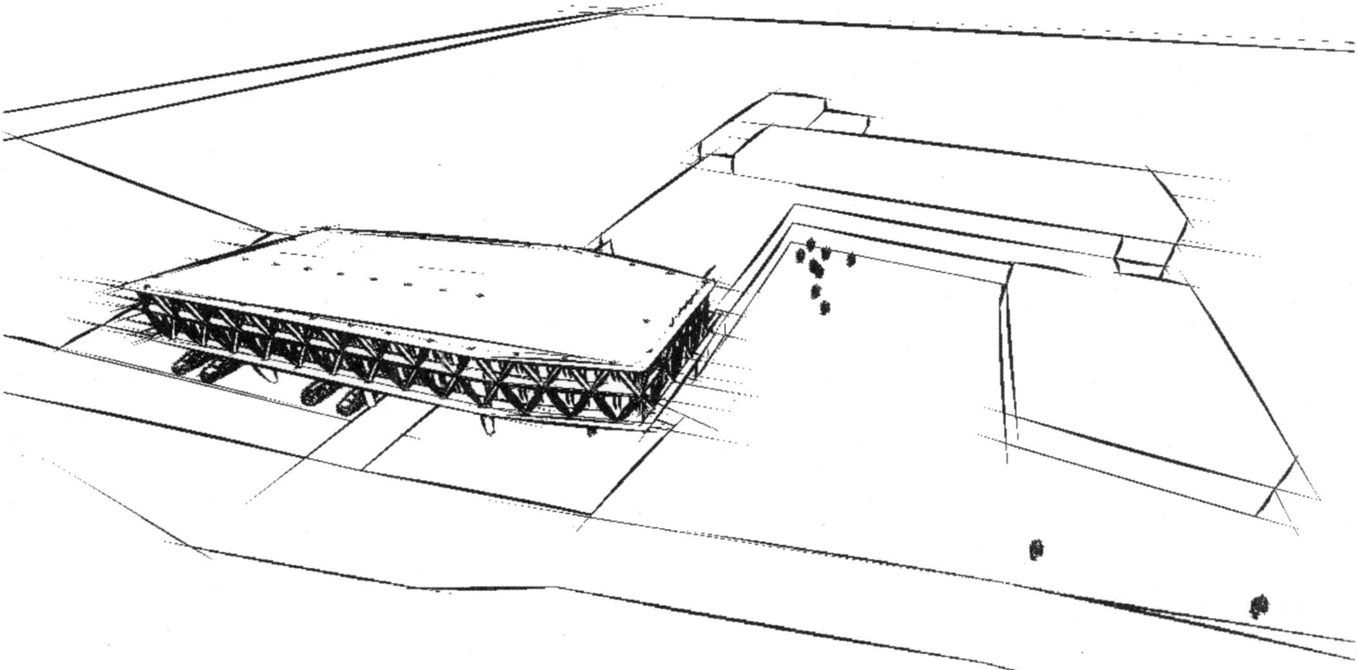

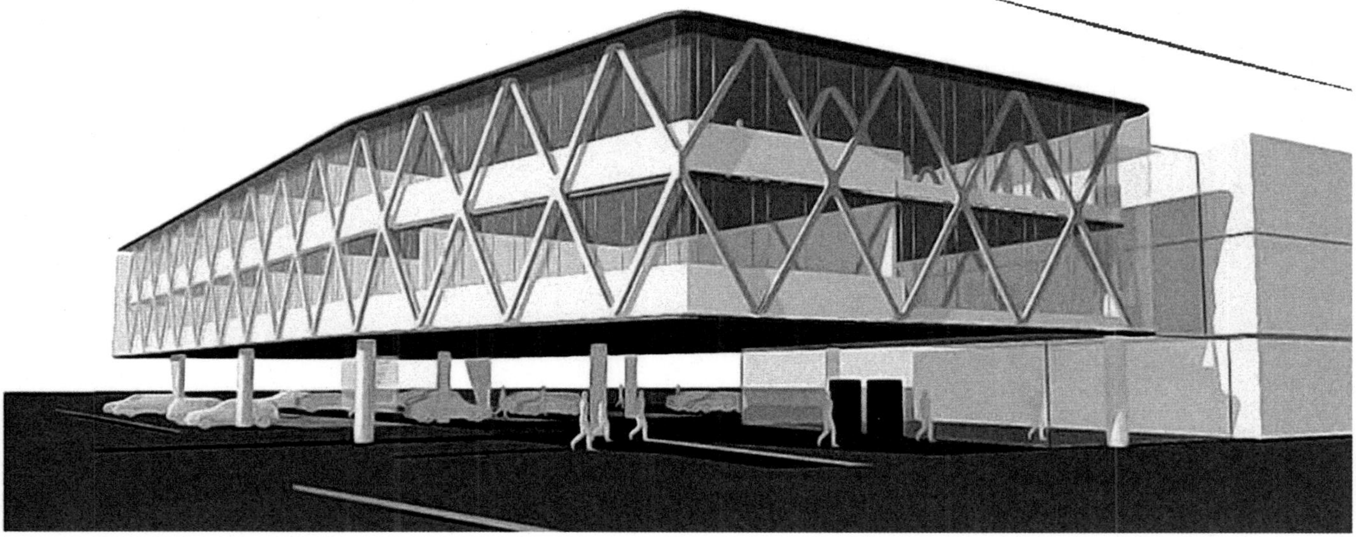

wettbewerb / competition
fremdenverkehrsamt / tourist office
1. preis / 1st prize riezlern 2001

fremdenverkehrsamt

das bestehende tourismusbüro in riezlern soll umgebaut und insbesondere die infotheke vergrößert werden. die erweiterungen im vorhandenen innenraum lassen sich kaum verwirklichen. doch caramel hat den wunsch des auslobers nach mehr infobereich für die gäste ernst genommen – und die neue infotheke durch die außenhaut bis auf den öffentlichen gehsteig verlängert.

it was intended to rebuild the existing tourist office in riezlern and in particular to enlarge the information counter. extensions within the existing interior can hardly be achieved at all. nonetheless, caramel took the client's wish for a larger customer information area seriously – and extended the new information counter through the outer skin and as far as the outside pavement.

3. pause, easy, eeeasy

hansi

tschuldigen, sind sie der hansi unterseer? wer? na, der berühmte hansi unterseer? ich kenn keinen hansi unterseer. na, der mit dem gesicht. der mit den haaren. macht eine charakteristische kopfbewegung. der mit dem markanten hüftschwung. ich habe ihn nie gesehen. nicht einmal von weitem. ja, dann auch nicht von der nähe. auch nicht von der nähe. ich hab mir gedacht, sie könntens sein. nett. wieso nett? na, dass ich so nah bei ihnen stehen darf. ich bin aber nicht der hansi unterseer. ah so, sie sinds gar nicht. na, so ein zufall. warum sagen sie das nicht gleich. jedenfalls freut es mich, dass ich sie gesehen hab. und dass sie so nett zu mir waren. das muss ich gleich meiner ganzen familie erzählen, die ist ein fan von ihnen. meine frau wird augen machen, dass ich fast den hansi unterseer gesehen habe.

excuse me, aren't you hansi unterseer? who? er, the famous hansi unterseer? i don't know any hansi unterseer. you know, the one with the face. the one with the hair. has a typical head movement. the one with a distinct swing of the hips. i've never seen him. not even from a distance. so not close-up either. not close-up either. i was thinking that you might be him. nice. what's nice? well now, that i could stand so close to you. but i'm not hansi unterseer. oh no, you're not him. well, what a coincidence. why didn't you say so right away. at any rate, i'm glad to have seen you. and that you were so nice to me. i have to tell the whole family right away, they're fans of yours. my wife'll be so surprised that i almost saw hansi unterseer.

friedrich achleitner

Triple Action
Colgate
NESCAFÉ

wettbewerb / competition
erweiterung / extension ars electronica center
preis / prize linz 2006

ars electronica center

das ars electronica center, »museum der zukunft«, sollte für das kulturhauptstadtjahr 09 eine erweiterung erhalten. die zielvorgabe war klar: die sicht auf die alturfahraner altstadtbauten darf nicht verstellt werden; also musste niedrig gebaut werden... oder hoch, dachte caramel und rahmte die altstadt ein mit einem linzer L. der altbau blieb mehr oder weniger altbau. daneben, selbstbewusst und eindeutig, die geste des für linz so wichtigen neubaues. caramel: »die statik war gefordert. werkraum wien löste das problem erwartungsgemäß mit bravour.«

the idea was to build an extension to the ars electronica center's »museum of the future«, for the city's year as cultural capital in 09. the brief was clearly defined: the view of the buildings of the old part of town known as alturfahr should not be impeded; which meant low-level construction... alternatively high-level, thought caramel, and framed the old town in a L for linz. the old building remained more or less old building. next to it, self-confident and unambiguous, was to be seen the gesture of the new building that is so important for linz. caramel: »the statics were stipulated. as expected, werkraum wien solved the problem brilliantly.«

wettbewerb / competition
privat museum / private museum liaunig
neuhaus kärnten 2006

privat museum liaunig

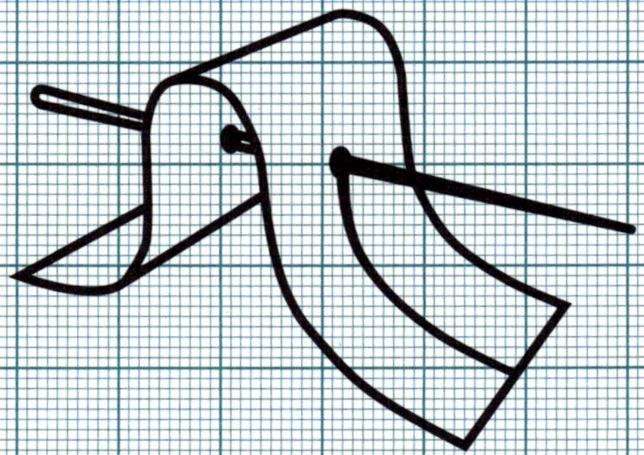

ein privatmuseum für eine fantastische sammlung österreichischer und auch internationaler, zeitgenössischer kunst der letzen 70 jahre in einer fantastischen landschaft an der kärtner südgrenze.
caramel beantwortet die frage nach dem umgang mit dieser bauaufgabe mit einem konsequent klaren baukörper, der, eingeschnitten in die hügelkuppe, als von oben belichteter white cube wie ein vom himmel gefallener monolith in der unverbauten landschaft liegt.
einem riesigen periskop ähnlich werden die öffentlichen bereiche mit dem veranstaltungssaal zur drau hin orientiert; ein weit in die kärntner landschaft blickender hinweis auf hohe kultur an diesem ort.

a private museum for a fantastic collection of austrian and international contemporary art of the last 70 years, set in a fantastic landscape on the southern carinthian border;
caramel responded to the question of how to approach this architectural brief by providing a consistently clear building structure, inserted into the dome of the hill like a white cube and lit from above, so that it seemed like a monolith that has fallen from the sky and is lying there in the undeveloped landscape.
resembling a huge periscope, the public areas and the events hall were oriented towards the drau; an indication of high culture in a location that looks out into the carinthian landscape.

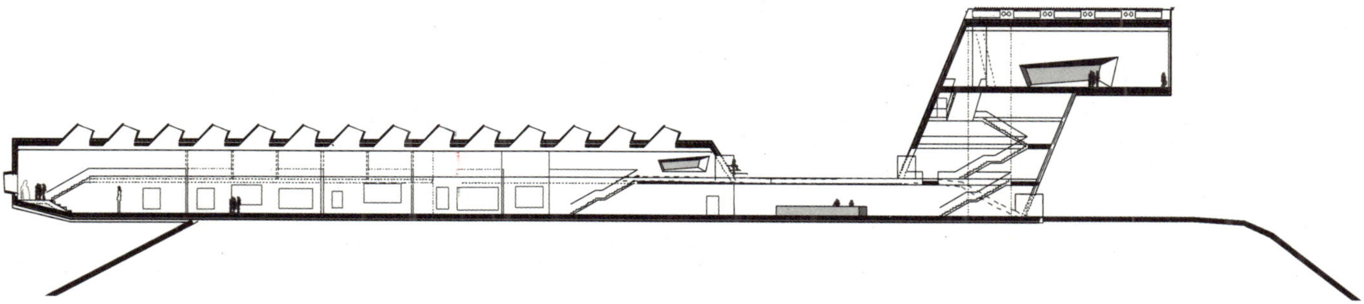

ein von der kärntner landespolitik wohl nicht verstandener hinweis; die vom engagierten sammler eingeladenen politisch verantwortlichen erschienen gleich gar nicht zur jurysitzung, was den bauherrn verständlicherweise dazu bewog, auf den öffentlichen teil seines privatmuseums zu verzichten...

an indication that was probably not understood by carinthia's regional government; when invited by the committed collector, the political figures responsible for such matters did not even bother to attend the jury meeting. understandably enough, this caused the client to give up on the idea of making part of his private museum public...

ausstellungsbeitrag zur ausstellung »die enzyklopödie der wahren werte« im
contribution to the exhibition »the encyclopaedia of true values« at »künstlerhaus«
wien 2003

die enzyklopädie der wahren werte

»... wunder eisenbahn religion treue erdäpfel kreuz lenin luxus ... das sind einige der worte, die wir aus zeitungen, rundfunk- und fernsehsendungen, politikreden, werbung, intellektuellen essays und persönlichen gesprächen mit freunden und experten entnommen haben. es sind begriffe, die das denken und handeln der jetztzeit zu bestimmen scheinen. auffallend ist, dass es begriffe (phänomene, dinge, sehnsüchte, emotionen, vorstellungen etc.) sind, die bereits vor jahren oder gar jahrzehnten gebraucht wurden und die nach einer zeit der latenz, gleichbedeutend oder neu auf die jetztzeit eingestimmt, wieder präsent sind. kurzum: es handelt sich um begriffe, die sich bewährt zu haben scheinen oder tatsächlich bewährt haben und die nun den alltag prägen. daher nennen wir diese worte wahre werte.«

textauszug von jan tabor zur ausstellung.

»... miracle railway religion faith potato cross lenin luxury ... these are just some of the words that we have taken from newspapers, radio and television programmes, political speeches, advertising, intellectual essays and personal conversations with friends and experts. they are terms that seem to determine the way people think and act at the present time. what is noticeable is that they are terms (phenomena, things, desires, emotions, ideas etc.) that were already in use years ago, or even decades ago, and which after a time of latency have once again become present, some with the same meaning, others newly attuned to the present age. in brief: they are terms that either seem to have proved their worth, or have really have done so, and which have now become part of everyday life. that is why we describe these words as true values«.

abstract of the text from jan tabor for the exhibition

studie / study
mobiles minihochhaus für / mobile mini high-rise building for new york 2005

new york turm entwurf

take-away sky scraper

bebauungssituation manhattan, new york city:
baulücken zu unleistbaren grundstückspreisen für preiswerten wohnbau – gleichzeitig lange brachliegezeiten dieser bauplätze und temporäre nutzung als mietparkplatz.
antwort caramel: ein mietparkplatz bietet einem mobilen hochhaus für eine familie raum; oder auch einem partyturm für menschen, die immer in bewegung sind. zentral gelegener wohnraum wandert von einer temporären baulücke zur nächsten.
die bodenfläche eines parkplatzes (250 x 500 cm) wird vertikal zu einer dreigeschossigen wohnung aufgestellt und mit den funktionen dance, eat, dj, staff, talk, lounge, work, sleep, dress, swim ausgestattet. das haus wird in horizontaler position als anhänger mit einer zugmaschine transportiert. bei der aufstellung des hauses wird der wasservorratstank an der bodenplatte gefüllt und sorgt gemeinsam mit solarzellen für ein einergieautarkes und bodenstabiles gebäude.

the development situation in manhattan, new york city: empty sites at unaffordable property prices for reasonably-priced apartment housing – at the same time, such gap sites lie undeveloped for long periods of time and are used as temporarily rented car parks.
caramel's answer: a rented car park plot provides space for a mobile high-rise for a family; or, alternatively, a party tower for people who are always on the move. a centrally located apartment space that wanders from one temporary infill to the next.
the ground area of a car park, 250 x 500 cm is developed vertically to form a three-storey apartment that can be used for dancing, eating, djs, staff, talking, a lounge, working, sleeping, dressing, or swimming. when in a horizontal position, the building can be transported on a trailer using a towing vehicle. in the process of erecting the building, the water storage tank on the base plate is filled up. in combination with the use of solar cells, this creates a stable construction with an independent energy source.

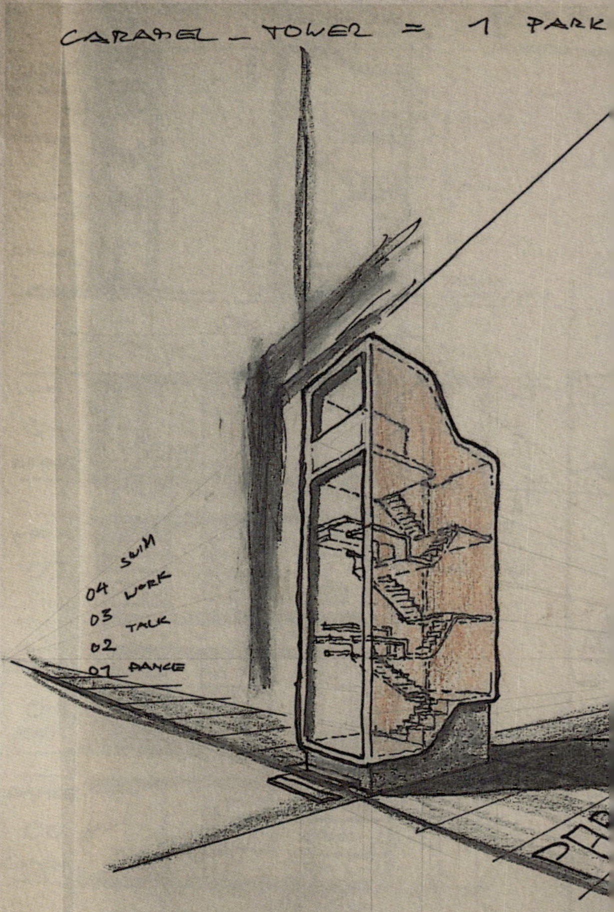

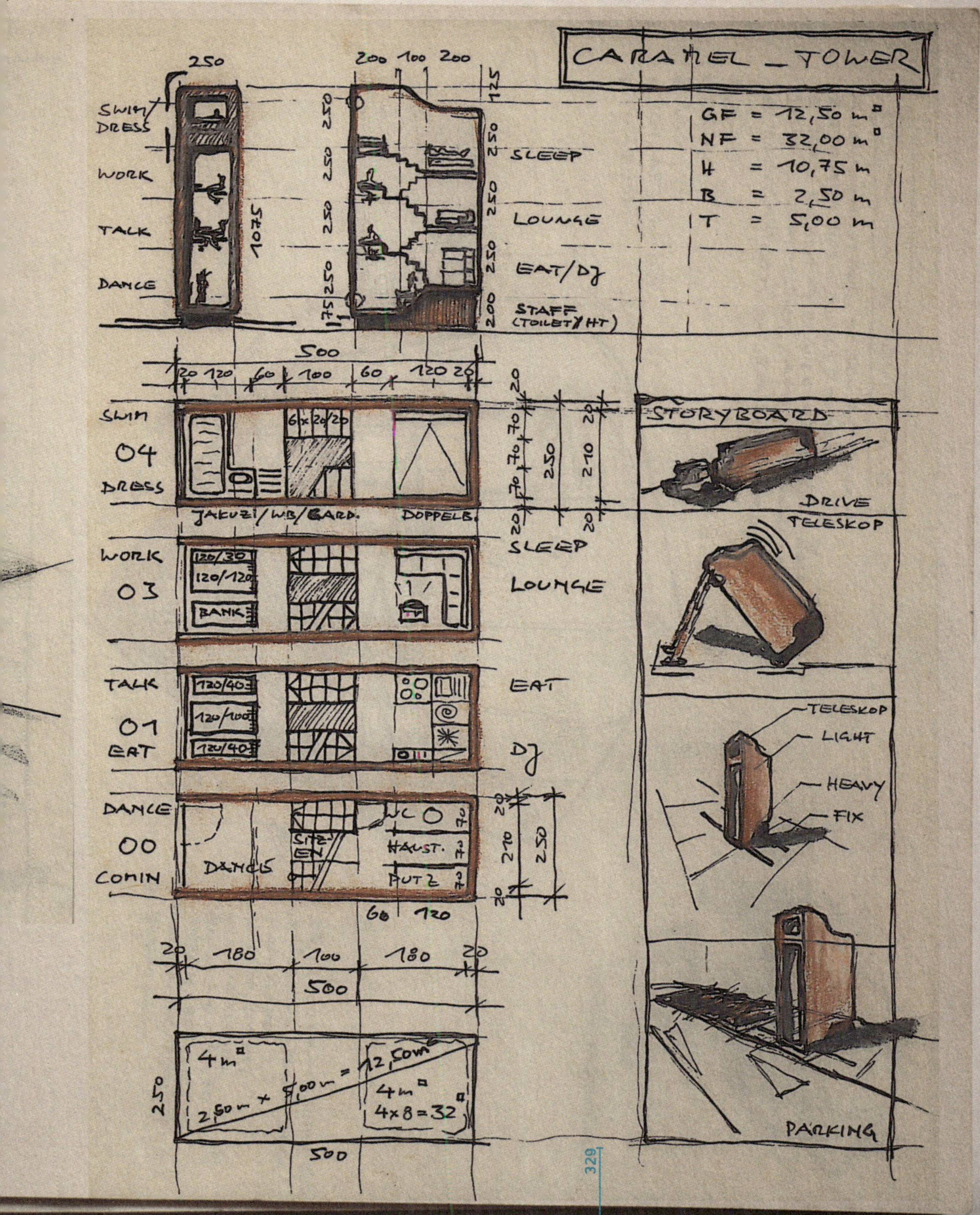
CARAMEL_TOWER
GF = 12,50 m²
NF = 32,00 m²
H = 10,75 m
B = 2,50 m
T = 5,00 m
SWIM/DRESS
WORK
TALK
DANCE
SLEEP
LOUNGE
EAT/DJ
STAFF (TOILET/HT)
SWIM 04 DRESS
JAKUZI/WB/GARD.
DOPPELB.
WORK 03
BANK
TALK 01 EAT
EAT
DJ
DANCE 00 COMIN
DANCE
SITZEN
WC
HAUST.
PUTZ
4 m²
2,50 m × 5,00 m = 12,50 m²
4×8=32²
STORYBOARD
DRIVE
TELESKOP
TELESKOP
LIGHT
HEAVY
FIX
PARKING

a new skirt for berlin

showrooms an der spree // showrooms on the spree

der vorgegebene städtebauraster schrieb den bauplatz als eine reihe von genau definierten quadern vor.
caramels antwort auf das »steinerne berlin« sah so aus:
»...die leichtigkeit der architektur widerspricht der schwere des ortes...« (auszug aus dem juryentscheid)
eine transparente und konstruktionslose membranfassade (etfe-folie als mittels überdruck gespannte außenschicht) kreiert einen schwerelos leuchtenden raum inmitten der massiv bebauten umgebung.
textile schichten im fassadenzwischenraum sind gestaltgebende verschleierung und enthüllung zugleich, der neue rock für berlin. die textilbahnen dienen den labels durch projektionen und bedruckungen zur eigenpräsentation. als nach innen gestülpter vorhang leiten sie den besucher in den schwerelosen kubus.
vom eingang aus schweift sich der blick von veranstaltungraum und gastronomiebereich über die terrasse auf die spree.
konstruktion: stützenfreie stahlbetonkonstruktion; plattendecken als »bubble«decken mit spannweiten von 20 m, ein stringenter vertikaler erschließungs- und infrastrukturkern. aus!

the already existent urban development grid determined that the construction site should be a series of precisely defined building blocks.
caramel's response to »stony berlin« looked like this: »...the lightness of the architecture contradicts the heaviness of the location...« (excerpt from the jury's decision)
a transparent and construction-less membrane facade (etfe-membrane as an external layer, stretched by overpressure) creates a weightless luminous space in the middle of the massively developed environment.
fabric layers in the gap between the facades create form by veiling and revealing, at one and the same time, a new skirt for berlin. the lengths of fabric serve as labels for projections and printing, as part of their own self-presentation. as curtains that are upturned towards the inside, they lead the visitor into the weightless cube.
from the entrance, the eyes roam from the events room and the gastronomy area, across the terrace to focus on the spree.
construction: support-free reinforced concrete construction; slab floors as bubble ceilings with a span width of 20 m, a stringent vertical core for access and infrastructure. enough!

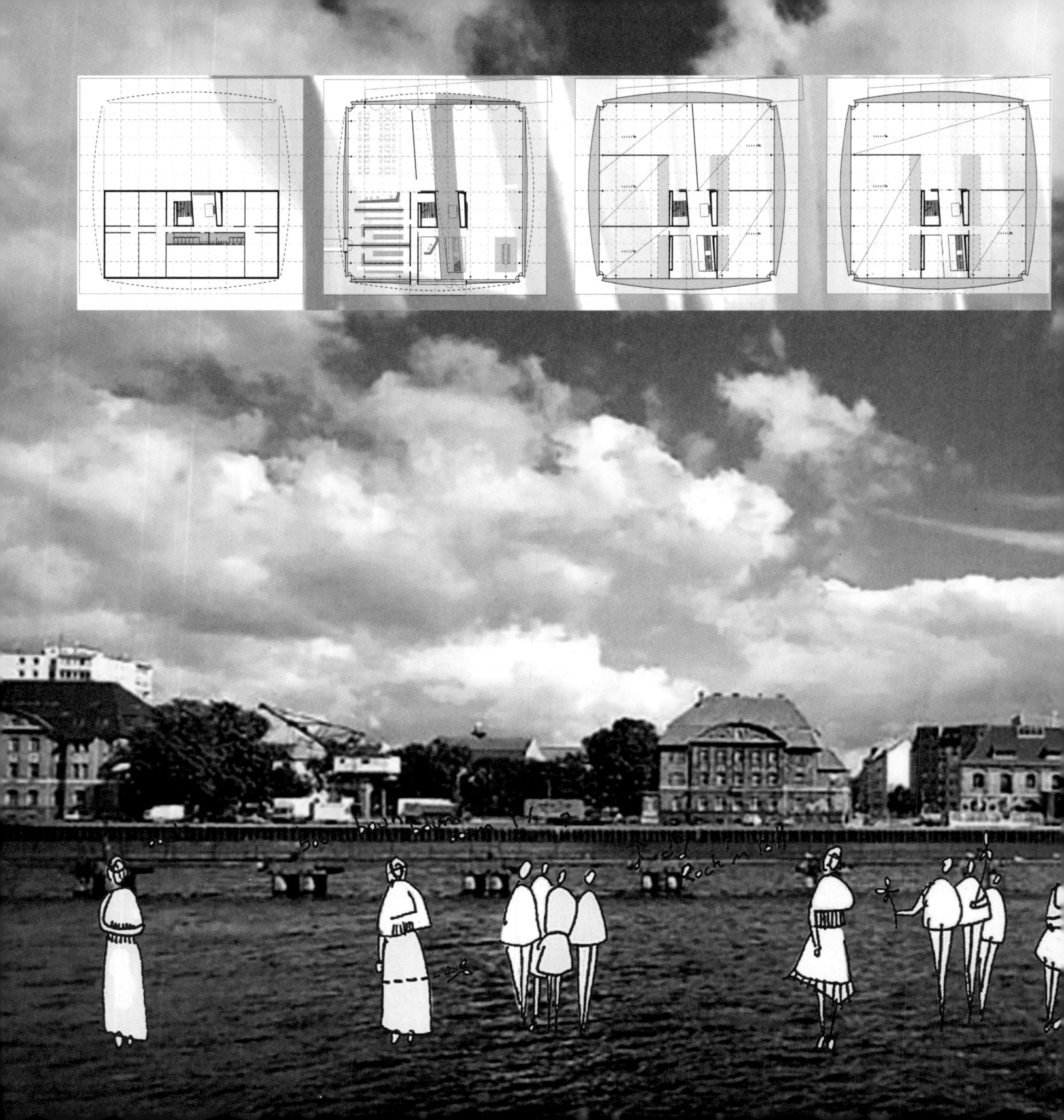
Rock'n roll

mobil

mobile

you'll be sorry if you forget mobil, schätzchen

»aus dem boden gewachsen«, anne bennent

das haus, aus dem boden gewachsen, mit einem eukalyptusbaum der den rundlichen, zum meer geöffneten hof beschattet. die küche ist der erste raum der gebaut wurde, vom bauern, daneben ein zimmer für das brautpaar. hinterm haus ein stall. dann wuchs das haus uneben, mit der zahl der geborenen kinder. zwei söhne. keine geraden winkel. niedrige decken. fast wie höhlen die kleinen räume, im sommer kühl, im milden winter stelle ich mir vor, dass die körperwärme der bewohner sich darin gut halten konnte und der erdige boden eine eigene wärme ausstrahlte. kleine fensteröffnungen, mit holzläden. ganz dunkel im haus. draußen das blendende licht griechenlands. es war ein lebewesen mit einem bauch, einem rücken, einer befindlichkeit, jeden tag schien es mir eine andere form anzunehmen und auch die farbe veränderte sich je nach tageszeit und wetter. der baum raschelte unaufhörlich, es war die sprache des hauses. nie werde ich das lebensgefühl vergessen, das dieses haus mir geschenkt hat, ich wollte nicht mehr fort. wenn ich an etwas wie architektur denke dann ist dieses mit mir atmende haus eine art anfang ... von wohnen. es ließ sich auch gerne streicheln ...
für mich sind gebäude lebewesen, die mit dem boden auf dem sie entstanden sind, der umgebung und den menschen die sie bevölkern sprechen und sich verändern. mein sohn wird wütend, wenn ich wieder einmal ausrufe: schau, das haus hat ein gesicht! wie baut man ein haus, es baut sich vielleicht fast wie von selbst ... mit den materialien, die in der nähe gegeben sind. zeit müssten die konstrukteure haben, zu erörtern und zu erhören was da ist, eine vision entstehen zu lassen von dem was da für wen wachsen soll. wo die sonne ist und was die schatten tun. manches mal, wenn ich spazieren gehe in gebäuden und auf plätzen, kommt es mir vor, als hätten die damen oder herren architekten kaum tage und nächte an den von ihnen gestalteten orten verbracht, nicht vorher, nicht nachher, vielleicht nicht wirklich neugierig auf das wesen des ortes. oft sehe ich da ein konzept stehen, ohne rück- oder vorsicht. begegne ziemlichen lebensfremdheiten und absurditäten.
zum beispiel ein denkmal für die deportierten jüdischen familien des zweiten bezirkes, auf der heine straße ecke zirkusgasse, das auf grund seiner form und seines inhalts monatelang als hundeklo benutzt wurde, weil niemand die dichte hundebevölkerung im viertel beachtete. nun ist ein hoher dreieckiger zaun daraufgepflanzt, der von kränkelden pflanzen beklettert wird. nicht schön. in österreich wundere ich mich über das oft fehlende lebenswürdig gestaltete auf plätzen. kein außenleben mit schattigen bänken zum rasten oder plaudern auf der straße, unter bäumen. kaum brunnen und fontänen. eher umzäunte, seltsam orthopädische spielplätze, wo ich mich als mama im rahmen zu benehmen habe. und die angst vorm außer haus ruhen, wir ahnen wo sie herruht, es könnte ja sein, dass irgend ein arbeits- und überhaupt fremdes wesen sich die freiheit leistete eine siesta im freien zu tun. beängstigender gedanke. wäre schön, wenn es so etwas gäbe wie durchlässige schlafgebilde in den sommerlichen städten, die man im winter wiederum zudecken könnte für frierende durchreisende, für alle nomaden.

überhaupt stelle ich mir gebäude, in unserer zeit, beweglich und verwandelbar vor. hybride häuser, die auch unter und über wasser schwimmen könnten, oder ein stück wegfliegen, mit kiemen und segeln. mit wind und sonnenrädern. zusammenfaltbar und jederzeit bereit, sich neu zusammenzufinden und zu wandern. feste gebäude gibt es ja eh schon viele, die wollen meist in ruhe gelassen werden. auch muss ich lachen oder weinen, wenn ich ein neues haus sehe, das gezwungen wird sich wie ein altes auszunehmen. im stil eines barockschlösschens oder eines alpinen bauernhofes. man kann solche ansammlungen disparater stile in zügen fahrend, in den umgebungen der städte in form von fertighaussiedlungen beobachten. ich möchte, wenn, dann doch lieber ein unfertiges haus, in dem ich weiter leben kann. das seine züge verändert und eher etwas spiegelt als etwas behauptet. in hamburg ist es eine lust zu schauen wie die fernen länder und ihre träume den stil der häuser von reichen seemännern beeinflussten. warum staune ich da und weine dort? werden dort fertigträume verkauft, die mit pauschalurlaubsreisen zu tun haben? wird man da vielleicht selber zum abenteuerlich schauenden? ...

»grown out of the ground«, anne bennent

the haus grown out of the ground together with a eucalyptus tree that gives shade to the roundish courtyard that opens onto the sea. the kitchen was the first room to be built, by farmers, next to it a room for the bridal couple. behind the house a building for livestock. then the house grew unevenly, together with the number of children that were born. two sons. no straight angles. low ceilings. the little rooms almost like caves, cool in summer, i imagine how the inhabitants' bodily warmth could be well-maintained inside during a mild winter and how the earthen floor would radiate a warmth of its own. small window openings, with wooden shutters. very dark inside the house. outside, the blinding light of greece. it was a living creature with a belly, a back, an existential orientation, it seemed to me to take on another form every day and also the colours changed according to the time of day and the weather. the tree rustled incessantly, it was the language of the house. i shall never forget the sense of life that this house gave me, i wanted never to leave it. when I think of something like architecture then it is this house breathing with me that forms a kind of starting point ... for housing. it also liked to be stroked... for me, buildings are living creatures that speak and change together with the ground on which they have arisen, their surroundings and the people who inhabit them. my son gets angry when i shout out yet again: look, that house has a face! how can one build a house, maybe it almost builds itself... from the materials that exist in the vicinity. the constructors need to have time to discuss and respond to what is there, to allow a vision to arise of that which should grow there and for whom. where the sun is and what the shadows do. sometimes, when I go walking into buildings and in squares, it seems to me as if mr or ms architect had spent hardly any days or nights in the places that were designed by them, neither beforehand nor afterwards, perhaps they were not really curious about the nature of the location. i often see that there is a concept that has not taken anything into consideration or taken any precautions. i encounter things that are pretty remote from everyday life and absurd.

for example, a monument for the deported jewish families of the second district, in heine straße, on the corner of zirkusgasse, which because of its shape and content was for months used as a toilet for dogs, because no-one paid any attention to the great number of dogs in the area. now a high triangular fence has been put up around it, which is being climbed by ailing plants. not very nice. in austria i wonder about the frequent lack of affectionate design in squares. no outdoor life with shady benches for resting, no chatting on the streets, under the trees. hardly any wells or fountains. rather fenced-in, strangely orthopaedic playgrounds, where as a mother I have to behave within a framework. and the fear of resting outside of one's house, we can guess where that comes from, it could be that some workshy stranger, perhaps a complete foreigner, might have the cheek to take a siesta outdoors. a dreadful thought. it would be nice if there were something like diaphanous images of sleep in the summery city, which in winter one could cover for freezing travelers passing through, for all nomads.

in general, i imagine buildings in our time as being moveable and transformable. hybrid houses that can swim underwater and on top of the water, or fly away for a while, with gills and sails. with wind and sunwheels. that can be folded up, at all times ready to come together again and go hiking. there are already many solid buildings, most of which want to be left in peace. i too have to laugh or cry when I see a new house that is being forced to look like an old house. in the style of a little baroque castle or an alpine farm. one can notice such collections of disparate styles when travelling in trains, on the outskirts of the cities in the form of prefabricated settlements. if at all, then i prefer an unfinished house, in which i can continue to live, that changes its features and tends to reflect something rather than assert it. in hamburg it is a pleasure to see how foreign countries and their dreams influenced the style of the houses of wealthy sailors. why am I astonished here and crying there? are prefabricated dreams being sold there, and do they have something to do with package holidays? will one perhaps become one of those who are looking adventurously?...

visitors bridge at voestalpine

ein besuchermodul für einen umweltfreundlichen konzern // a visitors' module for an environmentally-friendly company

lange zeit hafteten dem ehemals verstaatlichten konzern attribute wie unwirtschaftlichkeit, unflexibilität, aber auch simple rohstoffproduktion und umweltverschmutzung an. längst ist der konzern völlig umstrukturiert; das österreichische paradeunternehmen ist ein international tätiger verarbeitungskonzern mit eigener stahlproduktion. schwerpunkte der aktivitäten sind die produktion von höchstwertigen stahlerzeugnissen und die weiterverarbeitung von stahl und anderen werkstoffen; das thema umweltschutz wird dabei großgeschrieben um interessiertem publikum von schulklassen bis zu geschäftspartnern die betätigungsfelder »hautnah« zu zeigen, wurde ein gutachterverfahren für die entwicklung und umsetzung von besucherplattformen, die in unterschiedliche produktionsstätten einsetzbar sind, ausgeschrieben.

for a long time, the former state-owned company was notorious for economic inefficiency, inflexibility, but also for crude methods of processing raw materials and causing environmental pollution. the company has long since been completely restructured; now a model austrian processing enterprise, it is active internationally and has its own steel production. its business focuses on the manufacture of steel products of the highest quality and the further treatment of steel and other raw materials; the subject of the protection of the environment is one of its top priorities. in order to present its areas of activity »close-up« to interested audiences, ranging from school classes to business partners, a specialist report was commissioned with regard to developing and introducing visitors' platforms that could be used in a variety of production plants.

in zusammenarbeit mit / in cooperation with friedrich stiper

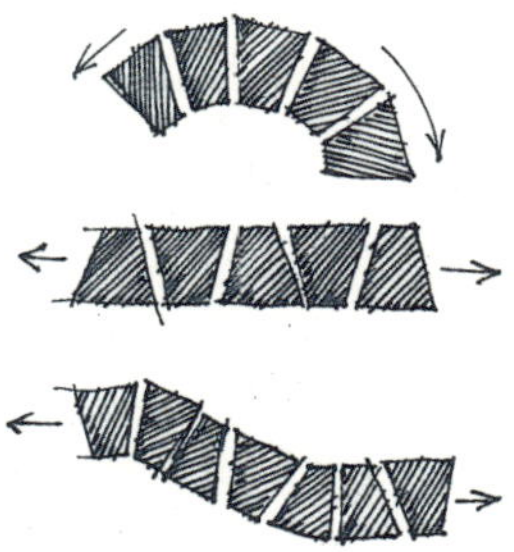

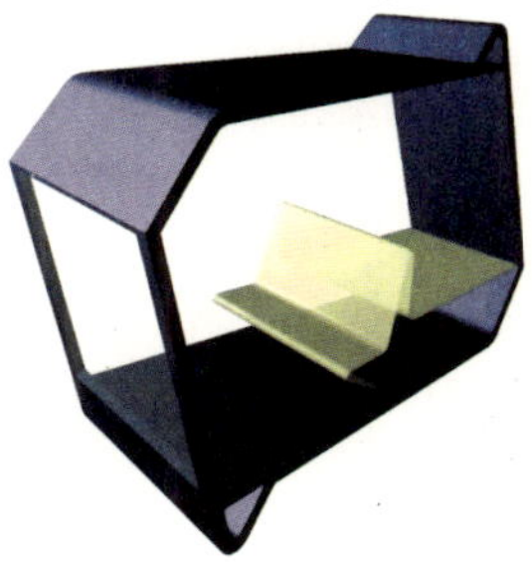

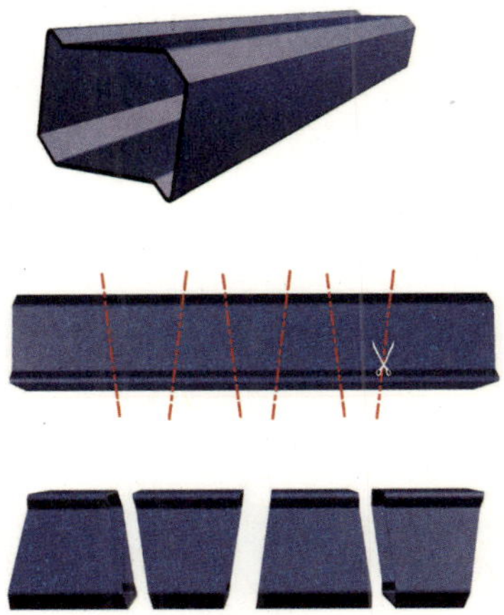

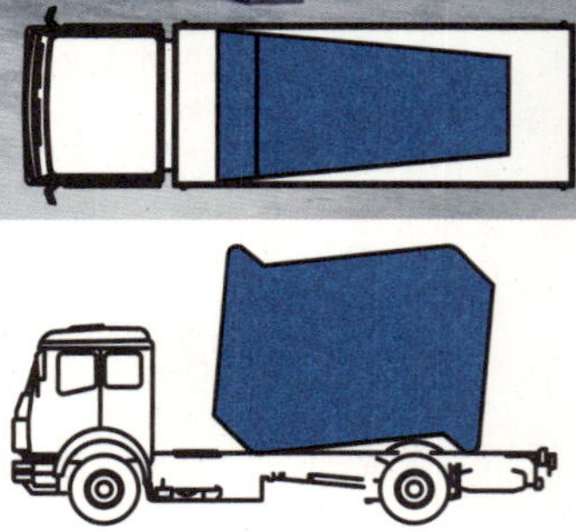

das ergebnis ist ein grundmodul, dass in unterschiedlicher addition verschiedene grundriss- und ausblicksformen möglich macht und in einfach transportierbaren einzelgrößen vorgefertigt zum einsatzort geliefert wird. die in logofarben gehaltene gesamtform kann an vorgegebenen knotenpunkten im jeweiligen umfeld montiert (gestellt oder gehängt) werden.

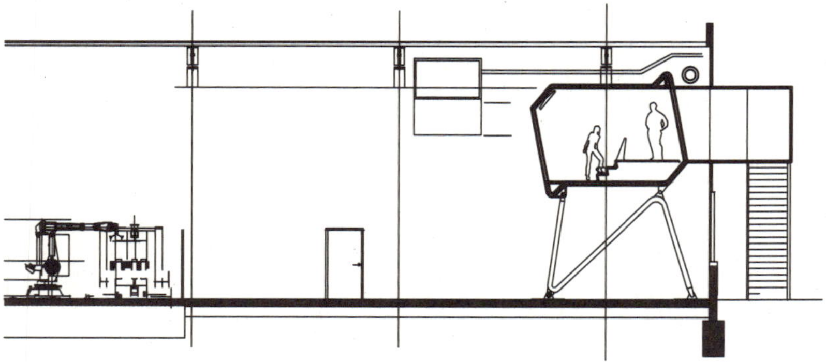

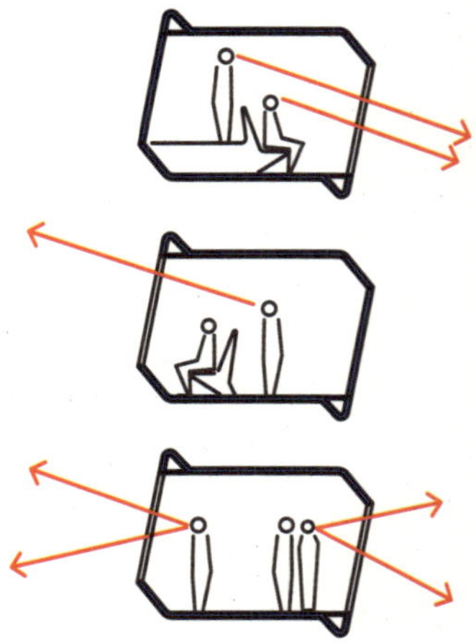

the result is a module that can be combined in different ways to fit in different situations and to offer varying views. the size of the module fits easily on any lorry. the construction, painted in the logo color, can be hung, aligned and mounted at specified places.

im inneren des symmetrisch aufgebauten stahlmodules wird durch einsetzen eines (hinterleuchteten) sitz- und stehpodestes eine mehrreihige bespielung des raumes erreicht; somit wird der gesamte ausblick auch von den hinteren reihen aus möglich. nach einem auf bündig montierten flachbildschirmen präsentierten vortrag werden die glasscheiben von matt auf klarsichtig gestellt und der besucher erhält unmittelbaren einblick in die produktionsabläufe.

inside the symmetrically constructed steel modules, a (backlit) podium for sitting and standing can be inserted so that the room can be used for presenting a programme to several rows of people; in this way, an overall view is possible even from the rows at the rear. after lectures, which can be presented using a flush-mounted flat screen, the glass panes can be changed from matt to clear, so that the visitors can receive a direct insight into the production processes.

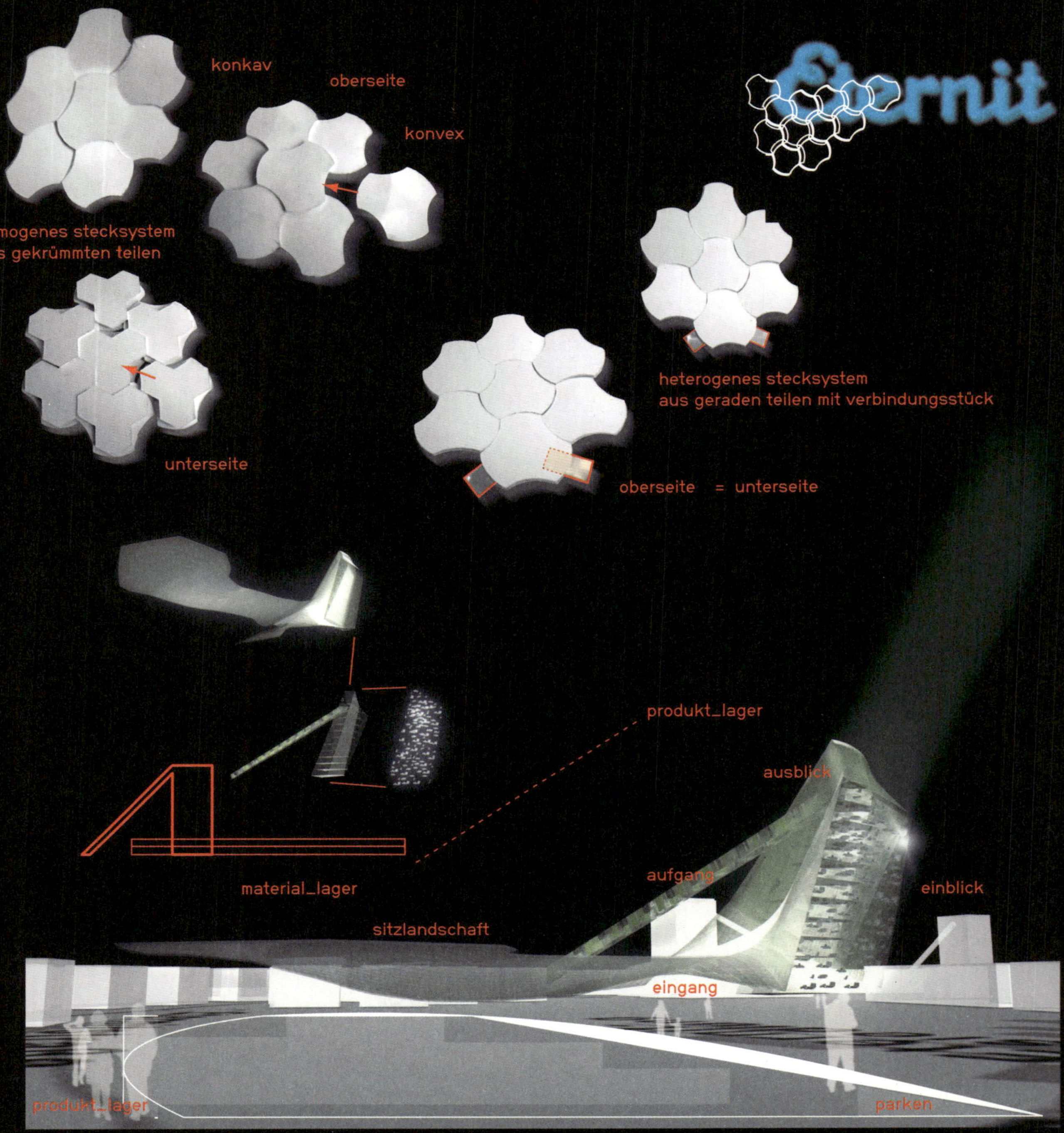
konkav
oberseite
konvex
homogenes stecksystem
aus gekrümmten teilen
unterseite
heterogenes stecksystem
aus geraden teilen mit verbindungsstück
oberseite = unterseite
produkt_lager
ausblick
aufgang
einblick
material_lager
sitzlandschaft
eingang
produkt_lager
parken

eternit

landmark für einen faserzement hersteller // for a fibre cement producer

schon an der bundesstraße verfängt sich der blick des ankommenden in dem ungewöhnlichen objekt, dessen vertikales schaufenster die produkte der firma präsentiert. geparkt wird unter einem mantel aus eternit-elementen am haupteingang, der direkt neben dem ein- und aussichtsturm liegt, schlägt der eternit-mantel eine welle. hier kann der besucher das werksgelände betreten, mit dem förderband zur aussichtsplattform hinauffahren, die ausgestellten produkte unter die lupe nehmen oder einfach in der sitzlandschaft aus eternit-elementen platznehmen und entspannen. der mantel, der das tor zum gelände der firma bildet, den parkplatz überspannt, auf der anderen seite die sitzlandschaft formt und schließlich den turm umhüllt, besteht aus einer zweifachgekrümmten struktur, die natürlich von eternit-elementen eingedeckt ist, teilweise opak, teilweise transparent.

even from the main road, one's eye is caught by the inconvenient object, with its vertical display window presenting the company's products. the car park is underneath a shell of eternit elements. at the main entrance, which is situated immediately next to the transparent observation tower, the eternit shell forms the start of a wave. the visitor can now enter the factory premises, ride on the conveyor belt up to the viewing platform, admire the products that are on show, or simply sit down in the seating area made of eternit elements and relax. the shell – which constitutes the gate to the company premises, covers the car park, forms the seating area on the other side, and finally envelopes the tower – consists of a structure with two curves, covered by the eternit elements. partly opaque, partly transparent.

infokiosk und buswartehäuschen

rast und rat für reisende // rest and information for travellers

riezlern liegt mitten in den bergen, umgeben von ausgedehnten wäldern. so wird der baustoff holz für kiosk und wartehäuschen als unverfälschtes konstruktions- und oberflächenmaterial verwendet. trotz der hohen schneelasten wirken die holzkonstruktionen leicht und schwebend.

riezlern lies deep in the mountains, surrounded by extensive forests. wood is therefore used as a building material for the kiosk and the bus stop shelter, providing a natural material for construction and surfaces. despite the high snowloads that they have to bear, the timber structures seem light and airy.

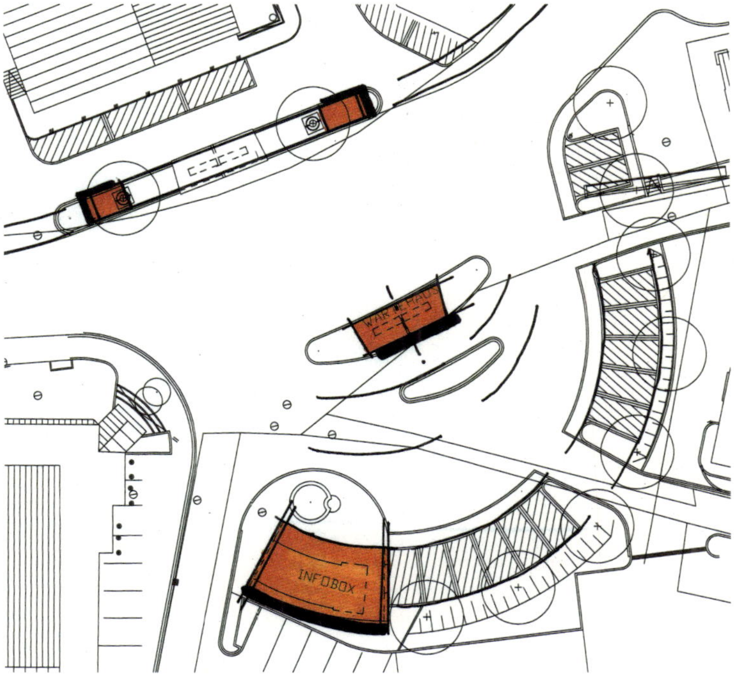

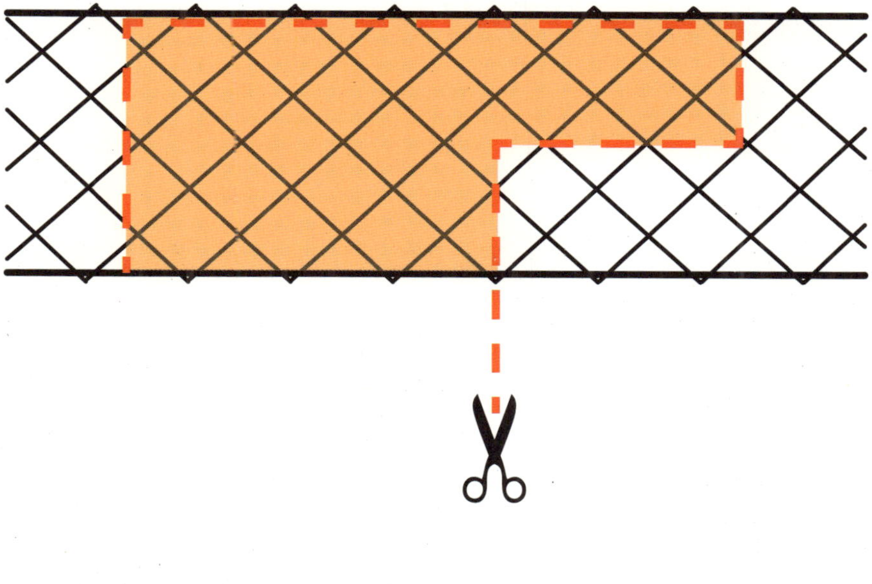

carport(able)

500 knotenpunkte verbunden durch muskelkraft // 500 knots connected with muscle power
konstruktionsablauf selbstbaugarage // do-it-yourself construction guide

_formrohre mit vorgebohrten löchern auf fundament befestigen!
_verzinkte rippenstähle mit muskelkraft von bohrloch zu bohrloch, also von boden zu boden spannen!
_500 knotenpunkte mit kabelbinder verknüpfen!
_stäbe auf richtige länge schneiden, die konstruktion in ihre endgültige form bringen!
_bauwerk mittels lastwagenplane überdecken!

_secure the tube to the foundations with pre-drilled holes.
_tension the galvanised ribbed steel rods using muscle power from drill hole to drill hole, i.e. from floor to floor.
_connect the 500 intersections with cable binders!
_cut the rods to the correct length and assemble the construction in its final form!
_cover the structure with truck tarpaulins.

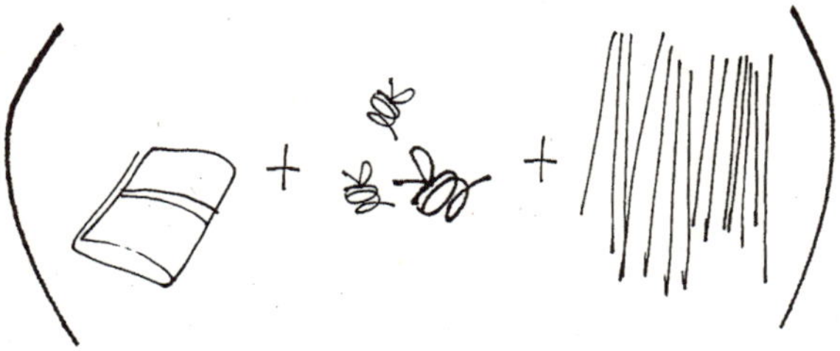

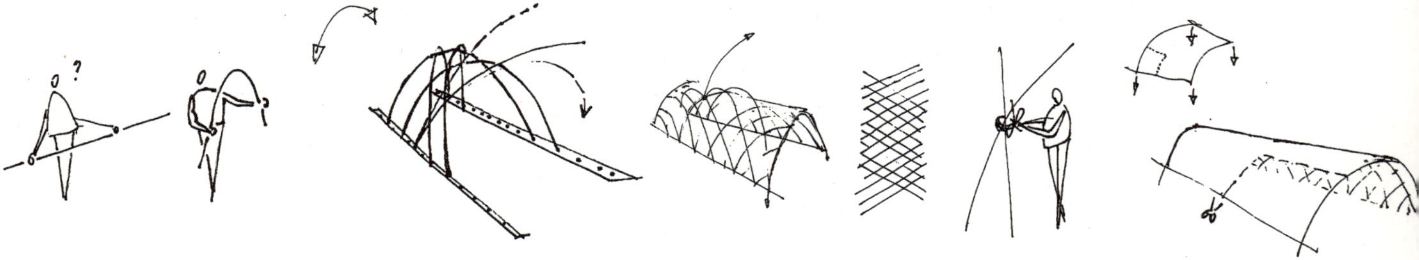

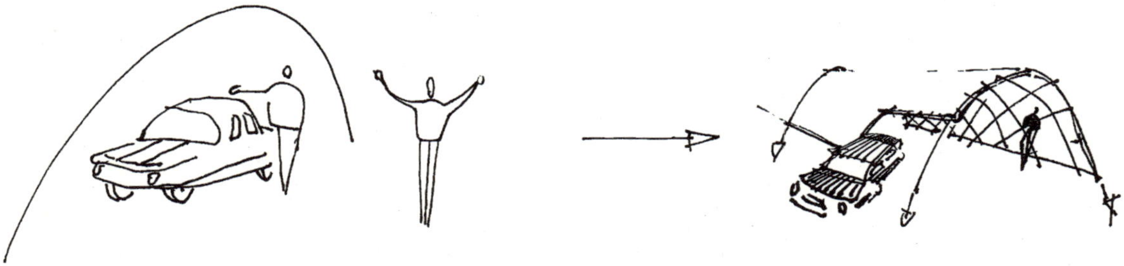

die einkaufsliste

- ein paar bewehrungseisen
  wenn gewünscht, auch bambus möglich
- ein paar quadratmeter LKW-plane
- ein paar (hundert) kabelbinder
- schere, schnur – und viel geduld!

the shopping list

- a couple of reinforcement bars;
  if desired, bamboo also possible
- a couple of square metres of truck tarpaulin
- a couple of (hundred) cable ties
- scissors, string – and a lot of patience!

VK 50 AY
W 24117

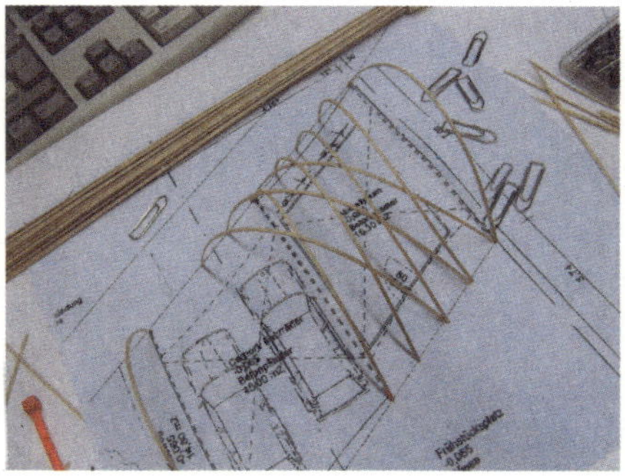

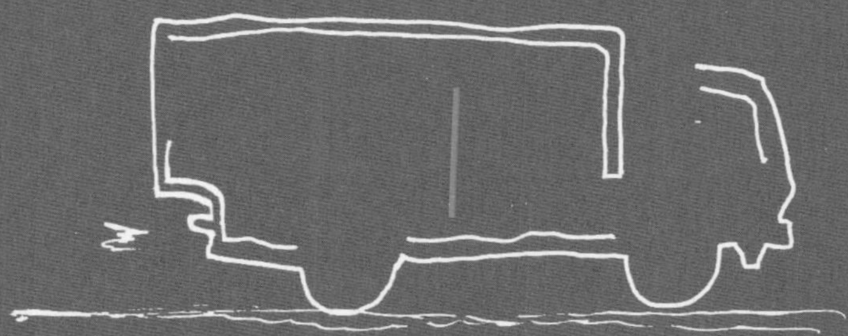

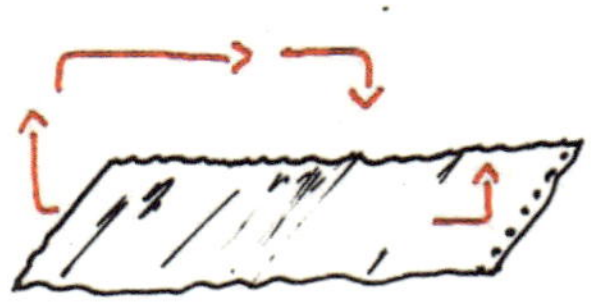

[1 - 3] idee / idea

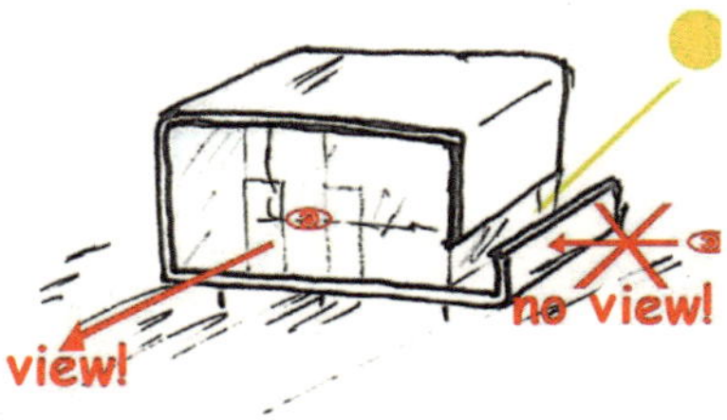

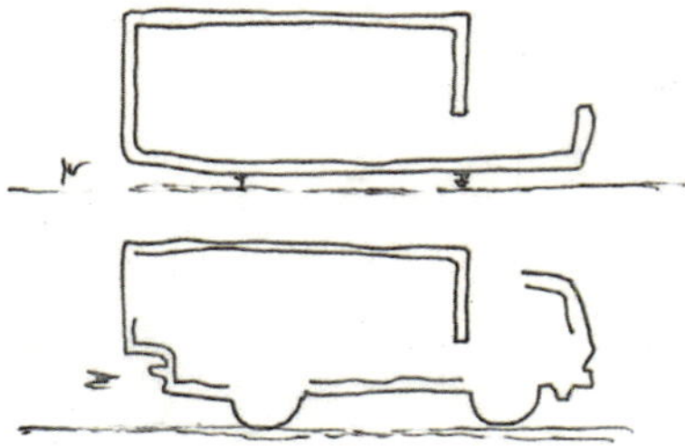

[4 - 6] entwurf / sketch

[7 - 9] lösung / solution

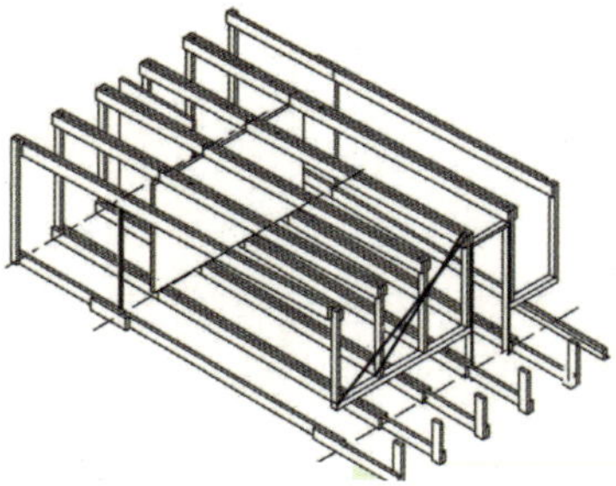

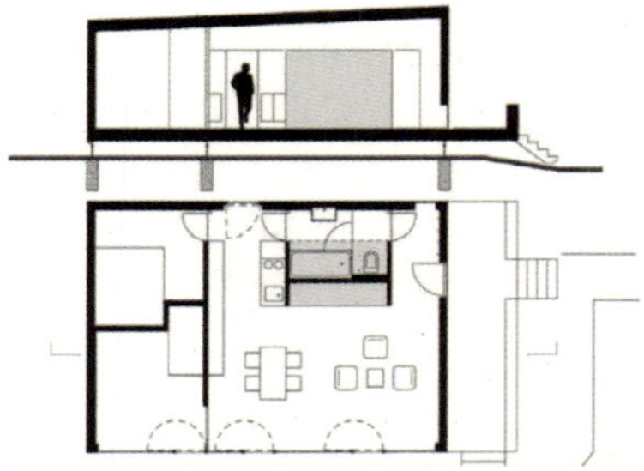

[10 - 12] konstruktion / construction

haus lina

riesig klein: der zur verfügung stehende platz und die finanziellen ressourcen beschränken den bau auf seine aktuellen, minimalen ausmaße; eine konsequent rationale planung sorgte für bauzeit- und kosteneinsparung. so wurden z.b. die abmessungen und der konstruktionsraster des baukörpers auf die liefermaße der grobspanplatten ausgelegt, die gesamtkonstruktion in leichtbau mit hohem wärmedämmaufbau geplant. die teilvorgefertigten elemente konnten so in wenigen tagen auf die zuvor ausgeführten stahlträger, die punktuell mit streifenfundamenten verbunden sind, aufgesetzt werden.
infrastrukturell an den benachbarten altbau »angedockt«, enthält der baukörper sämtliche primärfunktionen wie bad, küche, heizung und warmwasseraufbereitung.

extremely small: the building was limited to its present minimal dimensions by the space and financial resources available; consistently rational planning ensured that there were savings in construction time and costs. for example, the dimensions and the construction pattern of the volume were designed according to the delivery sizes of the panels of rough chipboard, and the whole building was planned as a lightweight construction with a great deal of thermal insulation. in this way, it took only a few days to set up the partly prefabricated elements on previously installed steel girders, which were connected at various points to strip foundations.
docked onto the infrastructure of the neighbouring old building, the volume includes all primary functions, such as bathroom, kitchen, and heating and water heating systems.

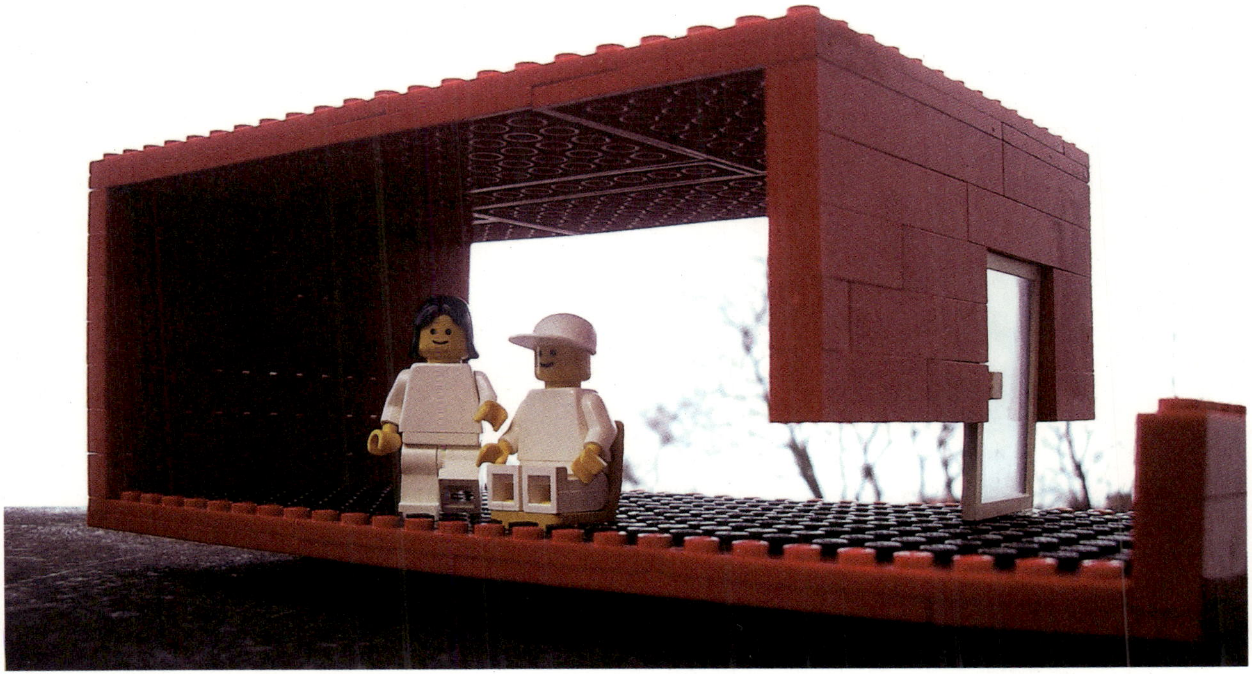

bebaute fläche: 69 m²
nutzfläche: 60 m²
umbauter raum: 202 m³

developed area: 69 m²
floor space: 60 m²
converted space: 202 m³

der bau wurde bewusst »nicht für die ewigkeit« konzipiert, er kann je nach zukünftiger lebens-situation leicht wieder entfernt, aber auch erweitert werden.

the unit was intentionally »not built to last forever«; it can be easily removed or extended, depending on the inhabitants' future living situation.

wettbewerb / competition
erweiterung und funktionssanierung bhak und bhas
extension and functional restructuring of a commercial college
preis / prize wiener neustadt 2006

seifenkistl

der äußerst heterogene bestand wird durch die platzierung einer neuen, homogenen baumasse beruhigt. die schule erhält mit dem rationalen baukörper eine neue identität; das hochgezogene, bedruckte sportnetz wird zum weithin sichtbaren merkmal, das neue zentrum der schule.

die aufständerung des neubaus führt zu einer großen, zusammenhängenden freifläche für veranstaltungen im erdgeschoss. die wesentliche erweiterung der spärlich vorhandenen sportflächen gelingt durch die situierung des sportplatzes auf dem schuldach.

the extremely heterogeneous nature of the existing building is maintained by careful positioning of a new homogeneous volume. this rational building structure gives the school a new identity; the elevated printed sports net becomes a feature that is visible from afar, and serves as the new focal point of the school.

the elevation of the new building produces an integrated large-scale open space for events on the ground floor. the fundamental extension of the barely existent sports areas is achieved by situating the sports ground on the roof of the school.

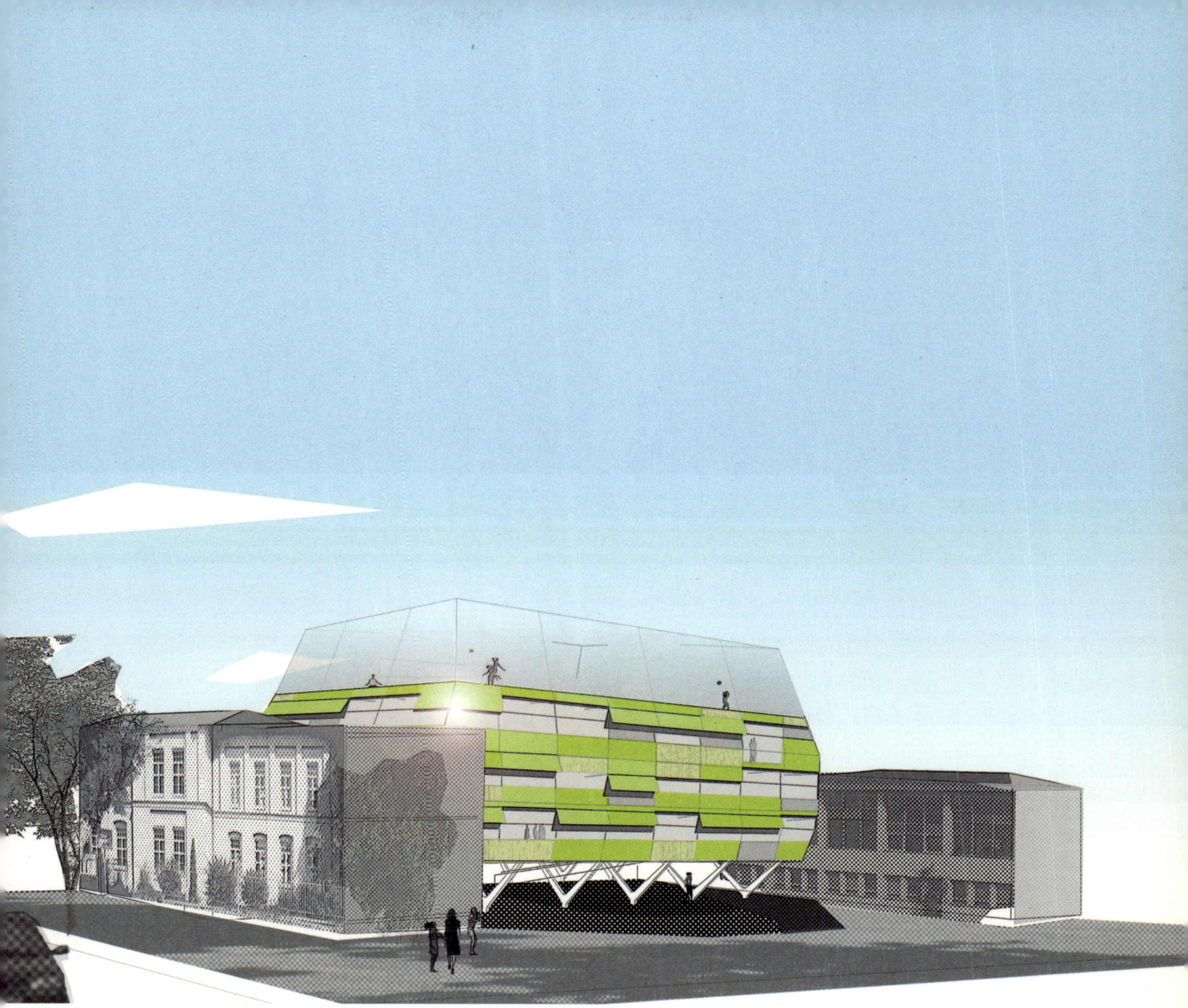

im inneren der schule bildet die neue aula eir lichtdurchflutetes zentrum, das über eine großzügige fußgängerrampe an den neu geordneten freibereich angebunden ist.

inside the school, the new school hall forms a well-lit centre that is connected to the newly designed open space by a spacious pedestrian ramp.

wettbewerb / competition
bundesgymnasium / state grammar school
gainfarn bei wien 2010

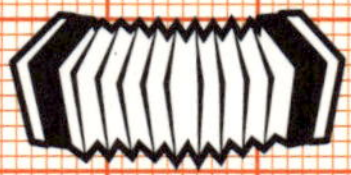

gainfarn

endlich luft für arme gymnasiasten… // at last! a bit of air for poor grammar school kids…

eine schulerweiterung mit 30 (frei)klassen.
als atmosphärische bereicherung der relativ gedrängten, bestehenden schulbebauung plant caramel die neu zu errichtenden schulräume als ebenerdiges raumfaltwerk mit ausschließlich zum freiraum orientierten lernräumen und vorgelagerten freiklassen. carpe diem!

an extension of the school with 30 (open) classrooms.
as an improvement in the atmosphere of the relatively crowded existing school building, caramel plans the construction of new classrooms as a ground-floor prismatic shell structure with the classrooms oriented solely towards the outside and outdoor classroom areas in front of them. carpe diem!

wettbewerb / competition
verwaltungsgebäude / administration building adidas
herzogenaurach 2007

adidas

warum nicht mal eine stringente funktionsmaschine? // why not a stringent functional machine for once?

ein webteppich als gebäudestruktur, der campus als gebäude; gedeckte und offene atrien alternieren mit flexiblen arbeitsunits.

a woven carpet as a building structure, the campus as a building; covered and open inner courtyards alternate with flexible working units.

unendlich erweiterbar: die struktur der flexiblen büroeinheiten mit dazwischenliegenden atrien. einzig begrenzt durch die grundstücksabmessungen.

endlessly expandable: the structure is that of flexible office units with inner courtyards situated in between. these are limited only by the dimensions of the property.

nomadisierende zellen

nomadisierende zellen gestalten als clan den stadtraum um. in einer vierwöchigen projektphase wird ein urbanes objekt entwickelt, welches im münsteraner stadtraum interveniert.
gemeinsam entwickelt mit den studenten der architekturklasse der fh münster, den wiener büros bkk-3 und sofa_architekten. organisiert von modulorbeat.

nomad cells redesign urban space like a clan. in one four-week project phase, an urban object is developed that intervenes in münster's city space.
organised by modulorbeat and developed together with the students of the architecture class at the technical college in münster and the vienna offices bkk-3 and sofa_architekten..

mehr inhalt // more content

deine geschichten haben zu wenig inhalt, sagte der kritiker und schaute mir wohlwollend, aber ernst in die augen. aha, inhalt, sagte ich, was ist das eigentlich? ich mag keine inhalte, die sind so vergänglich, die stecken so voller irrtümer und anmaßungen, voll von falschem. ich möchte geschichten ganz ohne inhalt schreiben, ganz leichte, die wie ein fisch im stehenden wasser schweben. merkst du die scheiße? jetzt wird's inhaltlich, sagte ich, nur weil du mehr inhalt forderst. der inhalt ist der feind jedes textes, von geschichten will ich gar nicht reden. inhalt - mir wird schlecht. ich muss aufhören.

your stories have too little content, said the critic and looked me benevolently but seriously in the eye. oh right, content, i said, what is that actually? i don't like contents, they're so transient, they're so stuffed full of errors and presumption, full of falsity. i'd like to write stories that are quite without content, very simple ones, that float like fish in standing water. do you notice the shit? now it's got content, i said, all because you demand more content. content is the enemy of every text, not to mention stories – i'm beginning to feel sick. i have to close.

friedrich achleitner

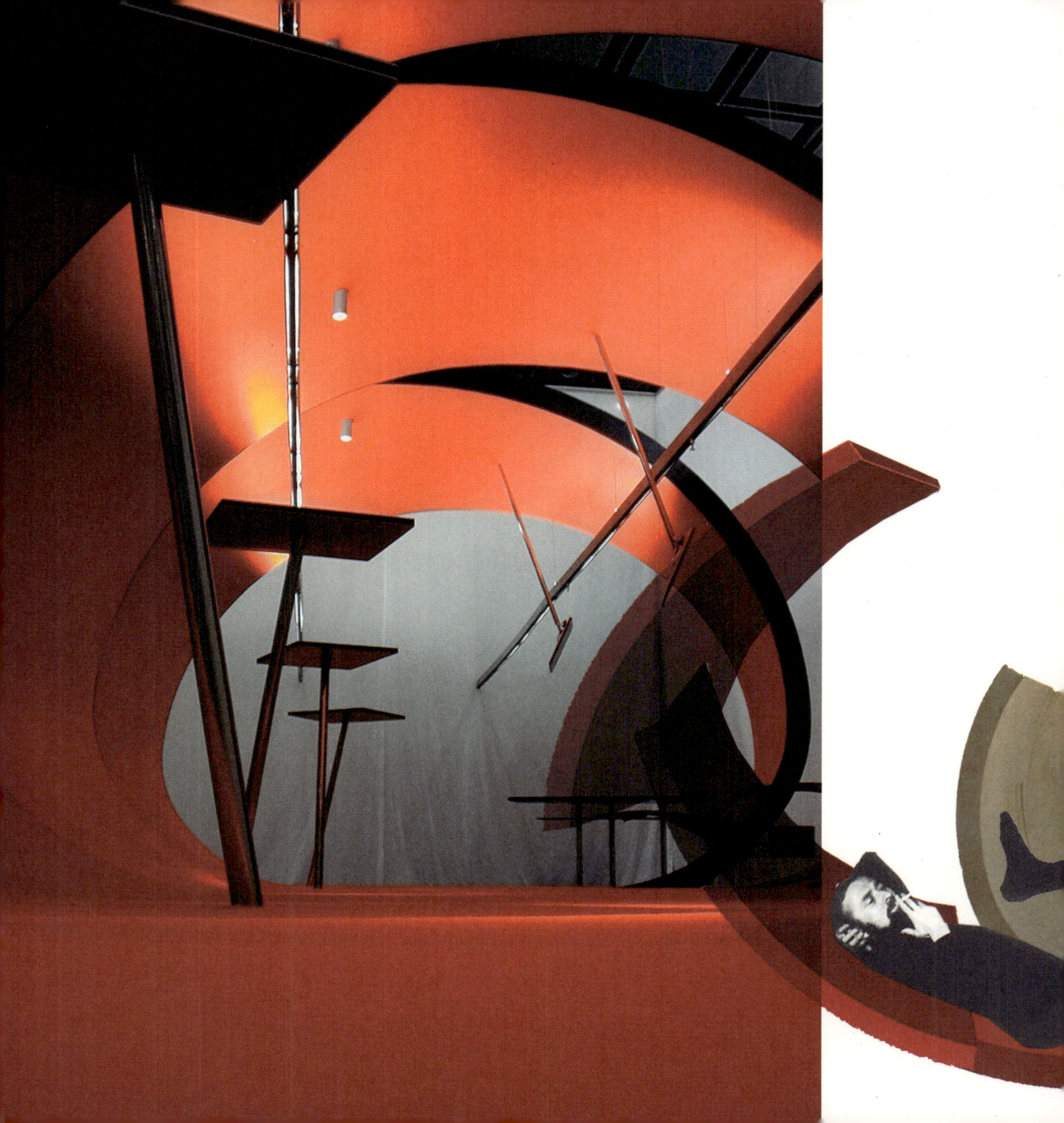

trade fair stand for ami

agrolinz melamine international - wiederverwendbarer messestand; konzipiert für k04 in düsseldorf, oktober 04 // agrolinz melamine international - a reusable trade fair booth; designed for k04 in düsseldorf, october 04

ein »raum im raum«, um der hektik und reizüberflutung großer messehallen entgegenzuwirken. ein ort, der durch seine farbgebung und seine akustischen eigenschaften geborgenheit ausstrahlt.
die farben der textilen oberflächen sind die des firmenlogos. die dreifache wickelung entspricht ebenso dem logo ami.
die beiden enden der spirale bilden die zwei zugangszonen; die assoziation »roter teppich« unterstreicht die einladende geste.
je nach blickwinkel gibt sich der geschaffene raum offen oder geschlossen. der raumkörper steht frei innerhalb der bewusst zurücknehmend gestalteten standabgrenzung aus weißem vorhangstoff, welcher lediglich die buchstaben des firmenlogos trägt.
im inneren kann man sich an stehtischen von unternehmensmitarbeitern informieren lassen. wer sich lieber in bequemer position »berieseln« lassen möchte, nimmt an einem der bildschirmterminals platz, info-chillen, gewissermassen.
den bildschirmen zugeordnet, »schälen« sich bequeme sitzflächen aus der innenschale der raumspirale. lichtpunkte auf den stehtischen korrespondieren mit linearem indirektlicht, das gemeinsam mit den vorgeschriebenen sprinklerleitungen geführt wird und blendfrei die oberseiten beleuchtet.

a »room within a room«, where one can get away from the bustle and sensory overload of huge trade fair halls. its colours and acoustic features indicate that it is a place of refuge.
the colours of the fabric surfaces are those of the company logo. the threefold coil likewise corresponds to the ami logo.
the two ends of the spiral form two access zones; the associations of the »red carpet« emphasize the gesture of inviting.
the created space can seem open or closed, depending on the angle of vision. the spatial volume is open within the confines of the stand, which is designed in a deliberately restrained manner, using white curtain material that displays solely the lettering of the company logo.

on the inside of the space, one can obtain information from company employees at stand-up tables. people who prefer to »absorb« things in a more comfortable position, can sit down at one of the computer screen terminals, where ami image films can be accessed. allocated to the screens, comfortable seating surfaces »peel off« from the inner shell of the spatial spiral. points of light on the stand-up tables correspond with linearly indirect lighting, which is conducted together with the stipulated sprinkler pipes and provides glare-free lighting for the upper parts of the sides.

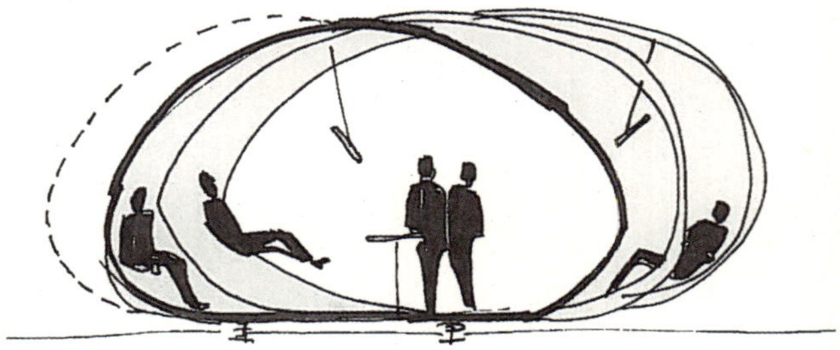

jedes einzelteil ist von 2-3 personen montierbar und enthält die leitungsführung. die einzelteile, die mit textilem, filzähnlichem belag bzw. schwarzem kunstleder beschichtet sind, lassen sich in kurzer zeit verbinden und sind wiederverwendbar.

every individual component can be moved by 2-3 persons and contains cables for the lighting and it. the individual components can be connected together quickly and are reusable. they are covered with a felt-like fabric coating, or with artificial black leather.

in zusammenarbeit mit / in cooperation with friedrich stiper

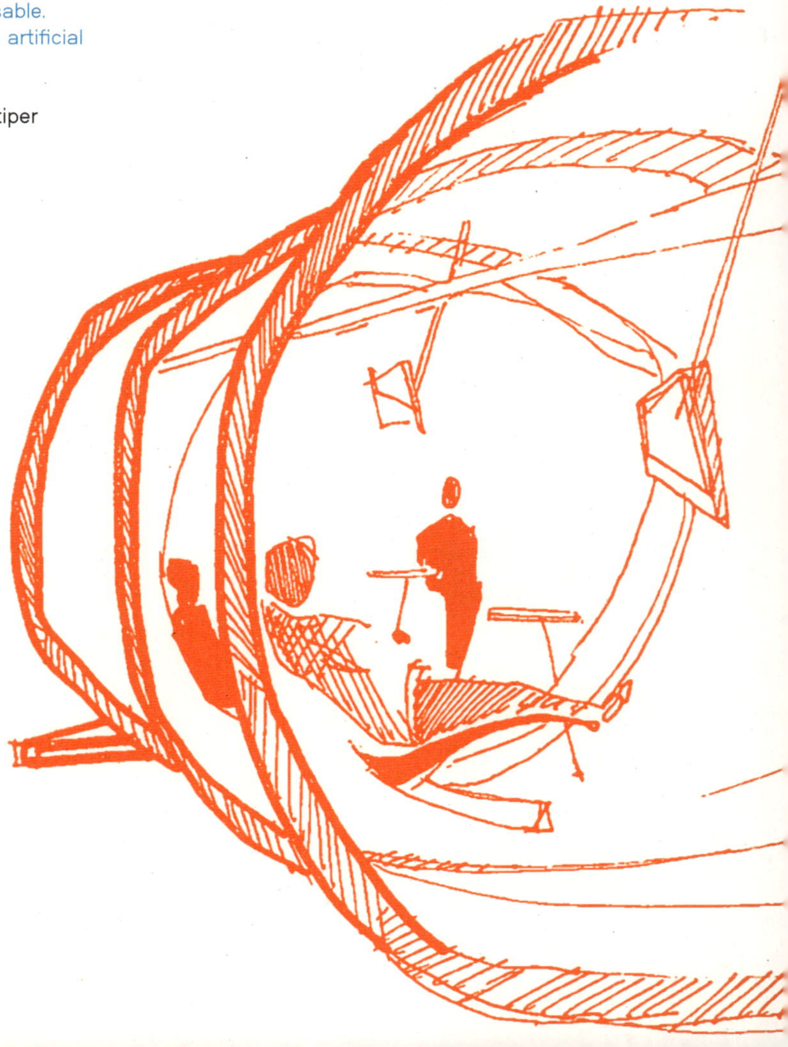

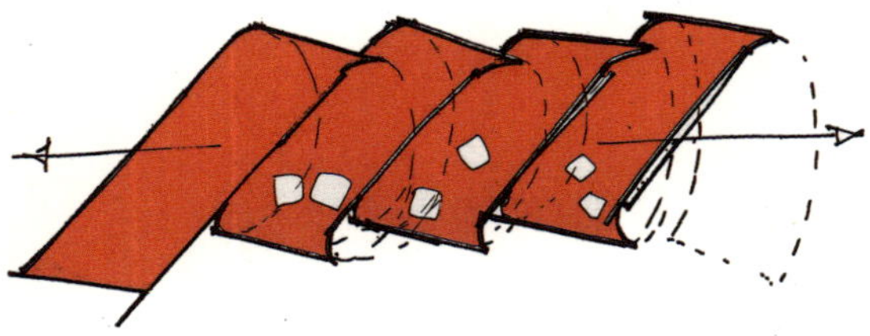

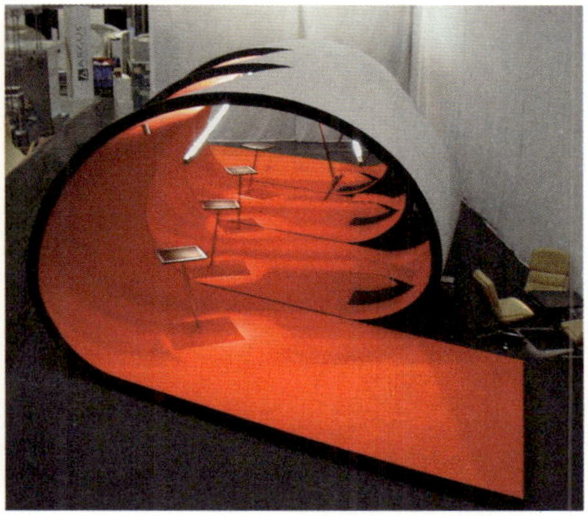

eine zweischalige holzleichtkonstruktion, aufgelöst in 5 vorgefertigte abwicklungsteile pro schleifenwindung, stellt das raumbildende element dar.

a double-shelled lightweight wooden construction, integrated into 5 prefabricated unwinding parts for each loop of the coil, constitutes the basic space-creating element.

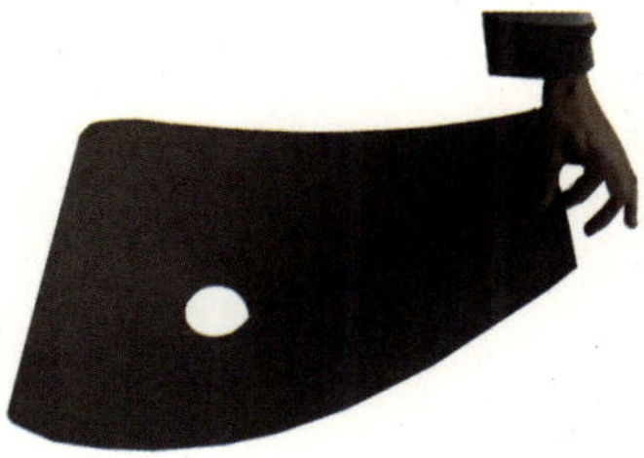

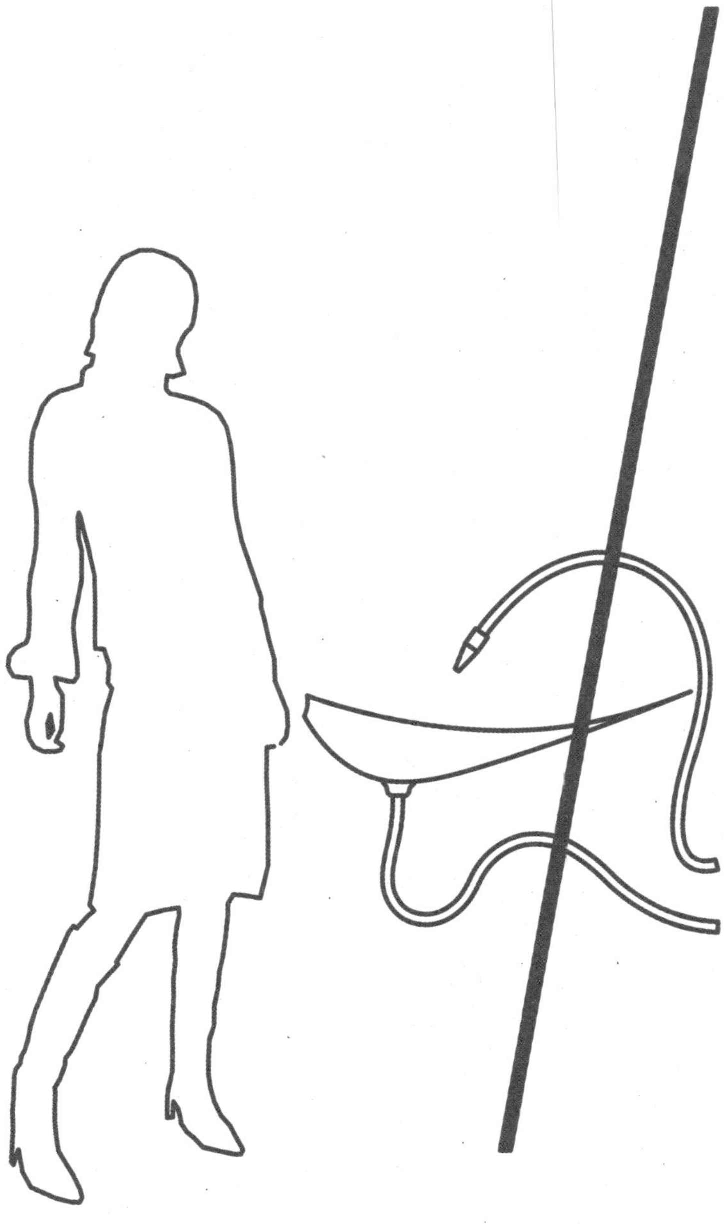

C funder-max

pfff...

grrr...

max waschmöbel

händewaschen nicht vergessen! // don't forget to wash your hands!

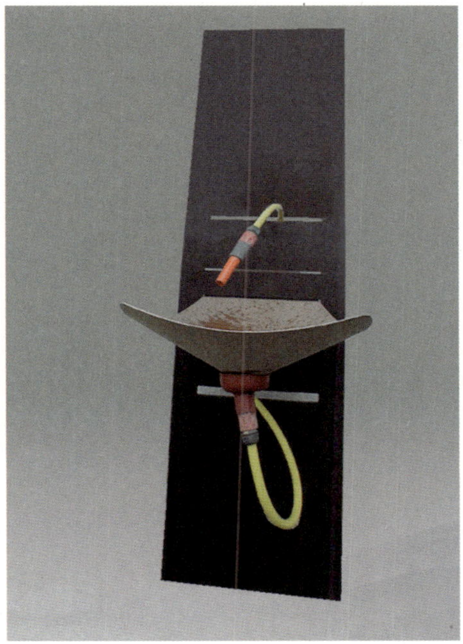

der hersteller von werkstoffplatten für das bau- und tischlergewerbe trat an caramel mit einer bitte heran: aus seinem produkt ein werbesujet zu entwickeln.

caramel erfand:
ein material- und arbeitssparendes teil.
als flaches paket liefer- und lagerbar.
leicht aufstellbar.
einfach wunderbar.

the manufacturer of material boards for the construction industry and carpentry trade approached caramel with a request to develop a way to advertise his product.

caramel came up with:
a component that saves both material and work.
can be delivered and stored as a flat package.
easy to put together.
simply wonderful.

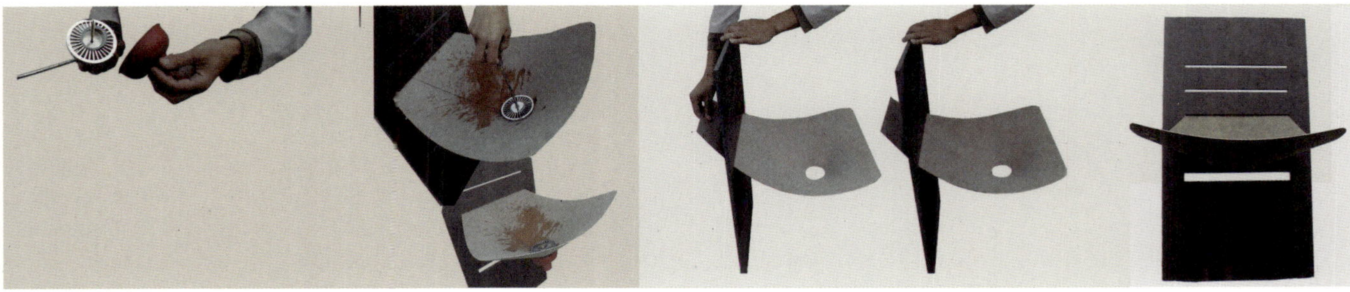

in zusammenarbeit mit / in cooperation with friedrich stiper

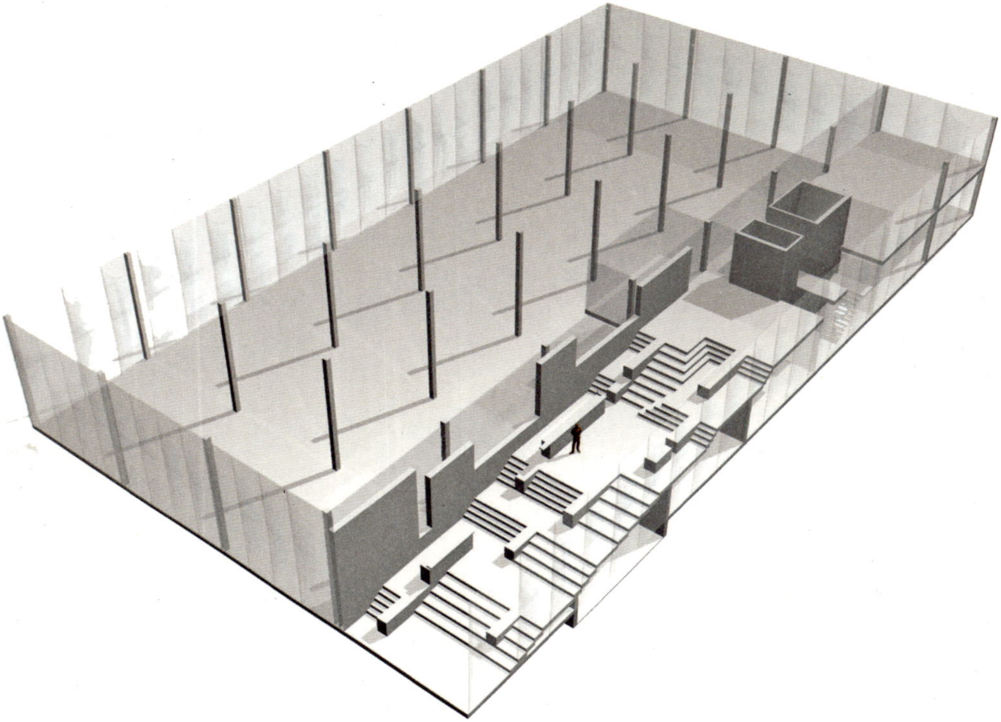

kaffee mitteregger

vakuumverpackt hält besser! // vacuum-packed keeps better!

fabrikationsgebäude für high-end kaffeemaschinen.
eine durch unterdruck gespannte pneufassade umhüllt einen reduzierten baukörper mit den funktionen produktion und showroom/degustationsbereich.

production building for high-end coffee machines.
an inflatable vacuum-stretched tyre rubber facade covers a rational architectural volume functioning as a production hall and showroom/degustation area.

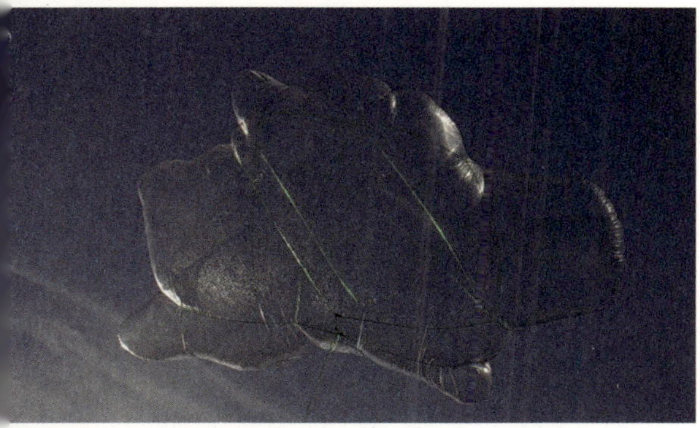

air_line by caramel

those who believed that rain is a present from the sky will be taught better by caramel, when this trio travels to venice, a cloud in their baggage and a serious attitude to cool things down

vorgeführt wurde eine steuerbare regenwolke (ca. 8x3x3m, mit helium gefüllt und von einem perforierten wasserschlauch umwickelt). diese überzeugte von 20.-26. september 2004 auf der architekturbiennale in venedig das publikum davon, dass niederschläge kein geschenk des himmels sind.
die wolke ist das ergebnis ausgeklügelter forschung und auseinandersetzung mit den elementen luft (helium, sauerstoff), wasser und festen materialien (pvc). nach genauen berechnungen wurde die kunststoffform von der spezialfirma schultes in wien hergestellt. der erfolgreiche testflug erfolgte im museumsquartier am 17. september 2004 und bescherte bei strahlendem sonnenschein »echten« regen.
auch in venedig wurde das publikum mit der unerwarteten erfrischung bedacht – vor dem österreichischen pavillon. »als architektenteam mit ausgeprägtem hang zum forschen und zum materialexperiment, ohne dabei den faktor spaß aus dem auge zu verlieren, fällt uns neben handfester architektur schon öfter mal so etwas wie die wolke ein.«
the subject of the presentation was a controllable rain cloud (c. 8x3x3m, filled with helium and wrapped in a perforated hosepipe). this convinced visitors to the architecture biennale in venice between 20-26 september 2004 that rainfall is not a present from the sky.
the cloud is the result of ingenious research and a study of the elements air (helium, oxygen) and water, as well as solid materials (pvc). on the basis of exact calculations, the synthetic form was manufactured by the specialist company schultes in vienna. the successful test flight took place at the museumsquartier on 17 september 2004 and produced »real« rain during brilliant sunshine.
an unexpectedly refreshing shower was also bestowed upon the public in venice, too – in front of the austrian pavilion. »as a team of architects with a distinct tendency towards research and experimentation with materials, who do not lose sight of the fun factor in the process, we often have ideas such as that of the cloud, alongside ones relating to concrete architecture.«

mit freundlicher einladung von / invited by alleswirdgut

AUSTRIA

air line by
Caramel

wettbewerb / competition
fh köln campus leverkusen
köln 2011

campus leverkusen

der städtebauliche charakter des areals wird bestimmt durch die langen werkshallen mit den typischen giebelfronten an den stirnseiten. diese werden als grundthema für das neue campusgebäude aufgenommen und bilden als fächerförmig angeordnete struktur einen übergang zwischen den bestehenden hallenausrichtungen der nördlichen und östlichen umgebungsbauten. die baukörperausformung übernimmt dabei die vorhandenen satteldachformen und übersetzt sie als skulpturale dachlandschaft mit giebelfronten in der dimension der umgebenden hallen.

the urban development character of the site is determined by the long factory halls with typical gable facades facing towards the front. these are integrated into the principal theme of the new campus building and, when arranged as a structure in the shape of a fan, form a transition between the existing orientation of the halls of the surrounding buildings to the north and east. in the process, the demoulding of the building structure continues the existing forms of the saddle roof, translating them as a sculptural roofscape with gable fronts to the dimensions of the surrounding halls.

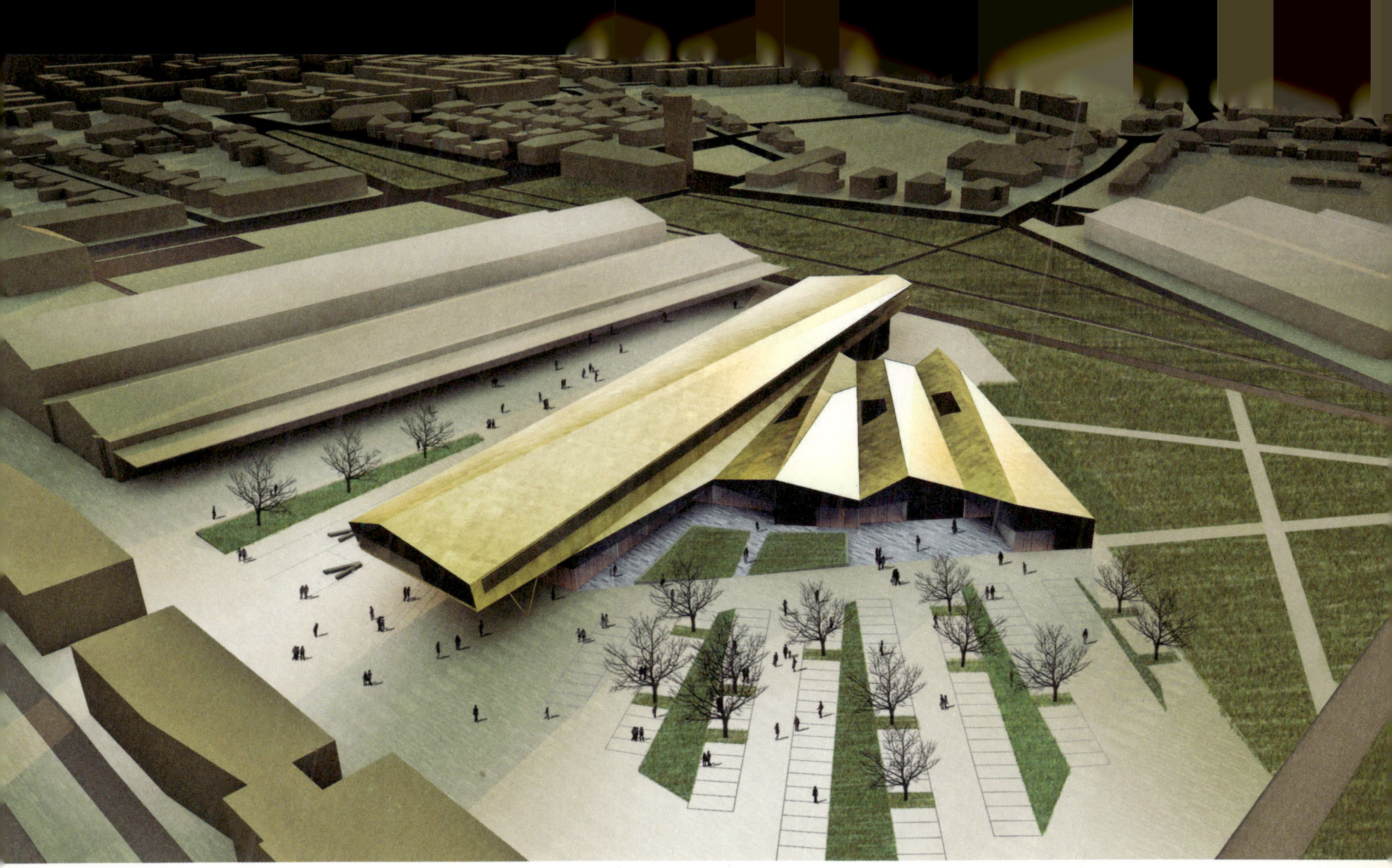

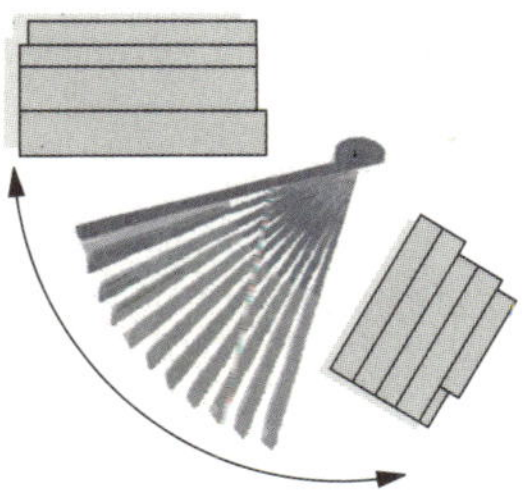

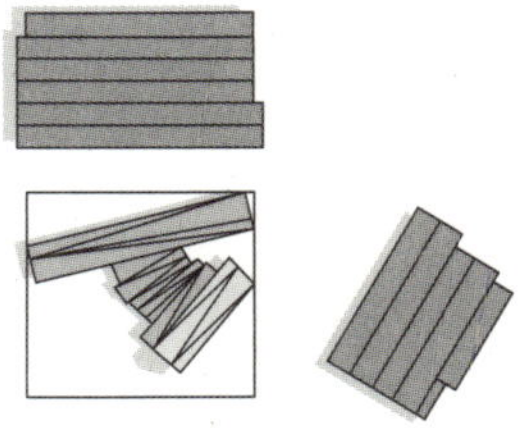

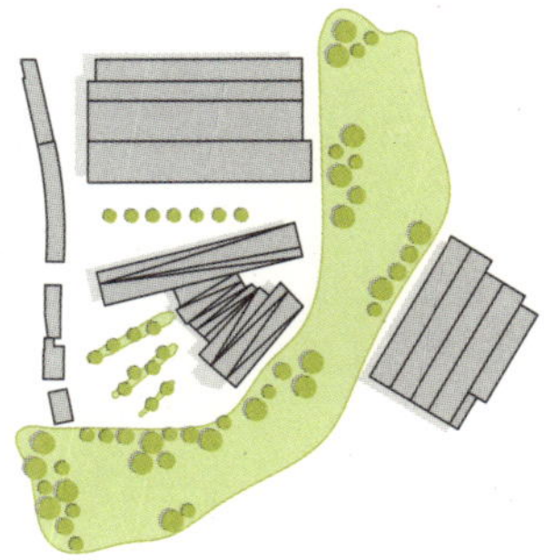

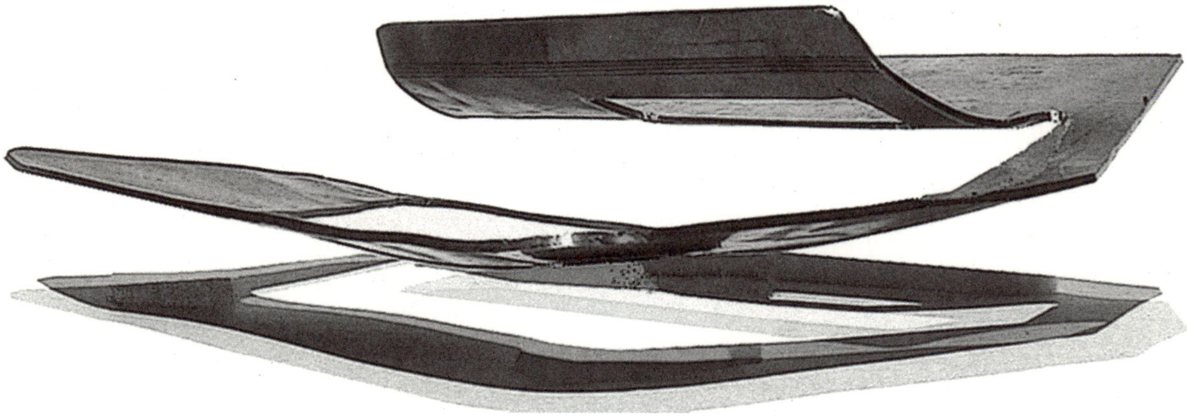

wettbewerb / competition
plenarsaal / chamber
hannover 2003

plenarneu

möblierter landtag // furnished regional parliament

ein »neuer plenarsaal für den niedersächsischen landtag in hannover« wird gebraucht: ein spiralmöbel als maßvoller eingriff in das bestehende bauvolumen bildet gleichzeitig einrahmung, erschließungsgalerie, eine geschossweise funktionstrennung und die geforderte erweiterung des plenarsaales.

a »new chamber for the regional parliament of lower saxony in hannover« is required: a piece of spiral furniture constitutes a restrained intervention in the existing architectural volume and at the same time creates a setting, an access gallery, a separation of functions on different storeys and the required extension of the parliamentary chamber.

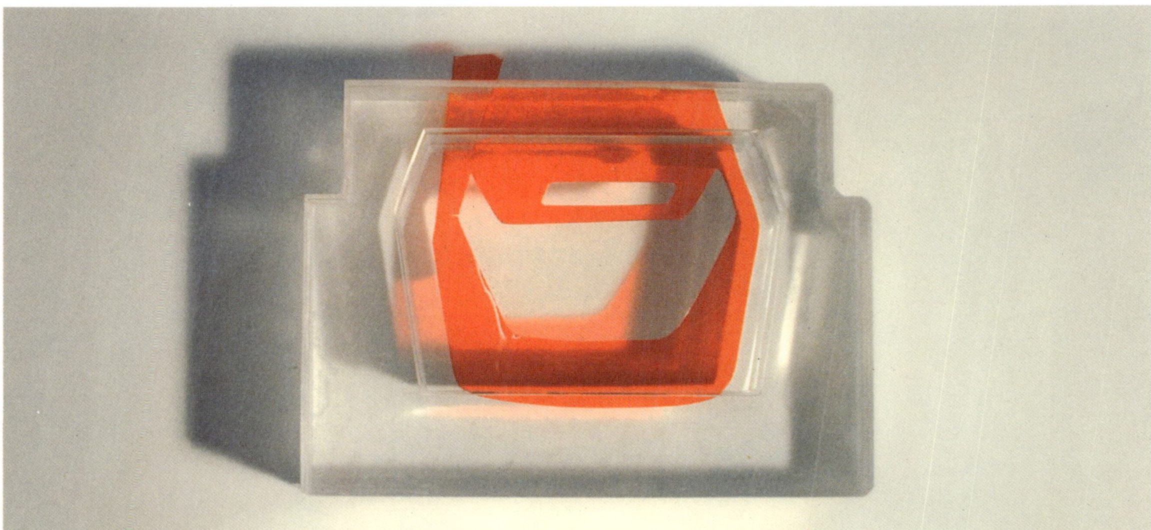

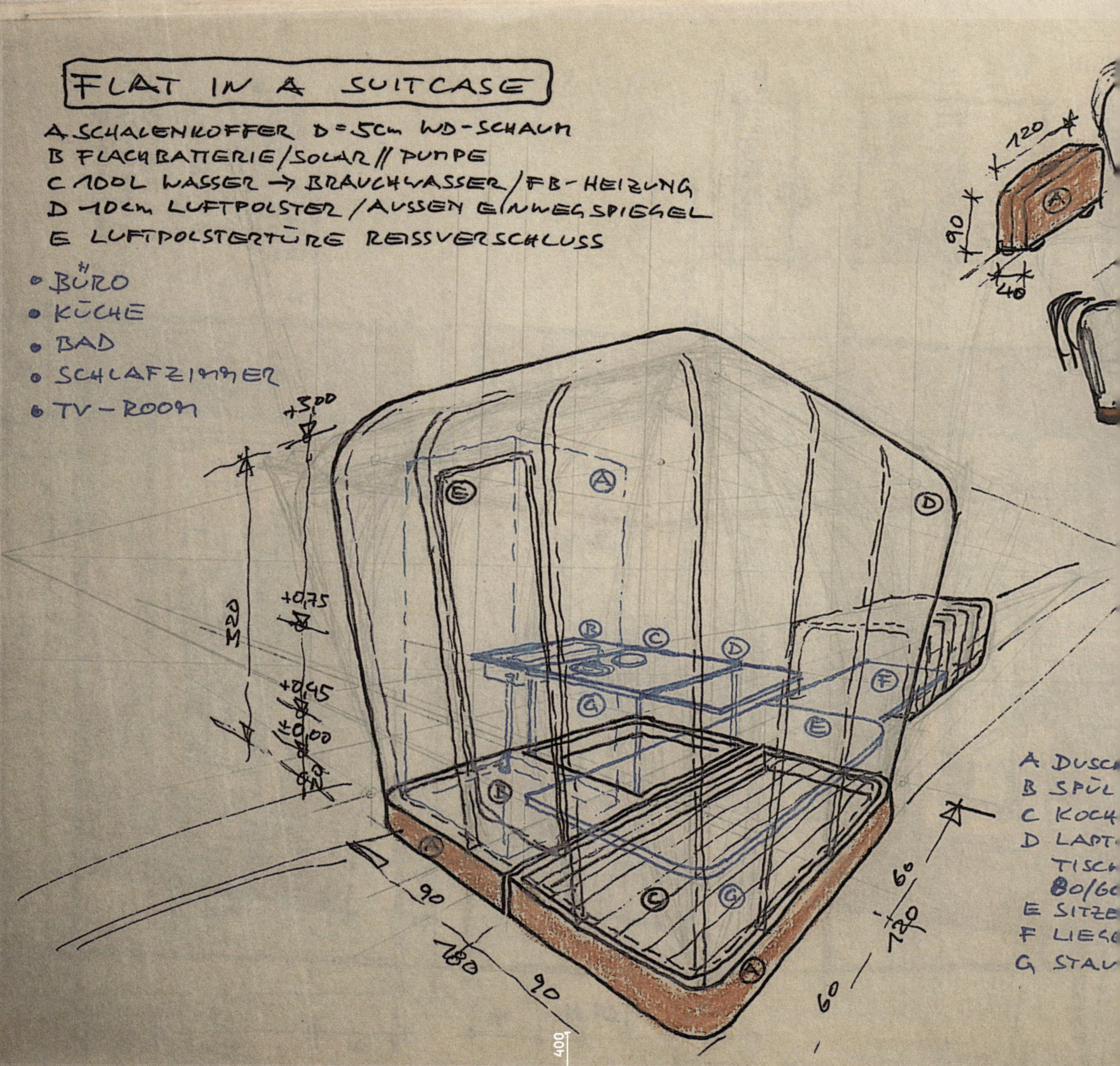
FLAT IN A SUITCASE
A SCHALENKOFFER D=5cm WD-SCHAUM
B FLACHBATTERIE/SOLAR// PUMPE
C 100L WASSER → BRAUCHWASSER/FB-HEIZUNG
D 10cm LUFTPOLSTER/AUSSEN EINWEGSPIEGEL
E LUFTPOLSTERTÜRE REISSVERSCHLUSS
• BÜRO
• KÜCHE
• BAD
• SCHLAFZIMMER
• TV-ROOM

flat in a suitcase

die wohnung aus dem koffer. studie 2006

die frage: kann ich meine wohnung mit auf die reise nehmen?
ja, ich kann. in einem 90/120/40 cm großen koffer hat eine komplette wohnung platz. beim aufklappen des koffers bläst sich mit der eingebauten pumpe ein mehrfach nutzbarer raum von 180/120/300 cm mit den funktionen büro, küche, bad, schlafzimmer und tv-room auf. die hülle ist durch einwegverspiegelung blickdicht, wärmegedämmt und durch den luftpumpenbetrieb formstabil. eine solar wiederaufladbare flachbatterie und ein wasserreservoir im kofferboden ermöglichen energieautarkie. und geben der wohnung durch ihr gewicht die notwendige bodenhaftung.
das ergibt: eine mobile wohnung für alle plätze dieser welt.

the question is: can i take my apartment with me on my travels?
yes, i can. there is room for a complete apartment in a suitcase measuring 90/120/40 cms. upon opening the suitcase, a space measuring 180/120/300 cms can be inflated using the pump included, so as to then function as an office, kitchen, bathroom, bedroom and tv-room. the skin is opaque as a result of the one-way silvering, is thermally insulated and is kept stable by the operation of the air pump. a rechargeable solar flat battery and a water reservoir in the bottom of the suitcase make energy self-sufficiency possible. the weight gives the apartment its necessary grip.
the result: a mobile apartment for anywhere in the world.

projekt / project
charity chair »dietiker«
wien 2009

chairity chair

instruction charity chair

»teilen ist besser als geizen«, will uns der charity-gedanke sagen. daher sägen wir den ono-stuhl in zwei. doch wollen wir nicht nur den stuhl, sondern auch die möglichkeit des ausruhens und sitzens mit mehreren personen teilen, ganz nach dem motto »mit luft und liebe viel erreichen«.
für die aufblasbaren kissen bedarf es nur die luft einer kräftigen lunge. um aber den mensch nicht überzustrapazieren, entschieden wir uns für eine schöne weiße druckluftflasche, angepasst an die klassische schlichtheit des ono-stuhls. aus eins mach vier! nun freut sich nicht nur ein stehender, sondern noch weitere steher aufs sitzen, plauschen und verweilen. ein stuhl an einem leeren ort ist unkommunikativ und macht einsam. mehrere jedoch schaffen raum für lustiges beisammensein. durch einfachste mittel wurde geteilt was nur zu teilen ging. zudem ist der stuhl ausbaufähig und wenn man möchte unendlich erweiterbar. zurückgeführt in den urzustand, durch verdeckt angebrachte verschlüsse, ist der ono-stuhl nicht nur leicht transportabel sondern sieht dabei auch noch gut aus.

the idea of charity tells us that sharing is better than skimping. that is why we cut the ono chair in two. yet we do not only want to share the chair, but also the possibility of relaxing and sitting in it with several people, in accordance with the motto »all you need is love and air«.
to blow up the four inflatable cushions all that is needed is a strong pair of lungs. however, in order not to put too much strain on people's lungs, we decided in favour of a nice white compressed air bottle, in keeping with the classic simplicity of the ono chair. from one make four! now not only one person, but several people who are standing around can enjoy sitting down, having a chat and passing the time. one chair in an empty place is uncommunicative and creates a feeling of loneliness. yet several of them create space for a sociable get-together. using the simplest of means, everything was shared that could be shared. moreover, the chair can be extended still further and, if one so wishes, extended infinitely. when returned to its original state by means of the hidden fasteners that are attached to it, the ono chair not only becomes easily transportable, but also still looks great.

1

2

3

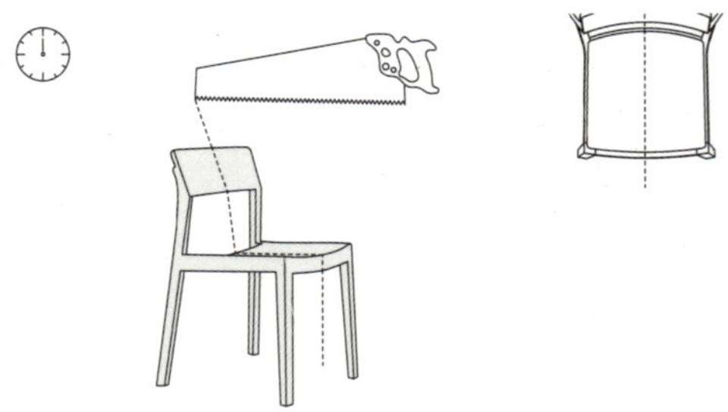

4

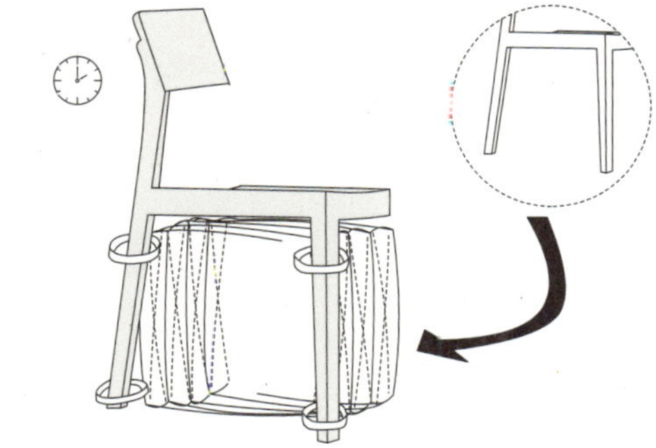

5

Hello

6

Just one more ...darling

7

20:15 - it´s time for loveboat
LOVE BOAT

wettbewerb / competition
mobiler pavillion / mobile pavillion
salzburg 2009

eventoskope

mobiles kunst- und kulturbauwerk // mobile art and culture structure, festival for new music, salzburg biennale 2011

ein veranstaltungsraum, der per lkw angefahren kommt und mit diesem auch wieder wegfährt. ein wirklich mobiles »eventoskop«, das sich automatisiert ausfahren und zusammenschieben lässt und dabei alle anforderungen an einen veranstaltungsraum mit nebenräumen erfüllt. eine schubladenkonstruktion, die sich von einer einzelnen person mittels seilwinde am lkw zu einem pavillon ausziehen lässt: von $33\,m^2$ auf $169\,m^2$. das kleinste raumelement ist mit einer elektrochromen glasscheibe als projektionsfläche für die bühne abgeschlossen. durch kippen und einlegen von bodenelementen wird eine ebene fläche für zuschauer und bühne geschaffen. die bodenelemente und die möblierung werden im verbleibenden volumen des transportzustandes mitgeführt. über den achsen des lkws befindet sich die haustechnik, ein standard mobil-wc, sowie ein behindertengerechtes wc. durch das aufklappen der beiden laderampen werden die eingänge geschaffen.

an events room that is delivered on a truck and is also taken away on one. a really mobile »eventoscope«, which could be automatically driven out and put together and meet all the requirements of an events room, including all the secondary rooms. a drawer construction that can be pulled out by one single person using a winch on a lorry to form a pavilion: from $33\,m^2$ to $169\,m^2$. the smallest spatial element is ready for the stage with an electrochrome glass pane as a projection surface. by tilting and laying floor elements, an even surface is created for the spectators and the stage. the floor elements and the furniture are carried in the remaining volumes of the transport condition. above the truck axles is the internal technology, a standard mobile wc, as well as a wc suitable for disadvantaged persons. the entrances are created by lowering the two loading ramps.

bewerbung mit / application with: markus scherer

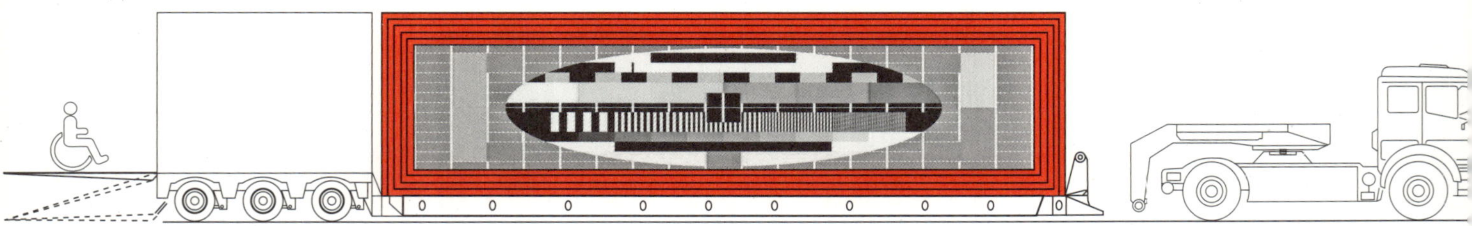

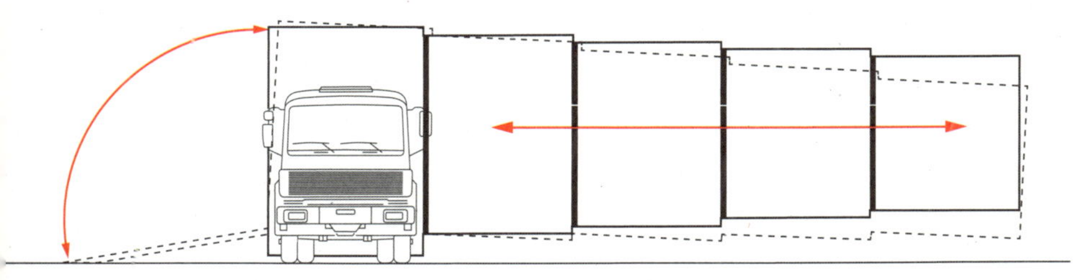

abspann

end titles

planet caramel

beitrag zur ausstellung »mega« im künstlerhaus, wien 2002
contribution to the exhibition »mega« at the künstlerhaus, vienna 2002

kurator / curator jan tabor

»planet caramel« ist der neue extraterrestrische planet am rand des uns bekannten.
»planet caramel« is a new extra-terrestrial planet on the edge of the known world.

team

2001-2011

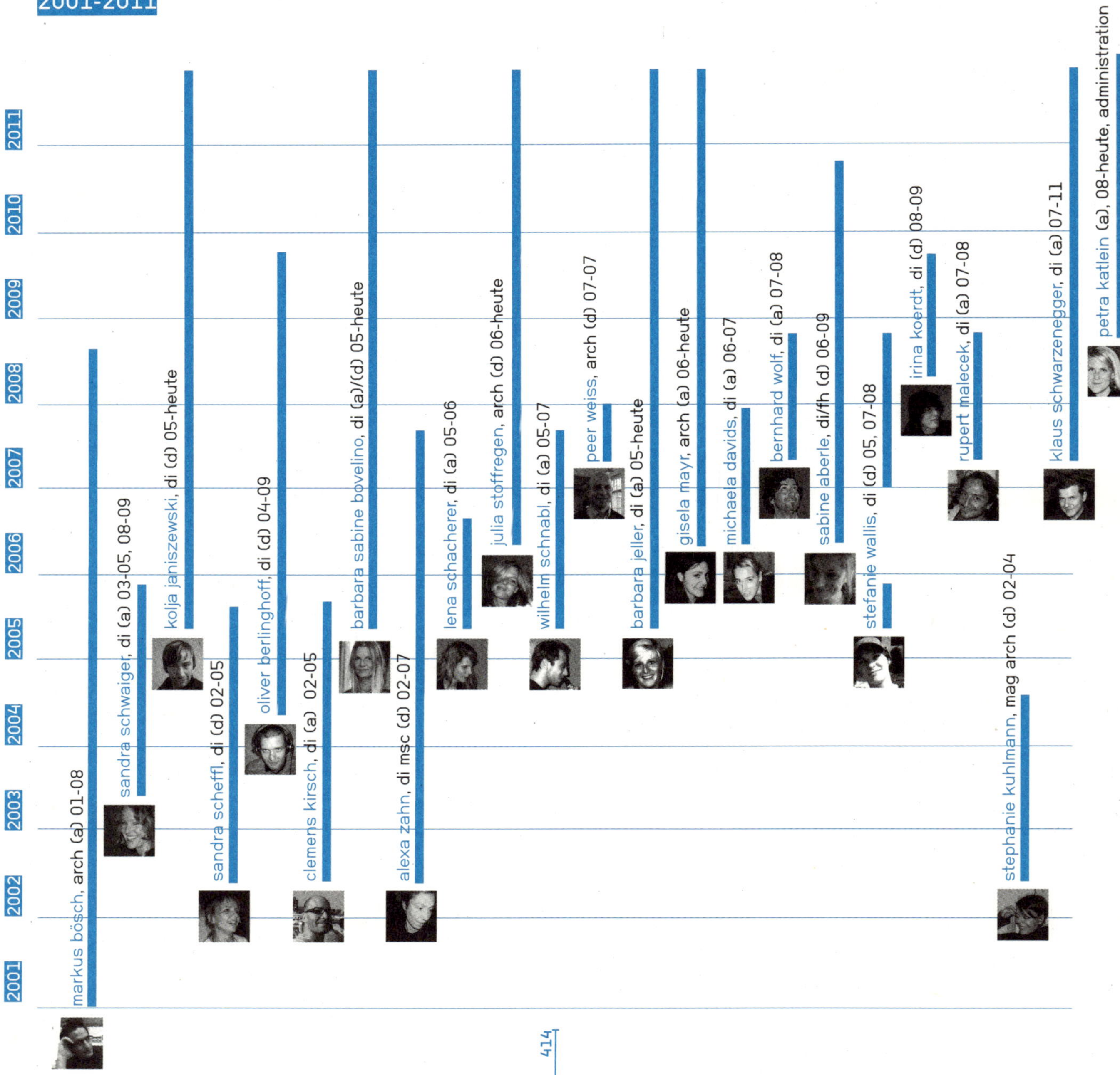

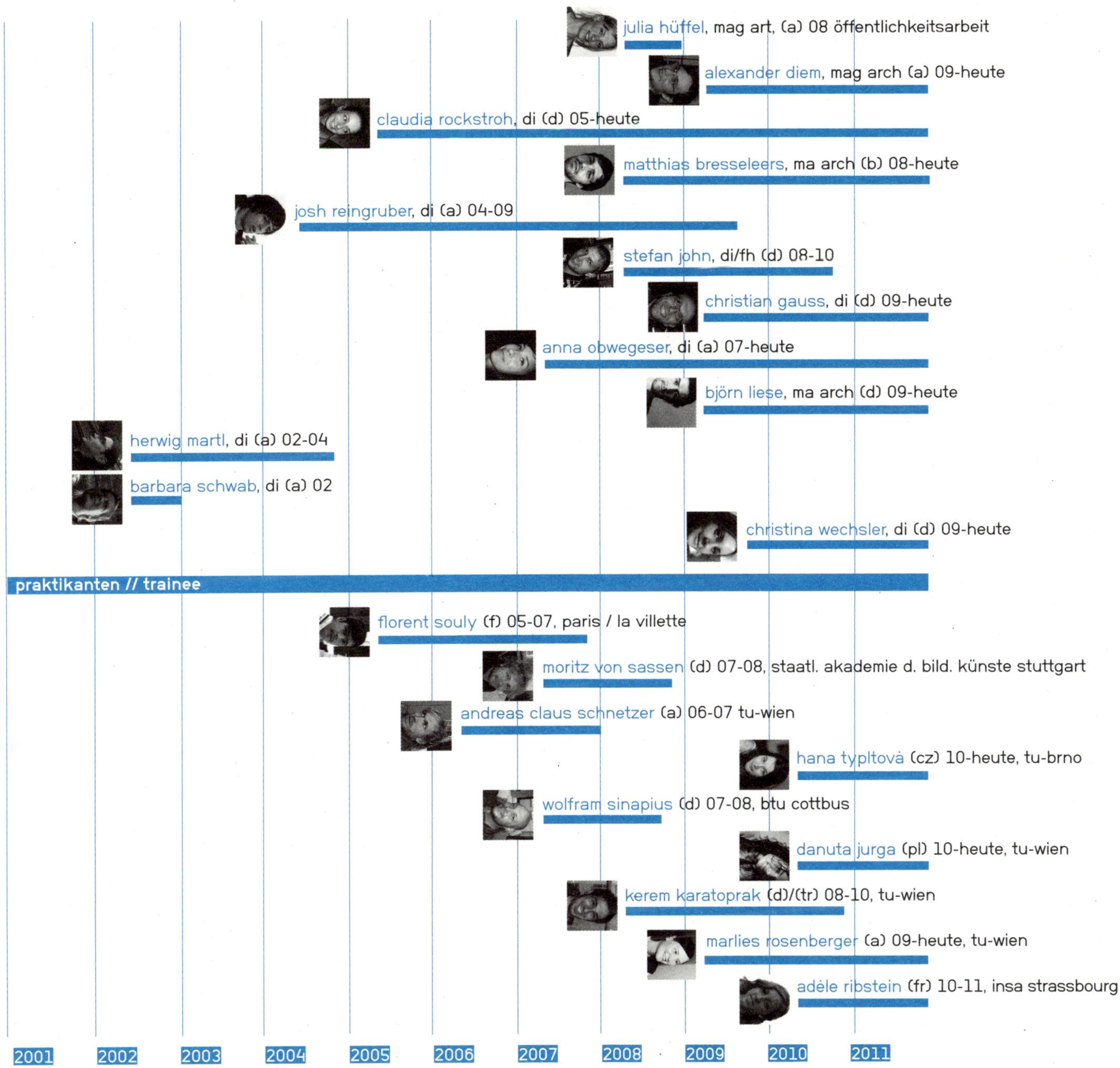
julia hüffel, mag art, (a) 08 öffentlichkeitsarbeit
alexander diem, mag arch (a) 09-heute
claudia rockstroh, di (d) 05-heute
matthias bresseleers, ma arch (b) 08-heute
josh reingruber, di (a) 04-09
stefan john, di/fh (d) 08-10
christian gauss, di (d) 09-heute
anna obwegeser, di (a) 07-heute
björn liese, ma arch (d) 09-heute
herwig martl, di (a) 02-04
barbara schwab, di (a) 02
christina wechsler, di (d) 09-heute
praktikanten // trainee
florent souly (f) 05-07, paris / la villette
moritz von sassen (d) 07-08, staatl. akademie d. bild. künste stuttgart
andreas claus schnetzer (a) 06-07 tu-wien
hana typltová (cz) 10-heute, tu-brno
wolfram sinapius (d) 07-08, btu cottbus
danuta jurga (pl) 10-heute, tu-wien
kerem karatoprak (d)/(tr) 08-10, tu-wien
marlies rosenberger (a) 09-heute, tu-wien
adèle ribstein (fr) 10-11, insa strassbourg
2001
2002
2003
2004
2005
2006
2007
2008
2009
2010
2011

further trainees

jürgen berner (a), tu-wien
hans zotter (a), tu-wien
florian kienesberger (a), tu-wien
ana martin del hierro (e), etsa sevilla
katrin fischer (d), tu-saarland
therese silberkuhl (d), tu-karlsruhe
kathi katherl (a)
laure fink (fr), tu-wien
simon valentin (d), fh kaiserslautern
moritz brembs (d), bauhaus univ. weimar
georg zschiedrich (d), htvk leipzig
bonny holland (d), fh regensburg
manuel oka (d), tu-wien
markus wilke (d), tu braunschweig
wolfgang bechtold (a), tu-innsbruck
ulrike wetzel (d) bauhaus univ. weimar
jana baumker (d), tu-wien
sven hedrich (d), univ. akad. der bildenden künste münchen
arnold wilfing (a), tu-wien
lisa görke (d), leibnitz universität hannover
julia ettl (a), tu-wien
max straub (d), georg-simon-ohm-hochschule nürnberg
benjamin gieseking (d), tu-wien
niklas ruprechter (d), tu-wien
simon köppl (d), uni. stuttgart
anja katharina ziehmann (d)
mareike fluhrer (d)
iryna miroshnykova (ua), kiewer nationale universität
rojiar soleimani (ir), univ. für angewandte kunst wien

petra richter (cz), die gute seele des büros

caramel partner

AND ...?
GOT IT?

NOPE
...
FORGOT IT!

022
info_point
linz09

029
ego shooter

030
transfusionsmedizin

036
oxygen tents

040
justizzentrum wien 3

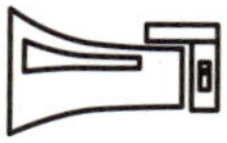

043
reklame

044
seniorenheim
gaspoltshofen

047
tapete belgrad

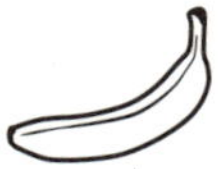

048
schulzentrum
krems

050
mak nite

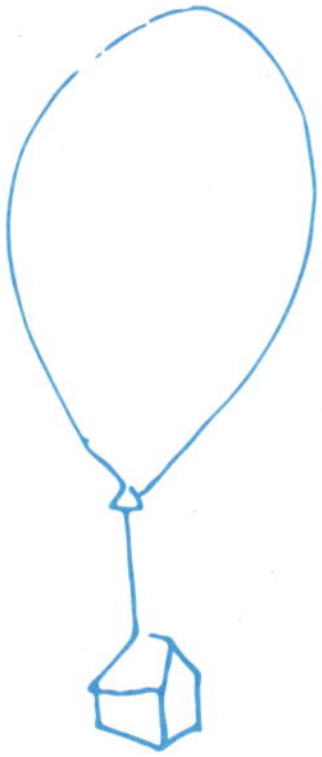

066
cube twister oslo

073
500 m² wohnzimmer

080
a higher school

082
technologiezentrum

084
schule eisenstadt

086
haus h

098
science center wels

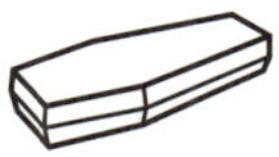

100
pathologie

102
downtown center

105
casino austria

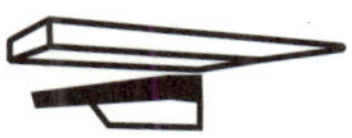

106
stadthalle wien

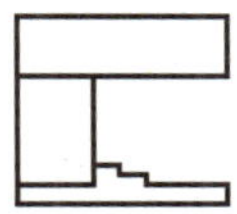

108
landesmuseum vorarlberg

112
design school
zollverein

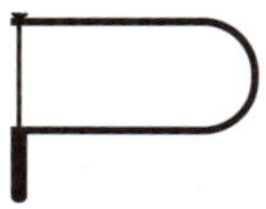

120
schlossmuseum
linz

122
schule wels

124
hauptbibliothek
wien

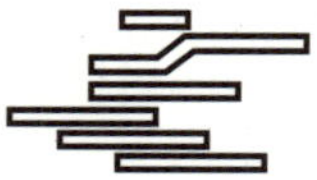

126
krankenhaus
schwarzach

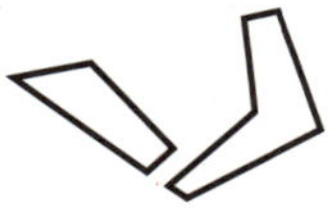

128
wifi campus

142
ma 48

150
fld & lgk

152
so_oke

156
betriebswerkstätte

167
bene

171
caramelbüro

172
kindergarten
tisis

175
schindlberg

178
haus kaps

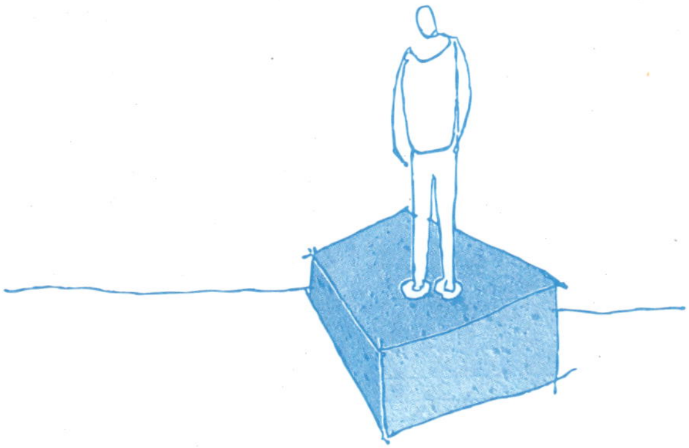

190
science park

204
musikschule

206
sonderschule

209
haus s

210
landscape-house-hybrid

212
erweiterung stadthalle
heidelberg

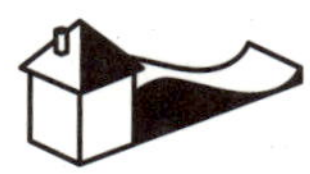

216
arbeiterkammer
wien

218
stadthalle
neunburg

220
fachhochschule
wels

224
haus p

234
öbb konzernzentrale

236
kunstuni linz

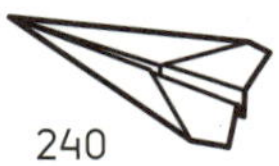

240
haus r

242
infobox hauptbahnhof
öbb wien

245
the infinite oasis

248
simmeringer markt

250
molekulare
biowissenschaften

252
landesbibliothek

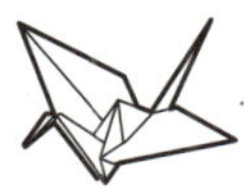

254
haus in der wachau

256
körösistraße 17

258
wohnbau
am krautgarten

266
schule
langobardenstraße

268
hotel kaprun

270
wirtschaftsuniversität
wien

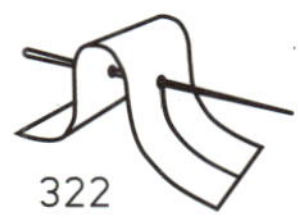

342
visitors bridge at voestalpine

348
eternit

351
infokiosk und buswartehäuschen

352
carport(able)

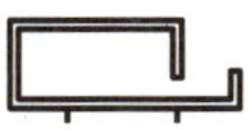
358
haus lina

366
seifenkistl

368
gainfarn

370
adidas

373
nomadisierende zellen

376
trade fair stand for ami

382
max waschmöbel

388
kaffee mitteregger

impressum / imprint

editor(s)
andreas russ-bovelino with kind help from caramel

printed in austria
springerwiennewyork is a part of springer science+business media
springer.at

layout and cover design: martin bruner, linz, austria
illustrations: martin bruner, adèle ribstein
translation from german into english: peter waugh, vienna, austria
printing and binding: holzhausen druck gmbh, vienna, austria

printed on acid-free and chlorine-free bleached paper

spin: 80029680

library of congress control number: 2011932989

with 559 colored figures

isbn 978-3-7091-0511-5 SpringerWienNewYork

dank/credits

fotografen und animateure/photographers and animators
ingo pertramer doris knecht s.018 dietmar tollerian linz 09 s.024-027, lentos s.038, 039, voestalpine besucherstege s.344-347, sporthalle krems s.293-299, linz 09 linz 09, s.025, s.027 ullstein verlag linz 09 s.025 katherina gossow transfusionsmedizin landeskrankenhaus (bürofotos) s.034, 035, 2.pause s.222, 223 pez hejduk reklame s.042, 043 matthias kessler casino austria s.104 samuel käppeli mak nite s.053-055, air_line by caramel s.392-395 katja hoffmann sibylle berg s.060 martin bruner cube twister s.069, landesbibliothek linz s.252, ein neuer rock für berlin s.330, 331 hertha hurnaus 500m² s.072-078, haus h s.088-097, ma 48 s.144-149, ansfelden s.158-165, science park s.192-203, haus p s.226-233, krautgarten s.260-265, carport(able) s.354-357 zoom vp areal eichstrasse stuttgart mitte s.102, 103, krankenhaus schwarzach s.127, öbb konzernzentrale s.234, 235, kunstuni linz s.237-239 zeche zollverein design school zollverein s.115, 116 marcel hagen wifi campus s.130-135 otto lechner otto lechner s.138, anne bennent s.338 janosz kalmar schindlberg s.174-177 johannes felsch kaps s.180-185 angelo kaunat kaps s.180-185 gerald von foris attwenger s.188 stefan fiedler die unendliche oase s.244-247 werner amann roberto yanez honecker s.274 herbert schwingenschlögl glasbau augsburg s.282, 283 otto hainzl haus m s.310-313 gaucho media privat museum liaunig s.324 frank drechsel infobox und buswartehäuschen s.350 wojciech czaja haus lina s.361 fh münster nomadisiernde zellen s.372-375 fundermax/robert striegl max waschmöbel s.385, 386 larry williams caramel partner (caramelfoto) s.417

alle übrigen und nicht aufgelisteten fotos und animationen sind von caramel und ihrem team.
all other photos and animations that are not listed are created by caramel and their team.

die pausentexte stammen mit freundlicher genehmigung von friedrich achleitner aus den bänden:
»und oder oder und« © paul zsolnay verlag wien 2006 – federieren, mehr inhalt, quartett
»der springende punkt« © paul zsolnay verlag wien 2009 – klo brille, kopf-rumpf, hansi
the intervening texts are printed by courtesy of friedrich achleitner from the volumes:
»und oder oder und« © paul zsolnay verlag, vienna 2006 – federieren, mehr inhalt, quartett
»der springende punkt« © paul zsolnay verlag, vienna 2009 – klo brille, kopf-rumpf, hansi

danke! thanks!
caramel team
adèle ribstein
fritz stiper
werkraum wien
peter bauer/peter resch
ursula klein
harald schmid
samuel käppeli
idealice
yes design
thomas gürtler
martin murero
heinz kasper
erich weismann
richard klinger
ernst hoffmann
dominique perrault
haushoch
peter kleinhans
nenad + markus
fröhlich & locher
ma.schin
andrzej orlinski
michl kaser
peter liebentritt
hable usability
gudi schwienbacher
andrea bina
sabine katherl
manisha jothady
scheibosan
roberta f.
juliane
ig-architektur
allen anderen all the others
und mama!